Marques Noah Marchand resides in San Francisco, California. *Junk Knowledge* is his first book. Marques's work focuses on the gritty truth that is addiction, and what it takes to recover and move forward. With a dark sense of humor, Marques will guide you through all the ups, downs and curves that have been in his life. Today, armed with a wealth of knowledge that his experience has brought him, Marques Marchand hopes to help other suffering addicts and the friends and family that are trying to help those that are currently caught in the grips of the madness—addiction. Please keep an eye out for his future work.

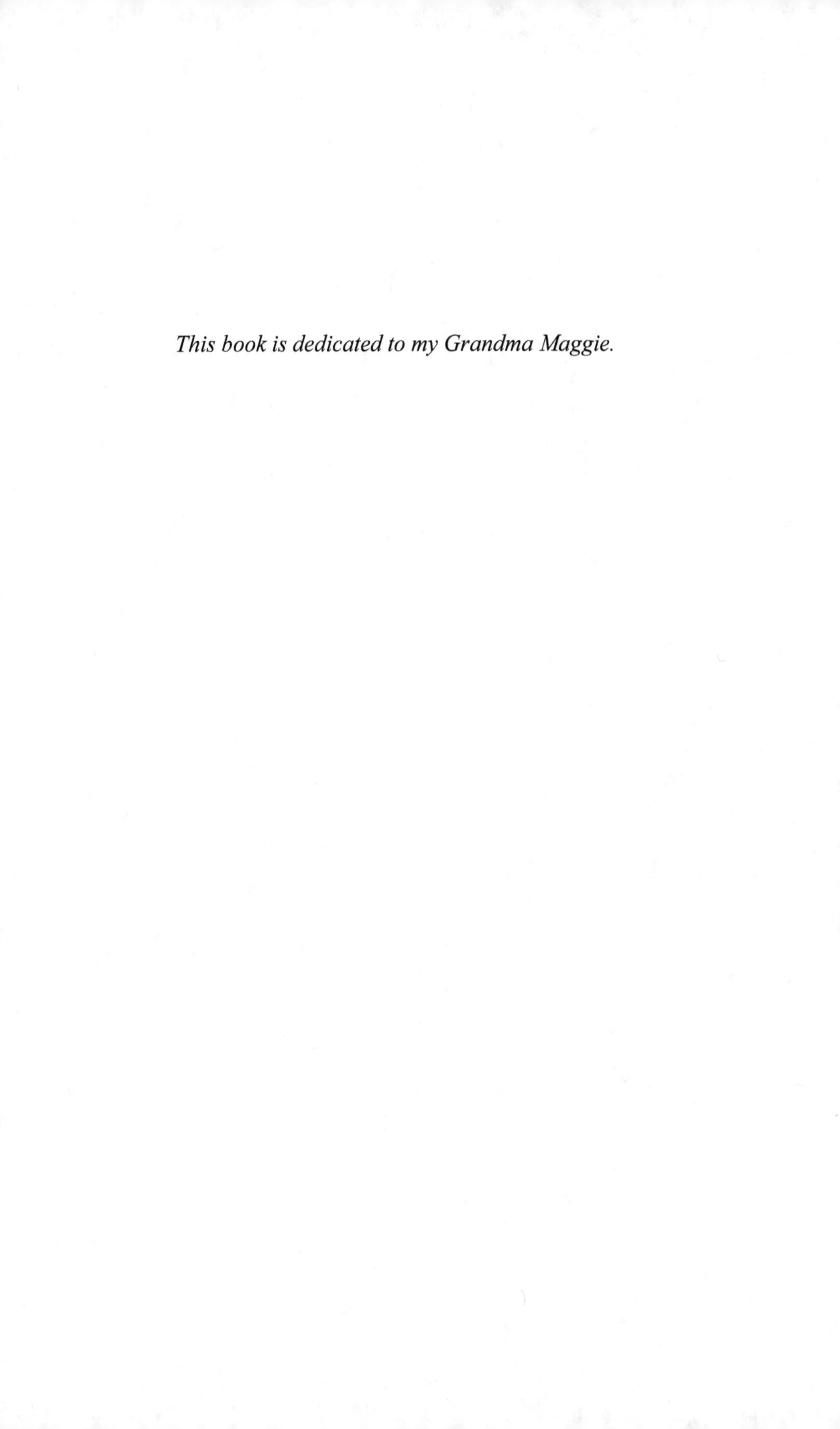

This book is dedicated to my Grandma Maggie.

Marques Noah Marchand

JUNK KNOWLEDGE

AUSTIN MACAULEY PUBLISHERS™

LONDON ∗ CAMBRIDGE ∗ NEW YORK ∗ SHARJAH

Ordering Information:
Quantity sales: special discounts are available on quantity purchases by corporations, associations, and others. For details, contact the publisher at the address below.

Publisher's Cataloging-in-Publication data
Marchand, Marques Noah
Junk Knowledge

ISBN 9781645752165 (Paperback)
ISBN 9781645752172 (Hardback)
ISBN 9781645752189 (ePub e-book)

Library of Congress Control Number: 2020912642

www.austinmacauley.com/us

First Published (2020)
Austin Macauley Publishers LLC
40 Wall Street, 28th Floor
New York, NY 10005
USA

mail-usa@austinmacauley.com
+1 (646) 5125767

There are some key people in my life that really made this book possible. I know that I spoke harshly about some people in my life. I basically told the world that I think my mother is mentally ill on more than one occasion. I might have made her out to be like Joan Crawford in *Mommy Dearest*. She wasn't that bad, but at times I saw her as a monster. I also spoke a lot about my stepfather. Did I compare him to Hitler? I really can't remember but I might have. I did not mention my biological father that much because I simply do not have that much to go on. I have described my father as more of a ghost than an actual person. I do not mean to come off cold or disconnected, but I simply do not know my father. My grandma, Maggie, will always be a saint in my mind. For all her faults, my grandmother can do no wrong. I will forever be in her debt. My grandmother pulled me out of hell more than once. She gave me food, shelter, and time. She allowed me to work on myself and become an actual human being, and for that, I will always love my grandmother more than life itself. I love you, Grandma.

I also want to thank every AA sponsor that I have ever had. I learned something from every man that has taken the time to work with me. To my best friend Peter. We have become bulletproof and we helped each other achieve success. We have both experienced hell on Earth and we clawed our way out. Thank you for being my friend, Peter. I have to thank everyone I ever met at every AA meeting I have ever been to. I have heard so many amazing stories over the years, so many amazing people that have shared their souls in crowded church basements and random Alano Clubs around the country and the world. Thank you to all the employers that kept me longer than they should have and thank you to the employers that fired me. It was the right thing to do. I also want to thank every asshole that I have ever met. In AA, the most important person in the room are the newcomers. In life, the most important person in your life will always be the biggest asshole in your life. You learn the most from assholes. I have learned patience, how to love unconditionally, and how not to judge others so much, thanks to the complete assholes of the world. Actually, I am still pretty judgmental, but I am getting better, I promise. I have learned how to say no, when to say yes, how to let the bad ones go, and how to fight for the good ones. Thank you to everyone that made any kind of impact on my life. I might not like you, but I love you.

I'm pretty sure most of this is true.

Preface

I decided to write this book because I am tired of people telling me that they left rehab because they hated talking about God. The number-one excuse for people leaving rehab early, not liking twelve-step programs and hating all the literature that comes with all these facilities is one little word, God. Oh, and rules, these people hate rules. I have been told by hundreds of men and women, young and old, that they simply do not want to talk about the whole God thing. I can't even fathom how many times I have heard someone say that they are not sure whether or not they actually are an alcoholic. Sure, they have been to rehab twice and recently court-ordered to go to AA meetings for the next six months but no, they don't have a problem. Meanwhile, these people can't keep a job, never pay rent on time unless their parents help them, keep losing their cars, their kids are one bad night away from being taken by the state, and they keep dating people that abuse them in one way or another. These people would prefer to go through all this rather than do whatever it takes to get sober and stay sober. Why? They say they don't have a disease and God isn't real. They aren't bad people. They just want to have fun but they take it a bit too far sometimes. That's all. Rehab is just a place for them to get away from the harsh world that doesn't understand them for a few weeks. Dad left when they were three, which gave them a major disadvantage. Life just hasn't been fair for these select few, so they deserve a little bit of leeway. These are the things they tell themselves to rationalize their negative habits, habits they sooner or later turn into full-on abuse.

I know I am coming off a bit harsh. The reason why I take a more brutal and straightforward stance on the issue of addiction is because I have not only seen what I consider the disease of addiction tear not only the individual addict apart but I have also seen the disease rip apart entire families. It has happened to me and both sides of my family. People in my family have died, gone mentally insane, or just disappeared only to return five years later as if nothing happened. I come from low-bottom junkies. I come from depression, anxiety, and denial. Maybe you don't. Maybe your family is successful, happy, and gainfully employed. But if you are reading this book, you probably found it in some twenty-eight-day spin dry center somewhere or you know someone that is an addict that read it and told you to check it out. Either way, things aren't perfect for you right now. Or maybe you are a good friend of mine and I forced you to buy my book. If that's the case, thanks for the ten bucks.

I want to make it clear that I am a no-bullshit, straightforward kind of guy. Some people like this and some people don't. But if you are going through a hard time, I might be your best friend. If you are an atheist and you are not sure if you are an addict and you don't want to talk about God, this book might also be for you. I wrote this book as an alternative to all the other books that you might be asked to read if you or someone you know is struggling with addiction. And trust me, for a hardcore junky like myself, there is no alternative to the Big Book of Alcoholics Anonymous. I have read everything you can read and the Big Book saved my life. I do however understand why someone would not want to talk about God or spirituality on any level when first trying to get sober. In the beginning, all you want to do is make it one day without drinking or using. Your body hurts, you keep throwing up, you have diarrhea all the time, and your mind is upside down. The description I have just given does not even come close to giving what withdrawal really is like any justice. The last thing you want to hear is, "Son, do you believe in God?" That question sends so many people packing. I can understand why so many people just say 'fuck you' to the whole God thing.

If possible, I want to give some form of guidance. In order to do this, I will talk about my using days, how great it was, how shitty it was, and I will talk about how and why I got sober. Some of this book will be a bit depressing. Some of this book will be funny. At times, I will come off like a genuinely bad person and that's because there were times in my life when I was a bad person. At other times, you might find me a bit endearing. I am a human being that has a real disease. I am an addict in recovery. No human being is one thing. Being human is complicated. Being a human being with a mental and physical illness hasn't been a picnic but it doesn't give me any excuse to be an asshole. I believe this to be true for everyone. No matter what you are going through, it does not give you the right to hurt someone. Yes, you might not have been loved as a child but that doesn't mean that you get to shoot up a grade school or stock pretty girls and rape them. Hopefully, this book can be one of the first steps toward a better understanding of yourself and the disease that has unfortunately inflicted you.

1. The Question

Maybe you are in some high-end rehab in Sausalito, California. Maybe you are staying in a shelter in Downtown St. Louis, Missouri. Maybe you moved back in with your parents. It really doesn't matter where you are. If you are a junky and you want to quit but you can't, I get it. I have been there more than once. But do you really want to get sober? Or are you just broke and need a place to crash? Maybe your girlfriend threw you and all your shit out because you get crazy and you black out and you threatened to kill her again. Maybe you finally got caught robbing your grandmother's house. Such scenarios are not fictions for addicts; they are standard. But when it comes to the point that everyone in your life has told you to get the fuck out, perhaps it's time to change.

As I write this, it is June 2018. I am thirty-nine years old and I have been sober for sixteen and a half years. I got sober when I was twenty-two years old. Many might think that twenty-two is rather young to get sober or wonder how things could have gotten bad enough at such a young age. My life must be perfect today, right? The truth is that my life didn't just fall into place once I got sober at twenty-two. My family did not become close, nobody won the lottery, and there was never a white picket fence.

So let's start at the beginning. I was born on January 2, 1979. Disco, Elvis, and any kind of denial that the United States once had that America was still this perfect place where anyone from any place could make a million bucks and marry a supermodel had all been killed off. Low self-esteem, greed, resentment, fear, addiction, you name it. These would become the new standard for so many today. It's all just mental illness. My mother and biological father met at a party in the summer of 1977. They had a series of one-night stands and mistook this for love, so they got married and I was born, metaphorically five minutes later. My mother realized a few months into their marriage that my father was severely mentally ill. Back in the day, they called it manic depression. My father would spend the rest of his life trying to get better. I visited my father three separate times in mental hospitals. My parents got divorced when I was eighteen months old and I would see him sporadically every four or five years but we never became close. My mother did her best to protect me from all of this. I would not start to figure out what happened to my father until I would reach my mid-twenties. This would be around the time that I would start to lose my shit as well.

My father got sober on my fourth birthday, but for some reason my father's life never improved, even though he put down all the drugs and alcohol. My father was about twenty-five when he got sober and he is about sixty-two today. He would never make a fortune or marry a beautiful, smart woman. My father lives in a one-bedroom apartment just outside of Portland, Oregon, and he has a miniature white poodle. My father does not date at all. For a time, I assumed my father was a closet homosexual, but over the years, I just realized that my father is just mentally ill and the medication that the doctors have put him on have probably just created a numbness in his soul and that will be the best that things will ever get for him. Maybe I am wrong about this. I hope I am. I hope things get better for my father. I can totally relate to this because I have experienced that numb detachment myself over the years. I am almost forty years old now, have been sober a while, go to my AA meetings, read my literature, swim my laps, ride my bike, drink my veggie drinks every day, and I take medication for depression and anxiety. I will be honest and say that my sexual appetite is shit and I have little to no interest in romantic relationships. I often wonder if it's the medications or whether this is normal for someone with a mental illness such as alcoholism. To be honest, I do not know. Doctors don't know. Nobody knows. On occasion, I will get laid or I will date someone for a couple of months or get an escort. But overall, I just do not have any interest in sharing my life with anyone.

Most of the time, this feels natural to me, but on occasion, I get very lonely. At times, I will feel such a deep gut-wrenching loneliness that I will be completely consumed by it. Eventually, the loneliness will fade away and I will just be myself again. I have dealt with this for most of my life. But overall, I prefer to live the bachelor life and just have sex on occasion. I prefer naughty massage parlors at eleven p.m., escorts on my days off, expensive spa days, and weekend getaways by myself. My mother calls me selfish. I used to feel so much guilt for my lifestyle, but over the last couple years, I have just come to accept it. Or maybe I am selfish. Maybe I do not have the guts to love someone else. My grandmother tells me that I have just haven't met the right woman yet, but in the back of my mind, I think that is just my grandmother's way of being nice when she really thinks I am just too fucked up to live the married life. To be honest with you, the thought of sharing my bed with the same person for the rest of my life makes me physically ill. Not being able to sleep in till one p.m. and eventually somehow finding myself in a condo ten miles outside of any major city of my choosing would kill me. I literally think I might kill myself if I ever got married. I know that is a harsh statement, but it's often the way I feel. My father lost his mind after marrying my mother and having me. I am so afraid that this would happen to me. Fuck that noise. I would rather feel lonely on occasion than attempt suicide every four months.

I remember when I first started thinking about alcohol. I would not call it an obsession yet, but I remember when I first became aware of it and knew that I really liked it. I was about three and a half years old. It was summer and I was at a barbecue in my grandparents' backyard. I was wearing jean cutoff shorts and my grandfather's favorite cowboy hat. It was hot and my family was sitting in a circle talking and laughing. I remember these times as 'the good old days.' Everybody in my family got along back then. Nobody was a junky yet. At least I don't remember anybody in my family getting too crazy. Everybody was just happy, smoking cigarettes and talking. The first sip I ever took was from a can of beer that I snuck out of my grandfather's hands. I took a quick sip, put the can back in his hands, and I just ran around the backyard in circles. I fucking loved it! I remember when my mother started drinking wine coolers. I would spend an entire evening at a family get-together just waiting for my mother to put her bottle down so I could take a quick swig. My mother would catch me and she would tell me to stay out of her wine cooler. This would become a kind of game between certain members of my family and me. Everybody thought it was cute. And compared to what was really going on in my family, I guess it was kind of cute. This was because things in my family would eventually become very dark.

2. The Dawn of Discomfort

When I look back at my life, I do not think that I became conscious of the world around me until my seventh birthday. Before my seventh birthday, I really didn't think anything was real. Everyone in my life seemed to make me one of his or her top priorities. Everyone just seemed to serve me. As an adult, this makes sense to me now. I was my mother's first child and my grandmother's first and favorite grandchild. I was always surrounded by women as well. I do not really remember being around men very often, so there wasn't a lot of rough housing. The beginning of my childhood was spent sitting around tables with my mother, aunts, and grandmother, and I would eat cookies and listen to them talk. I grew up in a fucking henhouse. My grandfather was always off working on the lawn or fixing something around the house. He was like a voluntary day laborer and the rest of us stayed indoors and just talked shit. I remember all the women in the house taking turns talking about one another. My mother would leave and my aunts and grandmother would talk about her. Or my grandmother would leave and mother and aunts would talk about my grandmother. It was a feeding frenzy. The women in my family were like sharks swimming circles around a boat with bloody fish in the water. Every shark was just waiting her turn.

I always assumed that I was safe from these talks that the women in my family would have. I never heard anything bad being said about me, but I wasn't safe from what soon appeared to be hypocrisy. The women in my family are more ambush predators. You will never hear or see them coming. All you know is that for some reason, someone is mad at you and you never know why. A week later, they will be nice to you. Maybe all women are like this. Most of the women I have ever met behave like this, so maybe I am thinking a bit too deeply about nothing. Or perhaps, as a man, I just don't understand women. I do wonder what kind of person I would be if I had been surrounded by men rather than women in my early childhood. Would I have become more butch? Would I have become more violent? Sometimes I believe that I am obsessed with the way I look, my weight, and nice shit because of all these damn women that surrounded me as a child. I have a half-brother that is almost seven years younger than me and he is a country caveman. He loves getting dirty, chopping wood, chewing tobacco, and big loud trucks. My younger brother was also raised by my mother and an extremely masculine alpha male as a father. He grew up learning to weld, shoot guns, and go camping. I hated that shit as a kid. I never understood why someone would want to wake up at 4:30 in the morning and go out to the mountains in thirty-five-degree weather and wait to shoot something while it rained. I'd rather just sleep in, have some quiche, and drink a shot of espresso. I mean, fucking relax!

Needless to say, in my household I was different. Or maybe I should say that I was 'different.' That's hillbilly for not being like anyone else in my family. I started noticing that I stuck out a bit by the time I was ten years old. One example would be that I felt like my mother never had the answers to any of my questions. From very early on, I felt that my mother was never really 'all there.' I noticed that the only thing my mother wanted to do was lounge on the couch, read trashy love novels, watch old reruns of Perry Mason, and drink Pepsi all day. Literally, this was all she did outside of going to the grocery store every Monday at three p.m. or going to the local mall. The house was always a mess. There were always huge piles of dirty laundry in the laundry room—slash—front door to enter the house, so the first thing you would see when you entered the house was mounds of laundry or there would be huge mounds of clean laundry in the living room that would take a few days to be folded. From very early on, I had a suspicion that my mother suffered from some kind of mental illness.

Today, I am hundred percent certain that my mother suffers from some kind of personality disorder. Looking back, this environment was where my extreme anxiety disorder and obsessive-compulsive need for perfection would begin. I ask myself, why didn't I offer to help my mother with chores around the house? Simple. Because I am and was a selfish little shit. Today, being in a room with a lot of clutter gives me panic attacks. If I spend more than thirty seconds in a room that is full of clutter with loud music playing, there is a good chance I will pass out. I didn't fully realize this until my mid-thirties when I would visit my parents for a weekend. I would spend a couple of nights there but when I would return home to my place in Portland, Oregon, I would feel completely exhausted and suffer from fatigue for a few days. During these visits, I would offer to help my mother while I was there, but she always said not to worry about it. To be perfectly honest with you, I would suffer from severe depression and it would throw me off for a while after visiting. Once I figured this out, I decided that it just isn't healthy for me to spend much time at my parents' house. The environment that they have created literally makes me physically and mentally uneasy. I think my mother knows this but is just incapable of improving things. It is very sad. Sometimes I wonder what people might think about the things that I say about my family. I love my family. I really do. I have just found that for my own personal mental, physical, and spiritual health, I cannot be around my family for extended periods of time. I wish it were not that way, but it just is. I have a sinking feeling that it will always be this way.

I think that most healthy stable people have a natural desire to be close to other people and that they want to always have a place to call home no matter what happens, a group of people or tribe to call his or her own. The word 'kin' literally means a group of persons descended from a common ancestor or constituting a people, clan, tribe, or family. Everyone wants to feel safe and be a part of something. But what if you just do not feel this way about the people you were born into? What do you do then? I think the only thing you can do is just be polite and accept it while at the same time creating and maintaining boundaries, kind of like Edward Norton's character in *Fight Club*. That guy was completely insane. One of my biggest fears over the years has been that my mind has been lying to me all this time. One of the first things that you learn in rehabs and twelve-step programs is that the addict brain is a sick brain and it does not have a firm grasp of reality. You also learn that addiction is a progressive disease whether you are using or not and that the only way out is a spiritual experience and a belief in a higher power. But what happens if you never have a spiritual experience or you just do not believe in a higher power? Are you fucked no matter what? And if so, why would an atheist drug addict ever want to get sober? I mean… you might as well just run it all into the ground, right? Like Nicholas Cage in *Leaving Las Vegas*. That is a perfect example of an atheist junky just going all in and riding it till the very end. To me, if you want to stay in complete control of your destiny and you have a serious chemical dependency issue, you will almost definitely end up like Cage in *Leaving Las Vegas*. I know this because I am a junky through and through, and I have seen many people fight their whole lives to be in charge while continuing to use and all of them are dead. Yet it's the ones who give up and collapse on their knees that always seem to live another day.

The way I got sober and why I stayed sober is because it all started out with sheer stubbornness. I felt like my addiction was telling me what to do and I hate that shit. Nobody tells me what to do. This stubbornness has made me homeless not once but twice in my life. My stubbornness is why I have had at least twenty-five jobs in my life. My stubbornness is why I left home at fifteen, giving up the comforts of the cozy upper-middle-class lifestyle.

With all the negatives of being a complete stubborn asshole, it has given me the first gasp of air towards sobriety. If God is real, and I am sure that He is, he probably played a major role in the first days of my getting sober. But from a twenty-two-year-old's perspective, I was just sick and tired of being pushed around. I was so sick of telling myself at two p.m. on a Friday that I was not going to drink for a couple days, and by ten p.m. that same night, I would literally be crawling up the walls. I remember one Friday night, it was about ten p.m. and the voice in my head that kept telling me to get out of the house became so loud that I just had to scream into a pillow. It was madness and I knew it was madness. I ran into the shower, got dressed, and ran out of my Downtown Portland apartment and just ran down the street until I saw a cab. I jumped in the cab perspiring heavily and like a lunatic told the driver to take me to second and Ash, which was where a handful of dive bars were located, and I knew I would have friends there to get obliterated with. I was twenty-one years old. On the outside, this was not a big deal but, on the inside, I knew something was happening. It was exciting and part of me actually liked it, but I knew I was about to run off the rails. I was still having fun but I knew that I could not do this forever. Alas! The fun would still win out for a bit longer…

I want to talk now about the conversation that changed everything for me. On my seventh birthday, my mother threw me a big birthday party at the house. Back in those days, my mother loved throwing family parties. I loved it too. Everyone would show up and everyone was still laughing and enjoying each other. It was great. I remember it was about 6:30 p.m. and mother told my stepfather to take me upstairs because she had a surprise for me. So we went upstairs. My stepfather then said that he wanted to talk to me before we went back downstairs. He told me that he knew that I was having fun now but that if I kept behaving the way I did, life would become very hard for me in the future. He told me that if I did not go to college, I would never make any money and women would not want to be a part of my life if I did not make a good living. He assured me that if I did not make good money and did not have a car, women would want nothing to do with me. Something changed for me right there. My life would never be the same after this conversation. A feeling of fear came over me. The same feeling of fear that I deal with from time to time today began at this moment. Self-doubt, self-hatred, judgment from others, and an overall sense of darkness would wash over me and it would take a lifetime to cleanse myself of it.

Looking back, part of what my father said to me became very true, other parts not so much, but for years I would believe it to be true. I believe that this conversation was the match that would start a fire that would burn for almost forty years. As an adult, I realize that my stepfather was just trying to help me. He believed what he was telling me to be the essence of existence. It was *his* philosophy and perhaps he was just trying to protect me from his experience. Or maybe he was jealous of my seamless ease and comfort at dealing with others. I was just a kid, but I wonder now if my stepfather just hated me. Was I competition for him, and if so, what kind of threat could a seven-year-old pose on a grown man? Personally, knowing what I know about human beings, I am pretty sure that it was a little bit of everything I just mentioned. Regardless of what was really going on, this single conversation was the beginning of a war that would go on between my stepfather and me for many years. The war I speak of was never a physical one. Sure, I would get mouthy once in a great while and my stepfather would pop me on the mouth, but I think this happened a total of four times in the ten years that I lived with him. No, this was more like a battle of the minds. My father, the mathematical genius and workaholic, versus me, the sweet-talking, overly polite when out in public, manipulative, always thinking one step ahead, borderline sociopathic child.

Who would win this insane battle and what was the fight all about? I will tell you what it was all about. Territory. What was the territory? My mother. This was all about ownership over my mother. I also believe that whatever was going on with my mother psychologically at the time became much worse over the years. I firmly believe that my stepfather and I helped my mother become much sicker than she ever needed to be. I also think that when I finally rejected my family and left at fifteen to live with my grandmother, it sent my mother over the edge. She would tell everyone that what was going on was normal, that it was all just a phase. My mother and I would talk about this over the years and she would always maintain that it was all just a phase. My mother would never have the mental tools to look at our family history honestly. She would never be able to look at what happened in the face because in her mind, it never even happened. It wasn't real. Everything was always fine. If this was a movie, I would think that the mother in that movie was nuts, except it's not a movie. It's our life and it's *my* mother that came apart. Now in my late thirties, I have learned to just let my mother believe what she needs to believe. Actually, that's not true. On occasion, I will bring this up when I am really pissed off at her and I feel like twisting the knife a bit. I am ashamed to admit that I have done this a few times over the years. I could just throw my hands up and say, "Hell! I am an alcoholic. What do you want from me?" That is partly true but I have also been sober for years now and I should know better. It has become a pattern that helps me cope, even though it is unhealthy and I do know better, but I still do it anyway. Sick! Sick! Sick!

So, does alcoholism or any kind of addiction just start one day? Does it start the first time you are physically abused by a family member? Does it start the first time a group of kids beat the shit out of you after school? Does it start when your ninth-grade girlfriend breaks up with you? Was it the first class you failed in college? Can one single conversation start what would become the beginning of your undoing? All of these questions are valid and many of you may have had such devastating experiences. Shit man, scientists, psychologists, parents, teachers, and everyone else with a dog in the fight has their theory on this, but nobody really knows. I have been living with this disease since the beginning, but what does that even mean? What was the beginning? I have always thought that an addict is simply born with the disease and the disease is just waiting patiently for something to give it a jumpstart so it can begin driving you away. This disease does not sleep. I don't think any disease does. I think it waits for you to feel so uncomfortable that it can plant a whisper into your mind. The whisper quietly says, "Psst, hey, yeah, you. I know what would make you feel better. I know what will make you feel great all the time. You never have to feel bad again." And then boom! Whatever it is that you gravitate towards presents itself to you somehow. You go to your first party and someone brings a bottle of vodka. You go to your uncle's house and he lets you take a hit of some weed. It's summertime and you meet a cute girl and she has a little meth. *Pop!* You are done. You can check the next fifteen years of your life right off the board. And sure, nobody has the same story. Some of us get really lucky and we figure shit out early on. Some of will use till we are well into our fifties, get sober for a few years, and die jogging up a hill. There are so many ways to live and there are just as many ways to die.

I have been presented a particular set of options and I have made my choices. The path to sobriety must begin with an acceptance of something new. I am not trying to sell you God or say that sitting in a circle with strangers will heal you. What I am doing is telling you that if you are an addict or junky, or whatever you want to call it, and you think you need to quit or you think you want to quit, you probably have a major problem. The simple math of addiction is that if your problem gets bad enough, you will die from it. That I will not debate. I will never say that if you decide to keep using, you might live a long and happy life. *No, you are going to die.* That said, do you have any question about what it is that I mean by this? If you do, then you are surely doomed. Sorry, buddy, but you do need some semblance of IQ to make it out alive. You do not have to be a genius to get sober and stay sober but you do have to know the difference between your left and your right. Unfortunately, some people do not know the difference and Mother Nature always has a way of weeding out those people. You can now take the time to get all offended by what I have just said but your disease does not care if you are offended. Remember that. Your disease actually wants you to get frustrated and angry. It's so much easier to kill you when you are pissed off!

At this point, my question to you is: what started it all off for you? How did you get here? Were you ever a happy kid or were you always miserable? What was done to you? What did that one person say that made you question your entire existence? Of course bad memories are painful, but if you can't at least try to begin to face the facts, the pain your addiction will give you will be far worse. If you can pinpoint those memories, you definitely have a fighting chance to get past your worst days. Once you can say, "Fuck! I have a serious problem and I don't want to do this anymore," and you even have an idea of what it all is. Maybe one day, you will want to talk about it with someone. Or if you have found some kind of contentment in being miserable and you are in jail right now and you don't ever want to get out, just keep reading anyways. You might just laugh your ass off while reading this. Whether you want to stop or not, I wish you all the luck in the world.

3. Phil

I was about four years old the first time I met Phil, the man that would become my stepfather. It was late afternoon, midweek, and the weather was very nice. He was very tall, very muscular, had a full dark beard, and spoke in a very deep voice. I was standing in my grandmother's kitchen watching her make coffee when Phil walked in with my mother. I was shocked. I just stared at him. He looked like a bearded superhero in normal clothes. I remember he wore prescription eyeglasses. I sized him up immediately. He frightened me but in the way you are frightened by your first rollercoaster ride. You have never seen this before but it is exciting in a way. I felt like my eyes were going to pop out of my head. My mother stood behind Phil, which I thought was very strange because my mother was always a strong, loud, and outspoken woman. But for some reason in the presence of this man, my mother shrank. She just stood behind him looking at the back of him and smiling. My grandmother was kind to him but did not seem fazed by him at all. My grandmother changed in his presence as well. Later, I would learn that my grandmother was very intimidated by Phil. I don't think any of us had ever met a man like Phil before. He was so manly, well-spoken, and physically in command of his environment. Phil was an alpha male and was in control no matter where he was. In the beginning, this would be very thrilling. Towards the end, I would find Phil to be a controlling, relentless taskmaster that would become an emotionally abusive man driven by fear and drowning in resentments. I don't think that Phil ever became as successful as he thought he would or should have become. He is an extremely well-educated man that grew up very Catholic and family is a huge deal for him and his relatives. When I left home to escape Phil, it must have been a major blow to his massive Italian, Roman Catholic ego. When a child leaves at a very young age, it is proof that something went wrong. It is impossible to hide this behind closed walls. It is all out there for everyone to see.

You may be wondering how Phil became a man that would need to be control all the time. What drove him to become such a perfectionist? Why did he isolate so much? Knowing what I know about the mind of an addict, mainly because I am one through and through, Phil's behavior is the behavior of a true addict. The difference between Phil and I is *what* we are addicted to and the fact that Phil, unlike myself, achieved success at a fairly young age. Phil was successful as an athlete, student, and entrepreneur. For the most part, he would become as much of a self-made man as one could hope to be in their lifetime. My mother and Phil were always talking about money, arguing about money, planning on making more money, and what they were going to do with all that money. Very early on, I felt a large amount of stress in the house. Even when Phil was out of the house, the feeling of stress would linger. When Phil entered the house, the feeling of tension would amp up immediately. I hated it from the very beginning and I would try to communicate my feelings to my mother, but I just didn't have the words. All I remember is wanting out. I wanted to go back to Grandma's house where we lived before my mother and Phil got married. Now I realize I was too young to remember what it was like living at my grandmother's house but I bet from a single mother's perspective, it just was not a position that my mother wanted to be in. I am sure my mother felt stressed out all the time. Having to work so hard, be away from her child so much, and rely on my grandmother for assistance must have been quite a burden. Everyone wants to be independent and just live the life they want to live. I am sure my mother felt like a bit of a failure. When I was born, my mother was only twenty-two years old. That is so young to be having children. How prepared could you possibly be to have children at that age? Plus, my mother grew up in a family that would be considered to be lower-middle-class and pretty much everyone was and is a drunk on my mother's side of the family. On top of that, my mother left home at eighteen because my mother and grandmother did not get along at all, which means my mother's personal financial situation could not have been that great. It's the typical Jerry Springer episode of babies having babies.

Knowing what I know about my mother and her childhood, I think meeting a somewhat successful man like my stepfather would in a way be like winning some kind of lottery. My mother's biological father, my Grandpa Dave was a physically abusive alcoholic if there ever was one. I am pretty sure that he abused my grandmother while they were married because she said the only reason why she would leave a man was if they laid a hand on her. Well, she left my Grandpa Dave and got remarried to my Grandpa Glen who was no prize either. Glen married my grandmother who already had four children when they met and they would have one more, my Aunt Michelle, who would turn out to be the worst out of everyone. If you have ever seen an episode of that television show *Intervention* where the mom has been homeless for years and smokes all day and has a gambling addiction, well, that's my Aunt Michelle. It's one of the saddest things ever, but if a person doesn't want help and they are that far gone, you kind of have to let them go. It sucks to be that kind of person, but for your own survival, you just have to let them go. It's even worse when someone like this leaves children behind and the only options that you have are that the children either have to live with an already-burdened family member or risk losing them to the system. It also really sucks that the innocent children of addicts are usually the ones who suffer the most.

So, back to Phil. Back to the subjects of war and taking hostages. I almost forgot about my half-brother, Joseph. Poor Joseph! I could not imagine being my brother, Joe. For one, I have always resented his existence. It's a mixture of jealousy, feeling I am better than him, and just being pissed off because once Joseph was born, I now had to share my mother with yet another asshole that I never really wanted around. (Sorry Joe—brutal honesty) I was excited about Joseph being born for about ten minutes. Once he was born, I was over him in less than a year. We looked nothing alike, we acted nothing alike, and we had nothing in common. I remember very few memories of living with my half-brother, Joe. I could only imagine what it would be like to have a big brother that never wanted anything to do with you. When I left home, I never once thought how that affected my brother. I just obsessed over how Joseph was so lucky because he got to have the life I always wanted just because he was born at the right time to the right people for him. Joseph got to be born to two parents that would always stay together and he would always have his own room and he would have a father that would love and support him no matter what. If I sneezed wrong, Phil would correct me and show me how one is supposed to sneeze. When it came to my brother, he could do no wrong. I would take the position of what you call the scapegoat child. No matter what went wrong in the house, I was somehow to blame. My brother loved animals and farming and getting dirty. We lived way out in the middle of nowhere surrounded by farms, so my brother was basically as happy as a pig in shit. Meanwhile, I was fucking miserable. Where were all the people? Where was all the action? I grew up on a street where maybe a tractor or a truck would go by every twenty minutes. I felt like Kevin Bacon in *Footloose* when he first moves to that shitty little Christian town where dancing was illegal and it was all run by that crazy preacher. Well, my new stepfather was my crazy preacher dad. It fucking sucked!

I appreciated nothing that was given to me back then. When my mother married Phil, we went struggling from lower working class to upper-middle-class overnight. Literally, our financial lives were improved to a level that I had never seen and may have never seen if my mother had not met Phil. What he did for us was truly amazing. But what I never understood back then and what I do not understand today is: why all the negative energy? Why did everything have to be so black and white, so cut and dry? Why couldn't our household have been friendlier and more relaxed? Over the years, I have gone to friends' houses where the families obviously had more money than my parents but the feeling in the house was much more pleasant. The houses were cleaner, the moms were in better shape, and the dads were nicer. My friends would actually have nice things to say about their families, which was foreign to me. My friends were not better students; they were not any more or less intelligent than I was. Why was my family so fucked up and intolerable to be around? I still wonder if this was all in my head or that maybe I was just some evil little fucker. Was I the cause of all this shit? My therapists and AA meetings have all assured me that I was just a kid and I am not to blame for all the things that went wrong in my family. Many kids from dysfunctional families have to learn the mantra, "It's not my fault. It wasn't my fault." I had a part in it, but I was not the only issue. Growing up, I was told countless times that I was manipulative and that I was doing everything wrong. So whom am I supposed to believe? Don't doctors just tell you what you want to hear as long as you pay them for their time? And Alcoholics Anonymous does have a bad reputation for being a place that attracts mentally ill people that cosign one another's bad behavior. I have personally witnessed this in my years attending AA meetings. Yes, I still go to AA meetings on a regular basis but everything has its pluses and minuses. Alcoholics getting together and patting each other on the back for an hour like they are little babies is definitely a minus.

I often ask myself what my stepfather thinks about my involvement with Alcoholics Anonymous. What is his opinion on my going to therapy off and on since I was sixteen years old? I take medication for anxiety and clinical depression. I grew up with Phil telling us that kids are overmedicated and basically that everybody is weak or dumb. I mean, this guy just didn't have any empathy for anyone. I basically became the kind of person that he has no respect for. I never finished college, I am mentally ill, I cry on occasion, I hate manual labor, and I hate guns, knives, bullets, and anything else that is sharp or will explode and make a loud noise. I just want life to be one big spa day. I prefer massages, facials, and expensive haircuts. I guess I am just a big pussy. Phil was always the type of person I would make fun of, mainly for being more successful than me but also for being so fucking socially awkward. And I think I was also the type of person that Phil would hate because our value systems were so different and because some of the things that came so hard for him came so easily to me. *Touché*, I guess. Life just isn't fair for anybody. But at the end of the day, I live in a tiny SRO in North Beach, San Francisco, and my stepfather owns two homes, hundreds of acres, and all the toys a man could want. From the outside, the better man won. From the inside, maybe both of us were and are still suffering.

4. The Other Neverland Ranch

Mental illness has played a major role in my life. It isn't easy to admit this but my struggle with mental illness started before anything else in my life. It started before puberty, before my first girlfriend, before my first cigarette, and my first hit of weed. In my case, I feel like my mental illness came before the chicken or the egg. I can't say exactly when but I started noticing that something was off by the time I was ten. I think the first time I experienced anxiety was during my sixth birthday. My parents allowed me to invite all of my classmates during my first-grade year and everyone showed up. I was after all the most popular boy in class and I would remain so all the way through the ninth grade, which was right before everything went south. All of my classmates were running up and down the stairs of my house and back and forth between my room and the bedroom that would eventually become my brother's room. All the kids were playing with my toys and almost breaking things and I was about to lose my mind. The chaos was too much for me: the screaming and shouting and the girls turning everything into a game of tug of war. All that energy inside our house! If it were outside, it would not have bothered me so much but the volume of the screams combined with the running in and out of hallways gave me what I would consider my first panic attack. Once we all got to Chucky Cheese for pizza, I was fine but that hour at my house was pure hell. It was as if I was born with post-traumatic stress disorder or something.

When I was ten years old, I started experiencing these random intense feelings wash over me to the point where I just wanted to disappear. I never had violent thoughts but I just felt that it would be so much easier if I didn't exist anymore. I would ask my mother why I couldn't live with my real dad. She would tell me that my real dad doesn't have any money and he lives in a very small apartment and he can't always be around. She would ask me if I wanted to live like that. I would just cry and say no. This was about the time where I noticed that at school, I was always very happy and the center of attention but when I got home, the other me would come out. All I would want to do was watch TV or go in my room. I never wanted to go outside and play. I always wanted all my mother's attention or I would beg my mother to take me somewhere like the mall or Grandma's house. I wanted to be anywhere but home. I hated home. At night, our house was scary. The house was an old farmhouse and it just looked like it was from out of a horror movie. On occasion, I would hear things under my bed or my bed would vibrate. Also, my stepfather would walk around the house naked late at night, which totally freaked me out. I always thought it was some weird kind of caveman thing to do. I found it to be a very threatening way to behave. I never felt comfortable in that house for the ten years that I lived there. I felt that there were forces that were against me and wanted me out. I would talk to my mother about it, but she would just push me off or tell me to go play, always lounging on her couch reading trashy novels. From the very beginning when I felt bad, my mom was checked out and my stepfather was always forcing things to fit the way he wanted them to fit, regardless of what it was.

Once I reached the seventh grade, my parents put me in private school. I really liked the kids and I became very popular very quickly and all the cutest girls liked me and showed me attention. Socially, I was a success but my grades plummeted. This drove my parents insane, especially my stepfather. My father was always having these long conversations with me about education, money, grades, and the way the world worked. It bored the shit out of me. This was when I really wanted to escape from reality but I didn't know how. I didn't have any talents to speak of other than the gift to gab. I liked talking. I didn't care whom I was talking to; I just loved talking. That was all I had. I would find someone to talk to and just tell stories. Some were true and some weren't, but this was the only time I was happy. I tried out for sports but they just didn't hold my interest and I found jocks to be idiots. When in conversation, I was always in charge. Even with adults, I could not only keep up, but also I could take the lead. I had questions and I wanted to talk about things that interested me at the moment. I loved talking about rock and roll, my favorite TV shows, movies, girls with big boobs, and the list could go on. I wanted to be Bon Jovi, Tom Cruise, or Arnold Schwarzenegger. *Anyone but me.* Actually, I didn't want to be in the life I was in. I wanted to be me but I wanted to live in a mansion and I wanted to drive a Lamborghini. Basic kid shit… except if *I* couldn't have what I wanted, I just wanted to die. That's the part that isn't normal. At least it wasn't normal when I was a kid. Today, kids are shooting up schools and theaters because they were told 'no' too many times. I know it's not that simple but you get my point. Today, in my late thirties, I look back at who I was and at my worst, I feel sorry for my parents. There is no handbook for raising kids but there definitely is no handbook for raising a high-functioning mentally ill kid with a really high IQ but with no skills to use it. What a fucking disaster! It's like putting a drunk teenager at the wheel of Porsche 911 and just letting him loose.

When I was about twelve years old, I spent a week with a friend during my summer vacation. His parents managed a golf course and they lived in a house on the grounds. It was such a fun week. Nothing went wrong. Once, we snuck out in the middle of the night and we drove one of the golf carts all over the course. We played with the sprinklers, nothing too crazy. On my last day when my parents came to pick me up, my friend and I drove the golf cart around one more time before I had to go. I put the golf cart in reverse and I smashed into some poor guy's van. But this wasn't just any van. It was one of those seventies' vans with a painted mural on the side. Of course, I hit the van and destroyed the mural. The owner of the van came running out, screaming. He freaked out. I was just stunned because none of it seemed real. The guy looked like a Hell's Angel gang member. He had long dark hair and a thick beard and he was pissed. Of course, my stepfather had to deal with the situation and my parents had to pay the guy cash or he was going to call the cops. Needless to say, Phil did not speak to me for a very long time. I never saw that friend ever again. This would be just one example of me fucking something up. I never got away with anything and punishments were swift. I spent a lot of time in my room from the age of ten until I finally left at fifteen. I was grounded pretty much all the time. Being stuck in my room for days at a time with no interaction with anyone really fucked with my head.

A lot of my days were like school, right back home after school and up to my room, downstairs for dinner, back to my room except for bathroom breaks and back to school, and wash and repeat for days and days on end. For some reason, this didn't fix the problem. This never fixed me. My parents tried so many kinds of punishments but nothing worked. In middle school, I began to think I was stupid. I was miserable at spelling and even worse at math. My stepfather would get so frustrated with me. We would go over the same problem over and over again and I never understood what he was talking about. I would get so frustrated that I would cry. We would stay up for hours on a ten-problem math assignment. I would go to bed dizzy, exhausted, and emotionally destroyed. This cycle stayed with me throughout school and did not change until I would reach college later in life. While my father was trying to explain some random math problem, I would have panic attacks. I had no idea what was happening at the time but they were definitely panic attacks. These were some of the worst days. It was like my father was speaking a whole other language that I was just unable to pick up. My stepfather is a math genius, so I bet it was extremely frustrating for him that I could not grasp something that came so naturally to him. My father is to math what Mozart is to music. He is probably the smartest person I have ever met but his emotional IQ is probably negative twelve. He is not able to have conversations with the average person. It's kind of like Albert Einstein needing assistance with balancing his checkbook. It was so simple that it was impossible for him because he thought on such a high level. I am the complete opposite of my stepfather. I have a very high emotional IQ but the part of my brain that is needed for math must just be shut off. That's probably just an excuse for my laziness or lack of interest. I know that dyslexia runs in my biological father's side of the family. My father and all his brothers have dyslexia, so I would not be surprised if I have it. I just never took the time to get checked for it.

I would have to say the year that I turned fifteen was the beginning of the end for my immediate family. Once I went into the ninth grade, everything just fell apart so quickly. My depression started to become very serious. I admitted to my grandmother that I was suicidal and I told her that I didn't want to live at home anymore. My grandmother could tell I was serious and that things were becoming very real. My parents were always fighting about money and me. I don't think they could afford two children. My mother was always yelling at Phil about money. It was so stressful. I would go up to my room and just listen to my mother yell at my stepfather. I always thought we were going to lose our house and become homeless. I would ride my bike to my grandmother's house, which was a two-hour bike ride away. I would immediately relax once I got to her house. I would arrive all sweaty but so relieved. Every time I approached my grandmother's front door, I felt like my life was being saved yet again. I just wanted it all to end. I think that my stepfather fought with me because it was always a fight he could win. My father could not win an argument with my mother. I just sat there and took whatever she would say to him like a grain of salt. Personally, I would divorce any woman that spoke to me the way my mother spoke to my stepfather. I don't know how he survived those years. Actually, yes I do. He worked in his workshop at least ten hours a day, seven days a week, and always had projects around the house. Our house and the property that our house was built on were full of unfinished projects. I lived with my parents for ten years and my stepfather never finished our staircase. For years, the bottom step was missing and only half of the stairs had carpet. It looked like crazy people lived there. Technically, crazy people did live there. My father was and still is a machine. He will wake up at five in the morning, mow a four-acre lawn, work on some random tech project for some random tech company, take an hour lunch break, clean some of his hunting rifles, practice the banjo, lift some weights, eat dinner at six in the evening, go back to his workshop and work on another tech project, come inside and watch a sci-fi movie with my mom, and then off to bed at exactly nine-thirty in the evening. Keep in mind that this is what my stepfather's day looks like every day. No vacations—just work, working out, and work projects. Who else can do this? Guys like Donald Trump, Bill Gates, and Tony Robbins do this. You can't get to know guys like this. It is literally impossible unless they either really like you or you are their flesh and blood. Other than that, you just do not exist. This is how my stepfather has been able to stay married to my mother all those years. He ignored her. That was probably why she was always yelling at him.

I found all of this completely nuts. My stepfather's addiction to work, my mother's denial and multiple personalities, and my half-brother's existence just weren't for me. I wanted to live in a day spa that would ideally be located next door to nice restaurants, parks, and other random things to do. I would beg my mother to get us out of that old farmhouse and somewhere with people and shit to do. Where we lived had a Wacko Texas vibe to it and my stepfather had a bit of a cult-leader thing about him. Towards the end of my time with my family, everybody's neurosis seemed to be getting worse. Everything and everybody was getting angrier and more intense. My mother wasn't bathing as much and Phil would wear the same work clothes for days at a time and he smelled like oil and smoke like he had been working in a coalmine all day. It was all so uncomfortable and I wanted out. During the Christmas holidays, I started planning how I would escape my family. I had no money and I knew my parents would not give me money if I left. Of course I was a spoiled asshole, so I did not want to work. I would not work. Needless to say, I never came up with a solid plan but I knew my time was almost up as far as living with my family was concerned. I started asking my grandmother if I could live with her for a while. At first, she told me that I wouldn't like living with her because she didn't have the kind of money that my parents had. I didn't care, so I just kept working on my grandmother. A month later, I would bike over to my grandmother's house and fill her in on the latest drama at my house, and finally my grandmother told me she would think about it. She would always say, "Let's just see how things work out." Once my grandmother started saying that I knew I was in.

My original plan was to move in with my grandparents at the beginning of my summer vacation. Now that I had a plan, my confidence was up and I started talking back even more to my parents. I became even more disrespectful. I kept adding up reasons in my mind why it was a good idea for me to leave. A few days before my ninth-grade spring break, I asked my mother if I could stay with my grandparents during the one-week break. Luckily, my mother said 'yes' without hesitation. I think she just wanted a break from everything, mainly me, since I was the source of most of the arguments. A couple of days later, my mother told me that my family was going to Dallas, Texas, to visit my godmother and they were bringing my grandmother with them, so it would just be my grandfather and me for the week. This was great news because I knew my friends would be having parties all week and my grandfather was so out of it that he wouldn't notice that I would be gone. Once my family left for Texas, I told my grandfather that I was going to stay the week with a friend of mine and he just said, "Whatever you want to do." Spring break 1995 would prove to be the silver bullet that would take down my family.

The Friday that kicked off spring break, my best friend Mike and I went over to a friend's house and a party began that would go the entire week of our break. The first time I ever smoked pot, got drunk off my ass, took ecstasy, acid, mescaline, and smoked heroin was all during this break while staying at that house. All of the family drama at home and overall uncertainty that a teenager feels disappeared during that week. I went from zero to one hundred miles an hour in five seconds flat. I completely lost it, but at the same time I was found. I was finally home. I wanted to feel the way drinking and drugs made me feel all the time and I would never go back to the way things were ever again. I would rather die. Once the week went by and all the money, booze, and drugs ran out, we all slithered away back to where we came from. It was Sunday and that night, my mother came by to pick me up from my grandparents' house. It was about a fifteen-minute drive back home and I told my mother that I needed to talk to her. We were about to have *the* talk. I gently told my mother that I thought living with my grandparents would be the best thing for all of us. My mother just listened. I gave her my sales pitch on how things would be more positive if I didn't live with them anymore. We talked for a couple hours and I could see in my mother's face that she was actually considering my idea. My mother said that she agreed that I had a point and that it would possibly be for the best. She also told me that in a few months, my parents were going to sell the house and buy a ranch in Eastern Oregon. I knew this was my chance to get out. My mother knew that I would not survive out in the middle of nowhere. Later, I would found out that my father sold our original house for the ranch because he knew I wouldn't want to go. My parents really wanted to end things just as much as I did. Nobody had any other idea on how to fix the mess that was our family.

Breaking it up and just cutting our losses seemed to be the only thing left to do. We simply just didn't like one another.

I would live with my parents for one more week after that spring break. My grandfather would pick me up early that Sunday afternoon. I loaded up four large bags full of clothing, an alarm clock, and my mother gave me $220.00 in $20.00 bills. She hugged me before I eagerly got into my grandfather's car. No words were exchanged during that car ride. My grandfather didn't really talk much, so I was not surprised. He never gave advice and he never tried to pretend that he had all the answers when it came to life because he had failed in very big ways over the years. During my time with my grandparents, I would learn more about the catastrophic financial mistakes that my grandfather had made that completely ruined their financial lives and would drive them into poverty for many years.

In the beginning, living with my grandparents was very surreal. I had become so accustomed to arguing with my parents, so much that I was relaxed yet a little uneasy by how quiet my grandparents' house was. My grandparents rarely spoke to each other. On occasion, they would tell each other what they were about to do. My grandfather would tell my grandmother that he was going to make a sandwich while my grandmother was working on a puzzle. Or my grandmother would tell my grandfather that she was going to the garden to pull some weeds while my grandfather smoked a cigarette in his chair in the living room. I did not realize how much my grandfather smoked until living with him but he easily smoked about two packs a day. He would sit in his chair and just chain-smoke for an hour and stare at the wall. What was he thinking about? It was a bit creepy. I learned quickly not to bring friends over because I would have to introduce them to my grandfather. I would say, "Grandpa, this is Mike!" My grandfather would nod and half-smile and then continue smoking his cigarette in his chair. He had very limited communication skills and was basically deaf from using power tools for years without wearing ear protection. I do not mean to be disrespectful but my grandfather was not a very intelligent man. Growing up with my genius stepfather and then living with my not-so-smart grandfather with next to no people skills and deaf on top of it all was a bit of a shock at first. It was one thing to visit for the day but to live with this was a bit strange. If my grandmother went out of town, my grandfather would not say a word until she returned. He could not cook, so all he would eat would be sandwiches or cereal, maybe soup to go with his sandwich. I found my grandfather to be a very bleak person. I felt sorry for him but also frustrated and embarrassed at the same time. My relationship with him was always very much on the surface. I can't remember having one deep conversation with him, ever, not because I didn't want to but because he could not hear me, and he was just so full of that kind of fear that so many men from his generation feel. I can't relate to it and I don't think many men from my generation or any generation after his could relate to the things they have been through and seen. I am completely aware of the fact that most men today, including myself, are total pussies. I grew up with my grandfather telling me to stop being so lazy or stop being a pansy. My stepfather was always telling me to stop primping in the mirror. Why in the fuck do old men always give a shit what you are doing with your hair? I never understood why older men were so offended by how long I took to get ready. Go fuck yourself!

That first summer with my grandparents was extremely rocky. I immediately started acting out. All I could think about was how much I wanted to drink and smoke pot and how my parents abandoned me. I would not realize until I was thirty how moving out of my parents' house was my idea. I was so self-absorbed and insane back then. My grandparents would give me simple rules to follow like, "Be home by ten," or "Lights out at eleven." I wouldn't do anything that my grandmother asked me to do. I just wanted to get high and fade away. I just wanted to disappear and get comfort. At this time, I did not even know where to get pot and there was never any alcohol in the house. On top of that, I was just not very resourceful. In August of 1995, I would take to walking the streets. I would look for kids around my age that looked like they might be partiers. The neighborhood I was in was full of senior citizens at the time or straight-laced couples in their thirties with very young children. There were no cool kids anywhere. I would walk around for hours and come up empty-handed every time. Finally, on a hot summer August day, I saw a couple of guys around my age playing hacky sack. They were both wearing tie-dye shirts. And the whole area around them smelled like pot. I knew immediately that they were exactly the type of people I needed to meet. I said to one of the guys, "Hey, do you guys know where I can get some acid?"

One of the guys said, "Yeah, do you smoke?"

I replied with, "Yeah!" I could barely contain myself. I felt like I was being asked to prom. I realized that the two guys that were playing hacky sack looked exactly alike, except that one had brown hair and the other one had poorly bleached blond hair. They looked like total stoner skater kids. I always wanted to be a stoner skater kid, so this was perfect. One of them said, "My name is Phil. This is my brother, Russ. Come down to our basement."

I said, "Cool, my name is Marques. You live right here?"

Phil's brother said, "Yeah, come check our basement out. It's awesome." I could tell immediately that Russ was the friendlier of the two and Phil was much more reserved and serious. I knew that Russ and I would become friends right away. The best thing was that I was on Fourth and Grant and they were on Third and Grant. We went down to their basement and the whole room blew me away. There were Bob Marley posters, five different bongs, glass-blown pipes, a bunk bed for people that partied a bit too hard and needed to crash over for the night—which I would do on a very regular basis. Phil and Russ' mother were always gone. She was a professor and a bit of a hippy. For some reason, she didn't care that we smoked pot all day and night. I would smoke so much pot with them that I did not even realize that they were also in college fulltime. They were both gifted students, and when they were sixteen, they were already finishing their second year of college. All I focused on was the pot and the mushrooms. I had no goals outside of getting high. I just wanted to see how far I could take it.

Phil and Russ were always able to balance the crazy parties and traveling with real-world shit. I just couldn't do that. I am an all-or-nothing person. In the summer of 1996, Phil, Russ, myself, and a bunch of our friends would travel the entire summer. We went to Rainbow Gatherings, Burning Man, week-long drum circle parties, and raves all over the US… You name it, we did it. It was amazing and I never wanted it to end. Phil and Russ would do their homework and find ways to sign up for next term classes while on the road. I would go on two-week ecstasy binges, forget to eat, and go to the hospital for dehydration and exhaustion. This would happen at least once a month. I met a girl named Clearwater in Washington State and followed her to Miami, Florida, only for her to tell me I was annoying her. Phil and Russ would tell me that we had to leave in the morning and I would end up meeting some people from Phoenix, leave with them, and finally come home six days later. I would come home and my grandmother would be furious with me. At the time, I was sixteen and seventeen years old and I was living like a modern-day hobo. I loved it, but my grandmother hated this about me. I just didn't live in reality and I had no respect for the feelings of others.

At this time, I had all but forgotten about my mother, stepfather, and half-brother. When people asked about my family life or my parents, I just told people that they were dead. My life was a bit of a mystery to my friends. Soon, I would meet other people that had voluntarily orphaned themselves: runaways, squatters, kids that lived in school buses for a year and just traveled the country. Those were my people. But even when I was in a crowd of these kids, I still didn't feel like I belonged. I was a bit smarter than all of them and the conversations bored me after a while. Every other word was 'dude' or 'bro!' I found it difficult to find my intellectual equals and this became a whole new kind of loneliness. All the acid, mescaline, and DMT really blew my mind open whether I liked it or not. It made reality even harder to deal with because now I was thinking about really obscure thoughts, out-of-body experiences, non-verbal psychic conversations with strangers, and Reiki. The only people thinking about this stuff were shamans or hippies in their fifties. I was just a kid. What the hell did I know?

My sophomore year of high school was horrible. The drugs were shitty and hard to find, and everybody seemed, well, stupid and extremely provincial. I had gotten used to hanging out in Portland and made a lot of friends of different ages in the city. I would crash on the weekends at an older friend's house and we would go to raves. Then on Monday, I was back to school. High school kids back in the nineties were lame and I am sure it's not any better now. I have never met a cool high school kid in my life. When I was sixteen, all my friends were twenty-five and older. Going back to high school every Monday was depressing. I knew that when my tenth-grade year was over, I would have to come up with a Plan B. My summer vacation before my junior year of high school was when the drugs really kicked in. I was starting to do everything and time was going by in the most abstract of ways. Eventually, I decided on going to community college. I found out that you could take really big class loads and just get all of your high school requirements out of the way. I would finish my next two years of high school in once year of community college. I did whatever it took so I could just party my fucking eyes out.

Fast forward to summer vacation 1996:

My relationships with Phil and Russ were still strong but Phil was getting a bit weird from all the mushrooms that he'd been doing, and Russ got a girlfriend in her late twenties, so he was busy getting his mind blown with incredible sex. I was still determined to take things to the next level. I wanted to achieve permanent bliss. In June of 1996, I would sneak my way into a commune in Springfield, Oregon. There were about eighty people living there—ages ranging from sixteen to about sixty. I was seventeen. My job was to keep the weeds out of the cornrows and pick seeds out of the marijuana. I would visit my grandmother a few times during my stay at the commune (that shall remain nameless). I told her that I was taking a live-in farming class at the University of Oregon. My grandmother knew I was lying but I could tell she knew I was safe somehow. I really hated tending to the corn, since that was a chore that I had to do when I was living with my parents and I promised myself that I would never farm again. As before, the whole getting-dirty thing didn't appeal to me. I did however love picking seeds out of marijuana. The problem was that I would smoke some of it and then just wander off and think about weird shit. I would leave the water hose running and just let it pour over me, and one of the head camp commune guys would see me doing this and start yelling at me. I was so disappointed because I had put so much energy into finding a place without rules but I realized that this place didn't exist. There is no such thing as *Neverland.* I was officially kicked out of the commune after about ninety days. It took me four days to get back home to my grandparents' house. When I finally walked through the door, my grandmother simply got up and started making me eggs and bacon with orange juice. For some reason, my grandmother thought that breakfast could fix anything. After the eggs and bacon, I would lie in bed for a few days and recuperate from my strange defeat. Little did I know that I would lose many more times in my life and I would lie in bed trying to come up with a new scheme or idea on how to succeed. But succeed at what? I had no skills. I lacked true ambition. I had no threshold for the pain it takes to get ahead. I just wanted immediate gratification. Drugs! I would just do more drugs. At this time in my life, drugs and alcohol appeared to be so reliable, maybe the only thing that was hundred percent reliable. I always knew what I would get when I did my drugs of choice. The drugs still worked. I had no idea that the drugs would ever stop working. It never seemed like a possibility.

During the summer of 1997, I found myself selling large quantities of marijuana, LSD, and ecstasy. It all happened so fast. I bought $400.00 worth of marijuana from Phil and Russ, and within a few days, I turned that into $1000.00, and a couple weeks after that, I had $7000.00. It all just kind of happened. A few months later, I had about $80,000.00 hiding in my room. For about a year, I turned my bedroom into a small pharmacy without my grandparents even knowing it. In late 1997, for a few months, I was Boise Idaho's main connection to high-end LSD. This was my scariest deal ever. Four guys drove up to my grandmother's house while my grandparents were watching *Wheel of Fortune.* I answered the door and saw that all four guys had really big guns with side holsters. I took a quick ride around the block with them and showed them $60,000.00 dollars' worth of high-grade LSD, and they turned that into close to $140,000. It was easy money for everybody. I was eighteen years old and a few months from quitting all this. I just didn't know it yet.

Even today, I can look back at my drug-dealing career fondly. There were only a few deals that really freaked me out. The first deal was when I was splitting twelve pounds of psilocybin mushrooms into quarter-pound bags and there was a knock at the door. It was one a.m. and something didn't feel right. My partner at the time shoved what he could in a bag and ran into our other friend's bedroom and hid under the bed as I answered the door. When I answered the door, there was a very shiny handgun in my face. There were two very tall men in black ski masks (of course), and they just barged in. I didn't have any time to think. I was in shock. I ran to the room that my partner was in and locked the door. Our other friend that lived in the apartment was running after them, which I knew, even while in shock, was a very bad idea. After about ten minutes, we went back into the living room where the craziness happened. Our friend started yelling at us and asked why we didn't help him. We didn't say anything. In the drug game, we committed a major sin. We were pussies and people would find out that we were pussies. Once people figure out that you are a pussy, a lot of other rumors would fly around. We knew it. This is just the nature of the beast.

A week would go by and there were no calls and no rumors getting back to us. In most cases, no news is good news but in this world, that isn't always the case. From what I had heard, no news can mean a lot of really bad things. We were all kids and living with our parents. There was just too much at risk from my point of view. My partner went right back to dealing a couple of days after the incident, but I was the cautious one. I had enough to buy my way out of this game. I had not gotten that big yet and I was close to my connections. But I knew that buying my way out too soon could be a mistake as well. I would just lie low for a few more weeks. Once my nerves had settled down and felt like things were safe, I decided that I would make the calls needed in order to get out of the mess I was in. I had an idea of what it would cost me and I had what was needed. That same week, I would receive a call. It was an old friend of mine from Jr. High. I called him Matt. Matt told me that he heard that I could get large amounts of acid and that he and some friends wanted to by ten thousand hits of acid. This would not be a problem at all. In the back of my mind, I felt that this was perfect timing because I could get acid for really cheap and make a killing off the turn around. This is called 'greed,' my friends. Very few people are able to tell successful stories about greed. I am barely one of those people.

At the time, I could get a hit of acid for a dollar for up to twenty thousand hits and then the price would go down to fifty cents a hit. I would sell the ten thousand hits for five dollars a hit straight across to Matt and make a nice profit and get the fuck out of all this. Matt and I arranged a time, date, and place. Everything but the place felt good. Matt wanted to meet on a Friday right after his last school period. Meeting in the middle of a high school didn't feel right to me, but I agreed. We were to meet in four days. I already had everything I needed, and after this last exchange, I'd drop the rest of my product off to my connection in Eugene, Oregon, and pay my exit deposit. At the time, I had about six pounds of high-quality marijuana, two pounds of mushrooms, fifty thousand hits of acid, and roughly one thousand tabs of ecstasy. This amount would never make me big time, but it was a small fortune for a seventeen-year-old. There would also be a lot of years in prison if I got caught. I usually had someone to make these runs for me but I wanted to save as much money as possible and runners cut into your profit big time. I would have had to pay the kid I usually paid five grand for this drop. Plus, the kid I normally used wasn't available, and although he had a recommendation for someone to take his place, there was no way I was doing that. I would just make this last run myself. I have always been a romantic and I wanted to take complete control of my destiny.

That next Friday, I would wake up, find three old schoolbooks, carve a four-by-four-inch hole in each book, place the three-by-three-inch sheets of acid in the book holes, close the books, and wrap them so they would look like gifts for someone. This was how I always shipped acid. I put the books in a bag and would eventually make my way to Matt's high school. When I arrived, it was about two p.m. I noticed right away that there were only a few cars in the school parking lot. Maybe it was a half-day for the students? I walked to the agreed meeting spot, the outdoor student square located right outside the student lunch hall. The place was empty. This was very strange to me, and while my brain was telling me that this was not right and that I needed to leave now, a middle-aged man came out of a separate building. I started walking away. The man yelled, "Excuse me, young man! Are you a student here?" I told the man that I was meeting a friend that went to the school but I think I had the wrong day. The man told me that I needed to stop. The parking lot was right behind the man who I would find out was the school's vice principal. I could see two police vehicles pulling into the large school parking lot. My face became very hot and I started to see black blotches and stars, like I had been staring at the sun for ten minutes too long. My stomach felt like it was full of battery acid and my mouth was so dry. I could taste aspirin in the back of my throat. The school principal said a few things to me but I was in complete shock. I could not speak. I watched one of the police officers open up his backdoor and a German Shepherd excitedly hopped out of the car. I knew I was spending the rest of my life in prison. I said nothing. This was a completely new territory for me and I had no tools to handle it. Within a couple of minutes, the four policemen and German Shepherd drug dog met up with the school's vice principal and me. They asked the vice principal what seemed to be the problem.

That was when I knew that I had been set up. Cops don't just arbitrarily show up to a school with a trained drug dog right as a school's vice principal is talking to a drug dealer. Fuck! Fuck! Fuck! The vice principal told the police officers that he was trying to figure out why I was at his school. The police officers asked me if I was a student at the school. I told them no and that I was there to meet a student to hang out after school. The police asked me what we planned on doing.

"What?" I asked.

The police officer repeated the question, "Why were you meeting this student?"

"To hang out," I said.

Everyone just looked at me like I was a total idiot. "What is the student's name?" one officer asked.

"Matt."

"What is Matt's last name?"

Shit, I knew he was going to ask that. "I don't know."

"You don't know your friend's last name?"

"No," I replied. I told them that I must have the wrong day. One of the police officers told me that they were going to need me to follow them to the principal's office. Fuck! We walked to the principal's office. They told me that they had a reason to believe that I had drugs on me and that I had intended on selling to someone at this school. I told them that I was just there to meet a friend. They told me they were going to need to search me. They began to search my bag. Before I knew it, I was in my boxer shorts, T-shirt, and socks. One police officer asked me what the presents were for. I said that I was on my way to a birthday party and those were gifts. "I thought you were going to hang out with Matt?" one officer asked me. I told them that after hanging out with Matt, I was going to a birthday party. We would go round and round like this for another ten minutes or so. The whole time I was just wondering why the police officers didn't just unwrap my books and take a closer look. The officer holding the books told me that they had not been able to find anything and that they couldn't hold me any longer. I could tell that they all knew I had drugs on me. This was just impossible. Why didn't the police officer check my books? Why did Matt set me up? What the fuck was this all about?

I put my clothes back on and walked right out of there. I was stunned. I walked to a friend's house that lived just ten minutes from the school and asked to use his phone. I called my connection in Eugene and told him I wanted out. We talked on the phone for about an hour. I was told to bring what I had left—my records and $85,000.00. This would be the easiest part.

This I could do. That Sunday, Phil and Russ would drive me to Eugene and I would drop everything off. There were no hard feelings or guns or anything dark like that. My connection was a retired professor in his late fifties. He had a long gray ponytail and beard to match. I mean, he looked like a Grateful Dead fan. But if you fucked up, who knows what would have happened. There were no rumors about my guy. It was as if nobody knew he existed. He was very smart and I am sure that was the way he liked it. He was a lot like Brad Pitt in the film, *The Big Short*, really calm and always gardening. He is the reason why I started getting colonics. He always swore by colonics, so I started getting them twice a year.

A few months later, I learned why Matt set me up. Back in Jr. High, Matt's girlfriend broke up with him right before summer vacation in order to start dating me. She actually told Matt this. I had no idea. We hung out a few times but she wasn't my type. I always liked short, thick women with a big booty and she was just too skinny and a white girl from the suburbs, which just wasn't my thing. So Matt decided that taking revenge on me was the best idea. Jesus Christ! People suck sometimes. I saw Matt one more time after all this, a few years later, at some random house party. I was a bit drunk at the time and walked up to him and smiled at him. I just stared into his eyes and smiled. Eventually, he walked away without saying anything. That was the end of that.

The reason why I am telling you this story about my dealing days is because dealing drugs fed my addiction even more than the drugs and alcohol ever did. Dealing drugs and being the big man on campus fed my ego. I believe that an addict's ego is the foundation of their disease. It has often been said that all addicts are narcissists. I believe that addiction is a three-part disease. Addiction is attached to your mind, body, and soul. Every inch of your being is involved. Drugs and alcohol gave me a little confidence and helped to quiet the negative voice in my head, but dealing drugs made me feel like a god. I had all the answers when I was a drug dealer. People came to me in order to be saved and they paid me very well for my answers. When I drank and used, I was just a spectator. As a drug dealer, I was all-powerful. But there was some good in me. I would give up that amazing feeling of invincibility in order to keep my loved ones safe. If anything happened to my grandmother, that would be the end. I owe my grandmother everything. But if I was going to quit dealing, I was going to use more. After all, I deserved it. I did something good and I wanted my reward.

After I quit dealing, my drinking and drug use skyrocketed. For about two years, I would smoke two eighths of weed a day, drink on a nightly basis, drop acid and ecstasy every weekend, and soon heroin started to show up. I would become a DJ and play at underground raves. I met a gorgeous Goth raver girl and she introduced me to her friends. They were into dark trance music, Wiccan magic, heroin, cutting each other, and group sex. The cutting turned me off but the heroin and group sex really blew my world open. I had always wanted to be a Jim Morrison cult figure type, and I felt that I was finally on my way. I was eighteen years old and everyone around me was thirty-something. I was going to the coolest parties and never getting home until ten a.m. At times, I would have my own place or I would live with six people or I would move back home to grandma's for a few months in order to get away from all the craziness. Whenever I came home, my grandmother would just go into the kitchen and make me more bacon and eggs with a side of orange juice. She never said anything. She knew there was no point. It would have been wasted air.

Eventually, I ended up meeting all the nightclub owners in Portland, Oregon, and I began getting offers to manage a night of my choice. For about six months, I managed a Thursday drum and bass night at a club in Downtown Portland. One Thursday night, I was attracted to a young woman dancing. I watched her dance for a solid hour. She was the most beautiful and free human being I had ever seen. Her movements, her exotic look, everything about her put me in a trance. Yes, I was a little stoned but this woman blew my mind. She stayed till the very end. Her laugh filled the nightclub. I watched as she walked through the room effortlessly talking with one person after another. It was incredible to watch. I could not work up the courage to talk to her. Eventually, she left the club. The next Thursday, this amazing woman appeared again, dancing in the same corner she danced in the week before. She would stop dancing to drink water and then just close her eyes, smile, and begin dancing again. Even the beads of sweat rolling down her arms and back put me under some kind of spell. I knew I was in love with her and I knew I had to talk to her. I eventually started dancing next to her and we would flirt, smile, and laugh for at least two hours straight. The way she looked at me was like nothing I had ever experienced before. To this day, I have never felt the intensity of those feelings again. Being around her was a rush. Finally, the music stopped and a few lights turned on. She looked at me, laughed, and said, "What's your name, babe?"

"I'm Marques."

"I'm Nicole." Then someone called out her name and she asked if I'd be back next week.

"Yes, I have to! I work here." I hoped she heard me because she just ran out of the room.

The next week, Nicole was back in the club. She showed up with a couple of others girls and an older-looking guy. He bought them all drinks throughout the night. He ended up buying me a drink as well. We started talking. His name was Ferdinando. He was visiting from Miami for a few months with his wife. I didn't even think to ask who his wife was. Eventually, Nicole would join us. The three of us talked for a while and eventually Nicole told me she was married to Ferdinando. We went up to my secret little office that overlooked the dance floor and we smoked some pot together. She then gave me all the details on her marriage. She was twenty at the time and Ferdinando was thirty-five. He was originally from Italy. They met in Miami when she was eighteen and became good friends. They got married so he could stay in the United States. For some reason, this gave me some kind of relief, like there was hope for Nicole and I to be together. As we talked, I knew I had to have her. After we stopped talking, she and her friends took off. We never made plans to see each other or talk again, but I knew we would.

Aside from managing random nightclub nights, I also worked part-time at a Starbucks in Hillsboro, Oregon, a suburb of Portland. One busy day, Nicole walked in and we both just started laughing. In my mind, I said, "Nicole, I love you." For months, I would say that to myself every time I saw her. I was completely head over heels in love with Nicole from the very first moment I saw her. I have probably already said this but it's true. I took my break and we would sit down and talk for a half hour. She told me that she lived in the apartment complex two blocks away from the Starbucks that I worked at. She told me that she moved to Portland two months ago for work but she really missed Miami. I could not imagine the kind of culture shock that came with moving from Miami, Florida, to a suburb of Portland, Oregon. Portland and Miami are two different planets. It made no sense to me. Soon, my break would be over and we made plans to go out dancing that Saturday night. We didn't have a destination but it was 1998, and in the late nineties, there was some kind of dancing event going on seven days a week. Eventually, Saturday came along and we met up at an underground dance party at around midnight. We each took a tab of ecstasy and danced all night only to take breaks for water and a couple of hits of weed. We both laughed and promised that we would do this for the rest of our lives! When she looked at me, it was just so seductive and primal. When she looked at me in that certain way, I would have done anything for her. I would have robbed for her. I would have killed for her. My feelings for her were dangerous.

At about six a.m., we decided to leave. She told me that we could stay the night at one of her girlfriends' place. I just followed her. I didn't care where we went. I would have slept under a bridge with her. She had the key to someone's apartment. There was nobody there, so we took turns taking a shower and then climbed into someone's bed and crashed. It was the greatest sleep of my life. When I woke up, Nicole was gone. I was in someone else's apartment, sleeping in someone else's bed. It was all very strange, but when I started going out with Nicole, this all became normal. She always had the keys to someone's car or the keys to someone's house or apartment. I have no idea how she managed all this. A night out with Nicole was simply exhilarating. She made me feel the way I felt when I was a dealer and I loved that feeling. Before I knew it, a year had passed. Nicole and I had become best friends and I was still secretly head over heels in love with her. Before and even after Nicole, I would become bored with a woman within a handful of months. Nicole was different. I actually enjoyed her company. She was fun and smart. She would tell dirty jokes and she could be sarcastic. She was everyone's best cheerleader. We talked about getting rich together and traveling the world. Nicole was perfect. There was only one problem. She was not available. I would find out later that Nicole was unavailable in more than one way.

One night after a long night of dancing, Nicole drove me home. Before dropping me off, she pulled over by a school running track. There was a small parking lot. We smoked a few cigarettes and we talked. She told me that her neck hurt. I had graduated from massage school a year earlier, so I started rubbing her neck. She closed her eyes and let out a light moan. The song *Wicked Game* by Chris Isaak was playing in the background. While she was sensually moaning, she said that she loved that song, and immediately I said, "I love you, Nicole." Her eyes opened and she told me that she was in love with me too. My eyes began to fill up with tears. I had never been vulnerable with anyone other than my grandmother before in my life. To this day, the only two people I have been completely vulnerable with are my grandmother and Nicole. For the others, I believe my detachment stems partly out of fear and partly out of lack of interest. After she told me she loved me, we kissed and kissed for a good thirty minutes. We didn't say anything. Eventually, she drove me home. I went to sleep that night with purpose. The next evening, I met Nicole at her work and when we saw each other, she instantly took my hand and yanked my body around the corner of her building and behind a tree and kissed me like no woman has ever kissed me before. Granted that I was nineteen at the time but to this day, nobody kisses like Nicole. Nicole's passion had no fear behind it. I was just a country boy but she was like a panther ready to tear me to pieces. It was the greatest thing I had ever experienced. For a few months, Nicole and I would sneak around, making out, hoping no one that knew us would see because we didn't want Ferdinando to find out. She wasn't ready to tell Ferdinando. We both suspected that Ferdinando had actual feelings for her, even though he pretended to be a party boy without a care.

One evening, Nicole called me and told me that Ferdinando was moving back to Miami. A few days later, he left. I immediately moved into Nicole's city apartment with her. It was the best six months of my life. Everything we did would lead to sex. Let's make some pasta… sex. Let's watch a movie… sex. Let's take a shower… sex. Let's go to our favorite café across the street and have sex in the bathroom. Let's talk about God and spirituality while we have sex. It was so amazing. We even went to Mexico for a month and just smoked pot, hung out in the ocean, and made love all the time. I always wondered where all her money came from, but I never bothered to ask. I would find out soon enough.

My girlfriend (as by now I could call her that) turned twenty-two on the Halloween of 1999 and everything changed. I was off the drugs and not really drinking at this point in my life. I had Nicole and would smoke the occasional spliff with her, but that was it. Nicole, on the other hand, started drinking a lot. She was getting sloppier, louder, and less present. We would make plans to stay in and make dinner together, but at the last minute, she would break our plans. I could never go to the clubs and bars because they were all twenty-one and over. She began to resent me and let me know verbally that my inability to go to bars with her was lame. I started giving her guilt trips to stay in and hang out with me, yet she just seemed put-out by this. I could tell she was bored. She was attracted to the action. We just were not on the same page anymore. On December 1, I came from work and saw Nicole was lounging on the floor listening to music but she seemed different. She told me she needed to go home for a couple of months. Her mother needed her. I asked if everything was okay and she answered that she didn't know. I wanted to talk more about it, but she shoved a spliff in my mouth and we got stoned and had sex. Later that night, we went to bed and I asked her about going back to Miami. She said it would only be for a couple of months but she would try to leave sooner. She assured me that she preferred being with me in Portland, and that made me feel better. We never got into why she needed to go back home.

A couple of days passed and Nicole told me that her mother booked her a flight back to Miami on December 17. I wasn't very excited about this but it was just for two months. For some reason, we never discussed what was going on. We just smoked weed, ate food, and fucked the issue away. December 17 came very quickly. Those last few days, I looked at Nicole a lot more. I just watched her walk. I scanned every inch of her body as much as I could. I couldn't believe that she was actually mine and now she was leaving. Every time I thought about it, my heart broke. On December 16, we walked to the park that we lived next door to and sat on the ground and just looked at each other, talked a bit, kissed, and looked at each other some more. We did this for hours. I still remember what she was wearing. I remember the exact length of her hair, I remember the smell of her shampoo, her heavier-than-usual eyeliner, her eyes looked more yellow and green than usual, and I could feel the pulse in her wrist. It had rained earlier that day, so it was very cold and quiet. The smell of fresh bark dust was by the playground. I remember everything. I truly believe that at that moment, Nicole loved me and I knew I loved her. The next evening, we took a taxi to the Portland Airport. We arrived a couple of hours earlier than we needed to. We just sat on the ground with Nicole's luggage. She buried her face in my chest, closed her eyes, and listened to my heartbeat. I could smell her hair. When it was time to say our goodbyes, I knew I had a strange intuition that I would most likely never see her again. That was my luck. I was an unlucky person. And I have always known that eventually everybody leaves. That is all I have ever seen in my life.

Nicole and I talked once a week for a couple of hours for the first month. We would cry on the phone. Her mother offered to fly me down to spend a week or two with them. Once February arrived, Nicole told me that she would need to stay in Miami until May. She said that I should move down to Miami and that we should just stay there. I could hear the excitement in her voice. She kept telling me how much I would love it there. The parties were amazing, the people were amazing, and everything was amazing. After about a month of this, I agreed to move to Miami. We made a lot of plans. Every time I would talk to Nicole, she was always at some party or club-style restaurant. I wanted to cool out on the partying and Nicole seemed to want to go full speed. This made me nervous. I wasn't interested in the rich coke crowd and I could tell that Nicole was beginning to move in that crowd again. I preferred the stoned lovey-dovey lifestyle and Nicole was neck-deep in being an extra in music videos, getting into modeling again and the 'go, go, go' pace of Miami.

A couple of weeks before it was time for me to move to Miami, things began to seem even more off. I started catching Nicole in random lies. I would call her at seven p.m. of my time which would make it ten p.m. east coast time and she would tell me that she needed to call me back because she was taking her little brother to get a haircut. What? Who takes their fourteen-year-old brother to get a haircut at ten p.m.? Then she wouldn't call me for a couple of days. Things just started to get weird and I knew something was wrong. Two days before my flight to Miami, I called her and she answered my call but then rushed me off the phone. Her voice was shaky and she just seemed troubled every time we talked. Finally at around one a.m., the day before my flight, Nicole called me. Her voice sounded like she had just finished crying. I asked her what was wrong. She told me that this wasn't going to work. I asked her what she meant and she said that we were just not going to work. She told me that she had met someone a month earlier and it had become very intense very quickly. I felt my heart tighten into a fist. I thought I was going to have a heart attack. You grow up hearing people talk about heartache or being brokenhearted but I never knew that a broken heart was a real thing. I fell back into my bed and I felt as if I was sinking into the ground. I felt like I was being buried alive. Nicole went on to explain that she wasn't ready to get married and that the man she had met had asked her to sail around the Caribbean for a couple of months. The man she had met was also years older than her and came into a very large inheritance. Looking back on all this, I would have done the same thing if I were in her place. I was only twenty years old and Nicole wasn't even twenty-two years old. We were retarded for talking marriage, but in the moment, it was the single most painful experience of my life. It would take me a decade to forgive her for this. Today, I am glad that she ended it because I would have gone through with the marriage and I think we would have killed each other eventually. We were both addicts, and if you have been in love with an addict, you know how horribly explosive it can all be.

I was so devastated that I immediately quit my job and just disappeared for two months. I rarely left my room. I just quit everything. I only kept in touch with two of my best friends. I would lie in bed till four p.m., get up, eat some eggs, bacon, and orange juice, lie on the floor and watch whatever my grandmother was watching, and by eight p.m., I would just go lie in bed till three a.m. and repeat this cycle for a couple of months. One day, the phone rang. It was Nicole. She seemed very happy. She wanted to see how I was doing. It was as if she expected my life to have become great in just a matter of weeks. She told me about Jamaica, Key West, and the Bahamas. I laconically just said, "That's nice," to everything she was saying. I was a complete zombie and Nicole was doing great. It made me very angry. Nicole could tell that I was not in the mood to talk. She said she would call me in a few months. We never spoke again.

Like my drug-dealing story, my story about Nicole has a point. Like my drug-dealing days, Nicole would make me feel invincible. In a way, I would make Nicole a kind of higher power. As long as I had her approval, I could do anything. If I was not getting the attention that I wanted from her, I would crumble. My emotional state, good or bad, was entirely dependent upon her. It would take me years to tackle this issue. I had no idea that I had a problem outside of drugs and alcohol. Denial and codependency would prove to be far deadlier for me than any bottle of booze or any drug. At least you can see and taste booze. But denial and codependency is odorless and you definitely can't see or taste them.

A few days after Nicole's phone call to me, I woke up with the need to do something. I had to do something extreme. I needed to change my life. The night before I watched the movie *Dirty Dancing* with Patrick Swayze, I woke up and my first thought was that I needed to become a dance instructor. I opened up the phonebook and I looked up dance studios. I found a page that listed a handful of ballroom dance studios. The first place I called asked me to come down and they would try me out. The very next day, I took the bus to the dance studio and met a man in his seventies. He started teaching me some steps and told me that I was picking up the steps quite nicely. He asked me to come back the next day. For the next six months, I would go to that studio Monday through Friday from noon to six p.m. and learn to ballroom dance. I was paid no money and I was broke the entire time. But my mind was off Nicole. I wasn't drinking or smoking pot or taking any drugs. I didn't even realize it but I had become sober. It was not a conscious decision. It just kind of happened. I finally learned (even if on a subconscious level) that I had the ability to completely immerse myself into something that I enjoyed. I could hyper-focus and forget the rest of the world, and this was exactly what I did do for those next six months. Eventually, the owners of the dance studio introduced me to a beautiful young woman who became my dance partner for the next four months. This was the beginning of the end for my dance career.

I was now twenty, almost twenty-one years old, and my dance partner Katherine was twenty-six. Katherine was originally from New York. She was the most refined woman I had ever met. Her sense of style was years beyond her age. She was very well-mannered, well-spoken, and had perfect timing with everything that she did. I never felt more like a country bumpkin when I was dancing with Katherine. My insecurities just came oozing out of me. Her clothes were all the latest fashion and I could barely afford bus fare to and from the studio. I was out of my league and I hated it. Briefly, things would change for me when Katherine began to show interest in me. She told me that I was the most genuine, raw, and honest person she had ever met. For some reason, this helped me. Katherine began touching me more after our dance trainings were over for the day, or in between breaks. She would kiss me on the cheek for no reason. After a few months, we really started to get our rhythm. We were starting to show our chemistry on the dance floor. Our dance teacher told us that watching us was like watching a love affair unfold right before his eyes. I will never forget that compliment.

By this point, we were asked to perform a tango routine for the upcoming annual Christmas Eve Ball. We were both so excited. We had one month to practice a three-and-a-half-minute tango routine. That month quickly came and went and the Christmas Eve Ball had arrived. We were the third act to go on and my nerves were getting to me. Champagne was everywhere and I hadn't realized that I had had four glasses of champagne, and we still had thirty minutes before we went on. Katherine told me to chill out on the drinking. Instead of switching to water, I had two more glasses of champagne and told Katherine that I loved her. She told me what I already knew was true and that was that I didn't love her but I did want to sleep with her and she knew the difference. She also told me that she didn't feel the same way and that I needed to get my shit together. As she walked away, I picked up another glass of champagne and threw it at her. I missed Katherine but I did hit the six-foot champagne waterfall that was surrounded by champagne glasses. My glass hit one glass and it started a domino effect of fluted glasses breaking in front of three hundred people. The owner of our studio saw all the broken glasses and then she looked at me. I just ran out of the ballroom. I ran outside and threw up and then I ran some more. I walked around Downtown Portland for a couple of hours and then caught the bus home. I knew I fucked everything up. I knew I could never fix what I just did, so I never went back. Dance career was over. This story is a metaphor for most of my life. A boy meets a girl. The girl rejects the boy. The boy becomes extremely depressed. The boy stays in room for a couple of months. The boy wakes up and gets a crazy idea. The boy manically rises to the top. The boy destroys everything. Wash and repeat. I would learn that I enjoy a near impossible challenge, but once I get close to my goal, I self-destruct because I do not believe that I deserve success. I am not worthy. Once I had thoroughly destroyed everything in my path, I would then retreat to my grandmother's house for a few months, eat some eggs and bacon, lick my wounds, and then eke out a mediocre existence for a while. Out of nowhere, an opportunity would fall into my lap and I would just do what I have always done—manic rise, fear, self-destruction, death, revival, and wash and repeat. It is an extremely exhausting way to live. Yet at least I am aware of it and I hope to stop this pattern in the near future.

I could keep telling you stories that pertain to my addiction but I want to change course. I could talk about my fucked up relationship with food and my obsession with exercise and healthy living. I could explore my preference for female escorts over a real relationship with a woman. I could talk about the fact that I like to sleep in. I could talk about my compulsive need to judge others in order to feel better about myself, and I am sure that I will touch on these things throughout the book, but my point is that it's all the same. Heroin, vodka, cigarettes, girls with big asses, cheesecake, eating pizza at two a.m., sleeping too much, not sleeping enough—my list can go on forever. It's all the same. Anyone of those things will eventually kill me. Some of those things I can't ever touch. Some of the things I listed, I struggle with them and some I just lost interest in. But how did I stop some of these things? The truth is that some of the things that I stopped which I needed a lot of help with once, I stopped. I have had to try so many things followed by so many crashes, followed by a lot of burns. And why did I try to stop? Why didn't I just let my addictions kill me? Because there was something inside me that told me I was worth it. It came from me. Something inside of me told me I was worth it and I wanted to find out what that something was. That was the beginning of my journey in a sense. It wasn't so much about quitting anything. It was about tracking down what was telling me to keep going. There was something inside of me telling me that life could be great. Something was telling me that I could live my dreams. I wanted that. I wanted to live a good life. But how? Nobody ever taught me how to live a good life. All I was ever told was what *not* to do. I was told to work hard, prepare for the worst, be afraid, and I was always taught that there was only one way to do something. I had no idea that there was another way. I had no idea that there were options. I had been so depressed for so long and been convinced by my own mind that I was broken. But there was one grain of sand in my being that disagreed with the darkness that had been going on inside of me for so long. Over time, I would become more and more aware of this positive grain of sand. I would become more curious. Eventually, my curiosity would become strong enough and I would start taking action. This curiosity would lead me down an amazing, sometimes very dark, path but it was all very necessary in order to get to where I am today.

5. Beaten Down

In my experience, nobody gets sober until they hit the bottom. For everybody, the bottom looks different. For some people, their bottom shows up in their child's eyes. You have been gone for five days straight, your wife has left fifty messages on your phone, and when you finally sneak in the door, your four-year-old daughter is asleep two feet from the front door with her favorite blanket. She has snuck downstairs every night waiting for you to come home. You open the door and there she is. Right as you close the door, she wakes up and she looks at you. Her whole world has finally come home. "Daddy?" she begins to cry and she asks you where you were. You start to cry as you hold her and walk up the stairs to put her to bed. Finally, you decide it is time to stop. You watch your baby girl sleep and realize how much of a selfish piece of shit you have been. Maybe you go to rehab. Maybe you try an AA meeting. Whatever it is you decide to do, you do it. You do whatever it takes to stop and make everything right. For some people, their bottom shows up in the form of a death of a stranger. You have been drinking and driving for years and you finally do what you always feared you might do. You hit someone crossing the street and kill them. You spend next to an eternity in prison. A couple of years into your sentence, you try to hang yourself and right before you fade away, a guard brings you back. You wake up devastated. Maybe you find God. Maybe you start talking to other guys that killed someone the same way you did. You find some way to make peace with it all. Maybe you sneak into your parents' house for the five hundredth time to steal some of your mom's jewelry. Your father walks in the door and catches you red-handed. He beats the shit out of you and drives you back downtown and tells you to fuck off one more time. You have finally run out of corners to run to. You are on the streets with no Plan B and a sixty-year-old man offers to give you a hundred and fifty bucks if he can fuck your tight virgin ass. You go back to his place and while he is in the restroom, something inside you snaps and you walk to the nearest emergency room begging for help. Three months later, you are taking a ninety-day chip from a six-foot-seven ex Hell's Angel Member named Rusty at some NA meeting in

Minneapolis. I could keep listing all the different types of bottoms but I think you get the point.

I have experienced a few different bottoms in my life. I have experienced my using bottom, my mental bottom, and my spiritual bottom. My bottom didn't come when I was sixteen and living on the streets off and on for three months. I never had to be homeless and living under or around the Burnside Bridge in Portland, Oregon. I could have gone home to Grandma's house at any time but there was one rule in the house: no using drugs. That was it. I couldn't come home if I was high. This would never work because I was always high. So instead, I would squat in abandoned buildings, sleep under the Burnside Bridge by the Skate Park, or crash on a friend's couch. People would ask me why I didn't just go home. I would always say, "Because I'm high." Whenever I needed a couple of days off from using, I would go home. Whenever I showed up, it was as if nothing had happened. My grandmother never said a word. She knew there was no point. My bottom wouldn't show up when I woke up in Phoenix and I couldn't remember how I got there. The last thing I remembered was that I was at a rave in Seattle. My bottom was nowhere in sight when I was drunk and talking shit to a bunch of MS-13 game members in Los Angeles. It was two in the morning and I was calling a bunch of gangsters with face tattoos 'faggots.' That's fucking insane. I was chased for over an hour in Downtown Los Angeles not knowing where the hell I was. If they caught me, they would have gutted me like a fish. No, I couldn't see my bottom even at that point and I would drink and use for a few more years after that.

My bottom is pretty mundane, to be honest. It all started on Thanksgiving of 2001. I woke up at around noon and a bunch of my friends and I met at a local bar that we all lived by. We drank mimosas and ate really bad Mexican food. We chain-smoked, talked, laughed, and drank more mimosas. It was like any other day. None of us was very close to our families, so we just decided to make a day of it. We hung out and drank until about ten p.m. Eventually, we all agreed that we needed a change of environment, so we all decided to go to another friend's house that was just a few blocks away. There, we drank grayhounds and smoked more cigarettes. We were what some would call the pretty crowd, so we all took turns sleeping with one another and dating one another over time. Eventually, two people would pair off and fade away into a corner somewhere and start making noises. I was going through a recent breakup and was not in the mood for any kind of action on this particular night. I wanted to get good and drunk. A couple friends and I switched straight to vodka and smoked a whole pack of cigarettes each. We talked about how crazy women were and made our best attempts at philosophizing about life. Finally at 5:30 a.m., I decided to take off and walk home. I only lived about four blocks away. After fifteen minutes of walking, I realized that I was kind of lost. This was extremely frustrating for me. I was in my neighborhood which I had lived in for years and I was lost! I started to panic. How could I not know where I was? I was dizzy and thirsty and felt like I was going to pass out. Eventually, I saw a light post that I recognized and right around the corner was my apartment. I stumbled in the door and just started ripping off my clothes. I made it to my bathroom and turned on the shower. I had one of those really deep old claw foot tubs. I climbed in and started soaping myself up. I slipped and fell out of the tub. Before landing on the bathroom floor, I hit the edge of the tub with my right side. The next thing I remember is waking up at two in the afternoon the next day. My head and right side were killing me. It hurt to breath and my face was killing me. The impact of my face hitting the floor knocked me out. I flipped over onto my back and said, "I gotta stop this shit." I was twenty-two years old, and for some reason it was over. I really don't know why. I slowly got up. In my mind, I saw myself walk outside to my front porch. What I do not remember doing was making myself a mimosa and grabbing a pack of cigarettes. The next thing I knew, I was sitting on my front porch with a mimosa in my hand and lighting a cigarette. What the fuck? I put out the cigarette and dumped out my drink. This really freaked me out. I sat on my porch the whole afternoon and tried to wrap my mind around what I would need to do in order to quit all this shit. I took a really good look at my life. All I had was my job, my drinking, my drinking friends, and my drugs. How could I get out of all this? It seemed so impossible. I knew I had to give it all up, so I called my best female friend Ronnie and I told her I was quitting drinking. She was quiet for what seemed to be forever and then said, "That's cool."

I knew Ronnie would tell all of our friends. I would never again receive a call from anyone of my friends. My phone stopped ringing that day. Then I called my grandmother and I told her that I needed to come home. She asked why and I told her that I was going to quit drinking. She knew I was serious. Nobody in my family believed I could do it. My mother said I would never quit. Everybody thought I wanted to move home so I didn't have to pay rent anymore, but I knew what I was doing and why I was doing it and my grandmother believed in me. I remember telling her that I might get really sick and that the next year might be really hard but I *was* going to quit. That same day, I took a cab to my job and quit on the spot. There was no way I could stay sober and work at a restaurant. There was no way I could stay sober and keep the friends that I had. There was no way I could stay sober and live in the city surrounded by bars and nightclubs. I knew that I had to get rid of everything and start over. It was just common sense to me.

I was twenty-two years old and I thought my life was over. I thought that there was a very good chance that I would just live with my grandmother for the rest of my life and hide—no friends, no money… just me, my sobriety, and my grandmother. At the time, this was fine with me. Once I realized that I was living in a horror movie called *My Life*, I was totally fine with becoming a monk and living in the suburbs with my grandmother. Four days after calling my grandmother, I moved back home. My grandparents seemed happy to have me. I put my things in my little room. I was shaky, underweight, and tired. I felt like I hadn't slept in a few years. I immediately took a long hot shower. I remember my grandmother knocked on the bathroom door twice to check on me. She told me a year later that she worried that I was going to kill myself for the first six months after I had moved back. She hated when I was quiet for long periods of time. I would always get a little annoyed by her knocking on my bedroom door every three hours but now I am grateful that she did. She had never helped someone go through drug and alcohol withdrawal before. This was a first for all of us. Luckily, my withdrawals were not that horrible. I just felt like I had a really bad flu for about five days. My muscles hurt really badly and I was always thirsty. At first, I would sleep for twelve to fourteen hours at a time and then I would have insomnia. My grandmother would make my meals, make my bed, and wash and fold my clothes. She would do this without complaint. Every time I tried to do something for myself, she would nudge me out of the way and tell me to let her do it. Part of the reason why she did this was because she had a system for how things got done and she, like myself, is an extreme creature of habit. I also think that my grandmother has been playing nurse to so many people for so many years, that this is how she finds her purpose. Taking care of people is what my grandmother does. God bless her! After a couple of weeks, I joined a gym. For the first month, I just sat in the steam and sauna. I smelled like vodka and cigarettes when I sweat for at least the first few days. I had so much shit in my system and it all needed to come out. Eventually, I started swimming a few days a week and then lifting weights. I developed an appetite. I learned to enjoy food. My relationship with my grandmother became really good. I would tell her what was on my mind. I started reading self-help books by Tony Robbins and I told her all about these books. Before I knew it, one hundred days would go by. As far as my body was concerned, I felt that the worst might be over. I would recover physically very quickly. What I did not know was that my mental and spiritual recovery would prove to be a whole other ballgame.

6. Sick in the Head

Once I got through the withdrawals and got my body back in shape, life was pretty good. After about eighteen months, I was able to move out of my grandmother's house and into my own cool little studio in NW, Portland, again, my old neighborhood where I felt most at home. I wasn't making a lot of money but I was getting by. By the time I was twenty-four, I was in the best shape of my life and getting laid as much as I wanted. I would get modeling gigs on occasion and travel to different cities. Things were getting glamorous for me. I would be in Vancouver, BC, then Miami, then over to Vegas, and then New York. I would spend every penny I made and then work would dry up for a bit. I would work odd jobs at Mom and Pop's Cafe to get by until more modeling jobs came up again. I loved the travel but I hated the modeling industry. It was really difficult to be in the skin industry while newly sober. Everybody smoked, did a ton of coke, and snorting heroin was big at the time. The models were stupid. Every bad cliché that you hear about models is true—no sense of humor, no talent, vapid, and lazy. I was no better. I had no skills, my ambition was gone, I starved myself, and I judged everyone. I was a complete waste of space.

When I was twenty-four, I moved in to my manager's condo overlooking twenty-third avenue in NW, Portland. My manager threw at least two parties a week and I grew tired of this quickly. He was forty years old and his girlfriend was fifteen. His girlfriend's father was the lead cameraman for local shoots. At the end of the day, he pimped his daughter out in order to get steady photo-shoot work. One weekend, my manager and his girlfriend got into a huge fight. All of a sudden, we had a different cameraman for local shoots. One weekend, I came home and there was a big party happening. I could barely fit through the front door. I noticed that in the last few parties, the girls were getting even younger. My manager told me that he wanted to branch out into the preteen market. This was before you would hear the term 'millennial' every five minutes but in a weird, creepy way, my manager was always one step ahead. I walked into my room and my manager was having sex with two under-aged girls on my bed. They could not have been over thirteen years old. He was into really tall, skinny Russian girls. I think in my drug days, I would have had an easier time looking past all this, plus the money was great, but the new sober Marques could not stomach all this. I looked around my room and there was coke on my dresser all lined up and ready to go and little baggies of crack and crystal meth. I went to my closet, got some clothes, and took a cab back home to Grandma's house. I really thought I was going to make a good life for myself and be completely independent, but it seemed like everything I touched turned to shit. Everyone I met was a con artist and just wanted to take advantage of me.

A couple of months after the modeling debacle, I met a couple of local movie producers and they asked me to move in with them in their mansion just outside of Portland. In exchange for free rent and a small stipend, I was supposed to write a screenplay for them. I had never written a screenplay before and had no idea how to begin to write one, but I jumped at the opportunity. I packed my stuff and moved in with the two producers without even seeing the house. The woman ended up being extremely mentally ill. She would drink vodka martinis with muscle relaxers and not eat all day. When she did eat, it was always fast food that her assistant slash pill connection would pick up and deliver to her. Her assistant really didn't do anything except listen to 'Amanda' complain. Amanda would slur her words and tell horrible stories about growing up wealthy. Her father co-owned a golf course and was a big wig in the Oregon lumber industry before it went bust. Amanda would go on and on about nothing for hours. She would nod off while talking to you and then yell at you for leaving. It was like living with 'mommy dearest.' She always wanted to brush my hair and give me homemade spa facials. After a couple of weeks, she would constantly tell me how she gave the best blowjobs and how her husband didn't like sex anymore. She told me that she was convinced that her husband was gay and seeing a man beyond her back. For the first two months, I could not write a thing. There was no time. I got sucked into Amanda's crazy, fucked up delusional world. Who knows which stories were real and which stories were bullshit? Eventually, Amanda and her husband went on a vacation for two weeks. I had the whole house to myself. I liked having my own private deck and the second floor to myself. Taking a break from the rat race and having nothing to do with the working-class world was a very odd experience. I was completely stress-free but isolated at the same time. For six months, I had no need for money. If I needed to go grocery shopping, there was a credit card for that. If I wanted to go clothes shopping, there was a credit card for that. I basically slept, hit the gym, and wrote a little here and there. A masseuse would come to the house once a week for me. It was an amazing and surreal time. There were always attractive women of all ages stopping by to see Amanda. On occasion, I would snag one of the women that stopped by. I could have anything I wanted, and I did.

It took me six weeks to write the first draft of my screenplay. I wrote it on large storyboards. I drew simple stick figures, described the scene, and wrote some dialogs. Six weeks later, *poof!* Amanda didn't even look at my work. She just wrote me a check of $10,000. We never even talked about it. It was so bizarre. Amanda's husband never brought it up either. Her husband was always gone. I think I saw him once a week. We only spoke three or four times during my six months there. My last three months at the mansion started getting weirder and weirder. Amanda would only bathe if someone came by to do it for her. She started having seizures in the middle of our conversations and I had to call for an ambulance a few times. I felt like I was beginning to lose my mind. The walls were beginning to close in on me. Everyone just used one another. I didn't know what to do. Everyone was too fucked up to talk business. Did they want another screenplay? Did they want me to leave? I had some money, so I didn't have to move back home, but where would I go? What would I do? How do you go back to work when you have been living like a Himalayan house cat for the past six months? I bet there are literally tens of thousands of people in that same predicament right now living in Beverly Hills. Again, no skillset to speak of, very little drive from having it too easy for too long, and surprisingly very little will left to live. As soon as anything goes wrong, you are fucked because you have no common sense and you are just hypersensitive to everything. Everything must be comfortable and perfect at all times.

Amanda and her husband finally returned. Once they got unpacked, Amanda's husband immediately took off again. Amanda would just lie in bed watching old movies that they had produced and directed together for two days straight. They only worked on a handful of movies together, which meant she would watch some of them more than once. I would check on her and we would talk. She would be very intoxicated. I remember telling her a story and she stopped responding to me. She just blanked out and stared at me. I would wave my hand in front of her face and it was as if she was not there. I would snap my fingers right in front of her face, and nothing. I called for an ambulance. When the medics took her away on the stretcher, she tilted her head slightly and just stared at me while being taken away. To this day, this would be the creepiest moment of my life. I have been shot at, I have seen a couple of dead bodies, and I have overdosed and almost died twice, but that stare tops my list.

That evening, I called a good friend of mine and asked her to let me stay on her couch for a bit. I wanted to get a job before I moved into my own place again. I ended up staying with my friend Stacy for four months. Stacy was an exotic dancer. Living with a stripper was to be a very interesting experience as well. Before I go deeper into my story, I just have to thank God for Stacy! We have helped each other over the years and this was definitely a time in my life when I needed help. I don't think I could have survived on my own during this time. My anxiety and depression were through the roof. Stacy also had an eighty-pound Rottweiler. I would wake up to him licking my face. If he wasn't licking my face, he was breathing his hundred-and-fifty-degree dragon breath on my face. I would wake up sticky from being licked all night in my sleep. At the time I thought I was in hell, but today I look back on this with fondness. I am happy to say that I would be able to return the favor to Stacy when she needed help.

Eventually, I got a job at a small café. At the time, I couldn't do much more than make double tall Americanos and wipe down tables (nothing against baristas by any means). It was just not what I wanted to be doing. I would work at a mother-daughter-owned café for four or five months but I wanted to move back to my neighborhood in NW, Portland, and the bus service to the city from the neighborhood I was working at was shit. It was almost 2004 and I was about to turn twenty-five years old. I had been sober for three years and my life was going nowhere. I was making minimum wage. I was depressed like usual and just stuck. I remember the economy was horrible at that time. I needed to make better money but the only way I knew how was to either deal drugs, buss tables, or bartend. That's all I could do. I would go from one hotel and restaurant to another and there would be a line of people in the human resources office waiting to fill out applications. I would go to a bar and the bartender would give me an application to fill out. Twenty minutes later, I would hand the application back to the bartender and they would put my application in a basket with a hundred other applications. I would go to a coffee shop and the place would be full of people filling out applications for businesses that surrounded the coffee shop. There were simply no fucking jobs in Portland. I would go downtown every day, five days a week. Finally, after five months of looking, I found a job making minimum wage at a tile factory working in what was called 'the seconds department.' I was so thrilled to have a job, but at the same time I couldn't help wonder how I went from modeling and making an obscene amount of money to writing a screenplay, to working at a café twenty hours a week, to now begging for a job working at a tile factory on the eastside of Portland, Oregon. What the fuck happened? Next to farming, that tile factory job was the hardest I had ever worked in my life for next to no pay. A lot of the people I worked with were ex-cons on some kind of work-release program. They would use terms like 'white nigger' at work, as in we were white niggers. I would hear this all the time and it really did a number on my mind. All the things that my stepfather told me were coming true. If I didn't go to college, I would be poor and nobody would want me. My stepfather always told me that I couldn't live off my looks forever. He was right, and I didn't know if I still had time to fix my life. About the time that I realized that I was approaching my first what-the-fuck-do-I-do-with-my-life crossroad, I suddenly got hit by a large SUV while riding my bike. I was on the way to a fitness photo shoot. I was excited about the shoot because I heard that fitness models were much cleaner and healthier than fashion models. I missed making good money, so I started networking in the fitness model market. I was having a really hard time getting any interest, but I got lucky and a local fitness clothing line needed models. I was only four blocks away when I was hit. To make a long story short, I would never have my photo taken for money ever again. My injuries took six months to recover from, and I think I just used that as an excuse to stay out of any kind of modeling. My need for glamour and being sexy and cool began to fade away. Plus, going to VIP parties really didn't do anything for me. Since I couldn't drink, I always felt out of place. I was always surrounded by coke and booze and emotionally stunted pretty people. I think it takes drugs and alcohol just to function in the skin industry.

So I returned to my tile factory job. I knew I wanted more, but I didn't know how to get where I wanted to go. One day, I decided that I would go to college. A few days before I decided to go back to school, I watched the movie *Pretty Woman* with Julia Roberts and Richard Gere. I always loved Hotel Manager Barney and how he took care of Julia Roberts' character, Vivian. Barney was Vivian's lifeline to this new world that she had been thrust into. I always wished that I had a Barney in my life to help guide me through the hard times. Whenever I would travel to other cities for modeling gigs, I was always lucky enough to stay at three and four-star hotels and I would always gravitate to the concierge desk. I grew to love hotel lobbies. Hotel lobbies and the hotel concierge became my sanctuary, relieving me from the loneliness I felt while traveling. I did not relate to the other models and I would be away from my friends in Portland for a week at a time. Being the new kid on the block and new to sobriety was hard. On the outside, it was caviar and roasted duck for dinner, and nightclubs into the morning, but to be honest with you, I was miserable and aimless. I knew the modeling jobs would run out. I was in my mid-twenties and that is old for the modeling business. Every job was my last. I fucked up my dancing career and selling leftover tile from old installation jobs was just not fulfilling any of my needs. I decided that I would become a hotel concierge. How hard could it be, right? I knew the city of Portland like the back of my hand, I loved talking to people, and I enjoyed helping people as well.

I started school in January 2005. By 2007, I would earn a two-year degree in tourism management. Sure, it was not as glamorous as catching an airplane and getting my picture taken, but it was something. I just needed a direction. I didn't know what kind of job I could get out of the degree I would earn, but I knew I liked wearing a suit, eating expensive food, and talking to strangers. I thought it might be easier to get a concierge job if I had a degree in a similar field. A few days after I started school, I got a job at an upscale restaurant. I would be their maître d'. I always preferred maître d' over 'host.' The job was fun and the schedule worked with my school hours. I soon found the perfect studio in my old neighborhood. My life was on track for the first time ever. My daily routine would be to wake up at eight a.m., go to school for four hours, go to work for six hours, and then hit the gym after work. I had two days off a week and I would use those days for having sex with women that I met online. I was back in school, working, in great shape, and fucking as much as I wanted. Sure, the girls I was sleeping with weren't models anymore, but a twenty-something male doesn't really care who he's sleeping with. At least I didn't. I found out that I preferred thicker women with big asses rather than the stick-thin models that I had become used to. I also loved that I could get four hours of sleep every night and not get tired. I learned that I preferred older women instead of women my age as well. By the time I turned twenty-five, all the women I would sleep with were over forty-five. Mommy issues? Probably, but it was so much fun. I would start seeing escorts more as well. Female escorts were where a lot of my money would go for the next few years. I still preferred what was naughty, a little darker, and maybe considered wrong by popular culture. But after a couple of years of this, I discovered that it was impossible to maintain an erection with normal women of my age. Every time I would go home with a twenty-something female, I would just listen to their pointless nervous banter and lose any interest that I might have had during the cab ride to her place. After a while, I decided to save myself the embarrassment of not being able to perform sexually and just keep having fun with my hot, curvy cougars. Older women could carry on a conversation, they always had amazing lingerie, their homes were much nicer, and I never had to pay for anything.

On occasion, I would meet a hot, older woman that lived in the city and we would really hit it off. We would go to the ballet together, amazing restaurants, and then out of nowhere they would start paying my rent. No, I was not into hanging out with women for their money. I just liked older women that dressed sexy. I have always loved leopard-print skirts, high heels, big hair, and big asses. For some reason, I seemed to attract middle-aged women that worked in some quasi-glamorous industry. They usually lived in highbrow neighborhoods right out of Downtown Portland. If I were the marrying type, I would have had it made at least six times over. But again, I just wanted to have fun, nothing too serious. I have had my share of amazing man caves with flat-screen televisions, private refrigerators, saunas, and hot tubs. But if you are not in love, none of it matters. I couldn't imagine marrying someone just for money. For me, that is a guaranteed ticket to suicide.

A year and a half into college, my panic attacks started up again and my depression was starting to pop its head out. I would be working at the restaurant on a busy Friday night, feeling good about life, and out of nowhere I would become dizzy and need to sit down. The room would start to spin and wouldn't slow down. I would need to go home early and rest. I didn't know what was going on and I didn't know what to tell people. The next day, everything would go back to normal. A month would go by and another panic attack would come back. Then two weeks later would come another panic attack and then a week later. I was almost done with school but the panic attacks wouldn't go away. I started going to hospital emergency rooms, which were extremely expensive because I didn't have health insurance. Every time I went to the hospital, it would cost at least a thousand dollars. I would wait for a few hours to be seen and then wait another hour for the doctor. We would talk for fifteen minutes and they would give me some Ambien for sleep. One evening, my girlfriend and I went to the movies together. We came home at around ten p.m. and crashed by one a.m. At four a.m., I woke up in a panic and walked to the hospital. From that evening on, I would stay in panic mode for four years. From October of 2006 to May of 2010, I suffered from anxiety and a deep clinical depression that would completely destroy my life. For four years, everything around me would spin. Even when I closed my eyes, I felt like I was on a rollercoaster. This wouldn't just come and go. This would last for four straight years. Whatever was happening to me, whatever it was, it was trying to kill me. During this time of my life, I would see acupuncturists, psychiatrists, psychologists, western doctors, eastern doctors, reiki specialists, psychics, and Greek palm readers that would perform candlelight therapy on me. Doctors put me on lithium, Prozac, Abilify, Seroquel, and Xanax. We tried everything and nothing worked. Some medications caused hallucinations. Some medications caused severe mania. Some medications made me sleep for thirty-six hours at a time. Needless to say, I could no longer work full-time. Before I could even get a real career started, mental illness had demolished me. I would eventually move back to my grandmother's house, yet again. I told my grandmother what was going on and she told me to come home. My grandmother never judged me. She was always willing to go through hell with me and I will owe her my life more than once. I already owed her for helping me to get clean and now I would owe her again for helping to put my mind back together again.

For a year and a half, my doctors didn't know what was wrong with me. My psychiatrist tried treating me for bipolar two, but eventually we found out that I was not bipolar. Then we tried treating me for borderline personality disorder. Then we discovered that I was definitely not suffering from borderline personality disorder. My doctor kept telling me that he thought I had the mixed bag that was clinical depression and generalized anxiety disorder. He put me on a small dosage of Depakote and Celexa. These two medications did help stabilize my mood and my anxiety would be cut down a bit. I was still miserable but I could go back to work full-time. I also had to battle with suicidal thoughts for a while longer. I wanted to live but I was in so much emotional turmoil and I didn't think there was any way out of it. Knowing what I know today, what I was experiencing was true poverty— financial, emotional, and spiritual poverty. I had no money, I had no love in my heart, and I didn't believe in anything. I didn't believe in God and I hated myself. That is just no way to live. The medication made it possible for me to get out of bed and walk in a straight line but the meds would never give me the love I craved. One thing that really pulled me out of the weeds was a small underweight pug named Frank. Yes, a dog would essentially help save my life. I remember the first time I saw Frank. He was about four years old, he had a terrible skin rash on his belly, and he constantly scratched himself. My uncle dropped Frank off with my grandmother and just never came back for him. (Again, Grandma to the rescue!) My grandmother put special doggy ointment all over Frank's belly and I would let Frank sleep on my chest while I watched MTV and the Food Network. For about a year, Frank was my only friend, and my saint-like grandmother took care of both of us because we couldn't take care of ourselves.

After getting my two-year degree, I took a job with the Portland Chamber of Commerce to help manage their tourism department. Ten of us would walk the streets of Downtown Portland and ask random people if they needed any directions or help with ideas on what to do in Portland. This job was perfect for my depression and anxiety. I don't think I could do anything else at the time. Every year or so, I tried applying for a concierge job that would pop up at the Portland Hilton, but I was rejected four times over a five-year period. I became obsessed with becoming a concierge. My manager at the Chamber of Commerce became a kind of mentor to me. I would tell him all about my past addictions and my mental illness. He would just be there for me and listen. Sometimes he would give me advice. He became a father figure to me in a sense. He was the only man that I had ever met that would talk to me and then listen to what I had to say. I had never experienced this before. A man had never just asked me how I was doing before. I didn't know how much I needed to talk to someone that wasn't a doctor and that had lived life, failed, and been able to come out the other side. My stepfather always worked too much to be around and when we talked, it was either to reprimand me or I just didn't understand what he was talking about. I started to feel a positive turn in my life right around the time Frank came into my life, and having a mentor really helped as well. I never had someone around to give me life options and positive feedback. If everyone around you just talks about how hard you have to work or your life will become shit, what is there to look forward to?

Once I got on the right medication, I could do more than just work and exercise. I was getting really bored with my routine and my life began to feel very small. Then I met a gorgeous forty-seven-year-old woman that lived in the heart of Downtown Portland, just two blocks from my office. On my lunch breaks, I would go over to her place a couple of times a week and we would have 'adult playtime.' We never went out, just sex. Afterward, I would shower, put my uniform back on, and walk the streets of Portland for a few more hours and go home. We did this for five years. It was a great time. Although I did attempt to have relationships with women my own age, after a few months they would crash and burn. I just couldn't go from sexy, classy, professional, forty-something women to neurotic, insecure, bratty, twenty-something girls pretending to be women. It would be like going from filet mignon to fast food. I am thirty-nine now and I tried going on a date with a twenty-eight-year-old recently and it was like I was talking to a really hot cartoon character on speed. But at thirty-nine, I shouldn't have anything in common with a woman in her twenties. If I do, then there is something very wrong with me.

All things concerned, life was beginning to fall into place as far as my temporary insanity was concerned. A few years went by. The medication was helping. Therapy was helping. Living with my grandmother was okay, and I had a job that I could do and I was good at it. I had never been good at working before. I would get into trouble at work on occasion. I would offend the mayor's personal assistant a few times and this would get back to my bosses and they would sit me down. Or I would get into trouble for going to the shooting range with some police officers in the middle of a Wednesday afternoon. I would take long two-hour lunches and just go to the gym, work out, and hit the steam room and relax. I never got away with anything but I also kind of got away with a lot at the same time. I began making friends with hotel employees all over the city, and on occasion, they would comp me a room. I would meet up with an escort on my lunch break and we would have some fun at one of the downtown hotels. My boss was having lunch with some of his old cop cronies and he would see me go into the hotel elevator with a woman. An hour later, we would exit the elevator. My boss had over thirty years of police experience, so he waited for me to come out of the elevator just to say, "Gotcha!" He knew exactly what I was doing. I got reamed for this one, but I never got fired. Working in politics was amazing. You could get fired for a bad text, but if you got caught having sex while on duty, people just looked past it. My boss told me that he thought I had a problem and that I should look into fixing it. The next day, I tried going to a sex addict's anonymous meeting. I went to a couple of SA meetings a week for five months. These meetings really made me look deeper into my need for acceptance and attention. I also learned that I wasn't a sex addict. I had low self-esteem and sex was one way of masking the bigger problem. I exercised too much and had sex with the wrong people at the wrong times for the same reason I drank and used drugs. I was almost thirty years old and yet, this was all just so new to me.

In 2007, I started volunteering a lot for non-profits like DBSA and NAMI. Depression and Bipolar Support Alliance and National Alliance of Mental Illness would change my life. Going to meetings through these organizations helped me so much. I learned that I wasn't the only person on the planet dealing with these kinds of issues. I wasn't the only one who had parents that didn't understand how to help, so they just ignored the problem and acted like nothing was wrong or like you didn't exist. I had hated my parents for years, but through educating myself and just growing up a little, I realized that parents are just people. Most people are not equipped to automatically know what to do when they find out they have a mentally ill child. All they know is that their child is acting out and behaving like a monster. This kid makes friends easily. He's smart and funny and looks normal, so what's the problem? He's just lazy. He is selfish. He doesn't care about anyone but himself. This sounds like a lot of kids, right? Well, a lot of kids are fucked up. Plus, a lot of people that surround that kid are fucked up too. I have met a lot of people that were sexually molested for years by a family member or a close friend of a family member and they never told anyone about it. Why? Maybe the person molesting them threatened to kill them if they said anything. If you were six years old and someone threatened to kill you if you told anyone a secret, what would you do? Or maybe your father or mother would beat you while in some kind of mental blackout and the next day they wouldn't remember a thing. This shit actually happens every day. In my case, I was perfectly normal except in one small way. I have the disease of alcoholism. I can't turn my brain off. I have an abnormally low self-esteem and have had depression and anxiety since the beginning. I don't know why. Is it genetics? Is it environment? I personally think it's a little bit of both. But then you can come from a family full of drunks on both sides and you can turn out fine. Go figure.

My parents did everything they could to shelter me from the bad things that people can do. They kept me away from violence and drugs and there was really never any alcohol in the house. My parents tried to give me the best education possible and college would have been mine for the taking, but there was something wrong. I call it the dark gene. I had the dark gene. I was born with this voice in my head that would tell me over and over again that I wasn't good enough, and for some reason alcohol and drugs killed that voice for brief periods of time. For me, it's as simple as that. How do parents compete with a disease that tells you that you are a piece of shit and the only remedy is to get as high as possible? What do parents do with that? Parents with resources tend to take their kids to doctors, but if your kid is a true addict, there is no MRI scan that will detect it. Addiction is like the ocean. We have only explored three percent of it. No good, honest doctor will claim to understand alcoholism or drug addiction. They will have theories or perhaps personal experience on some level of their own with it. Maybe they are alcoholics or they had a few family members that are addicts. But if all you have is a degree telling people that you are a doctor and you specialize in addiction—well, you might as well go into pottery. It's harsh but true. If you have a doctor of any kind and he has no real personal experience with addiction and that doctor is treating you, run away. Go find a doctor that has suffered from the disease and lived to tell his story. My point on all this is that if someone has told you that you might have an addiction problem or you think you have a problem with the things that I have been talking about, then chances are you might be a true addict. Addiction is not just a physical disease. Addiction is connected to your mind as well. Your brain is wired in some weird way just like mine is. You can keep living the way you always have, but if you do, things probably won't get better for you. If you are in rehab right now, you will eventually get out. But if you keep doing the same shit when you get out, you will end up in another rehab and this is the best-case scenario. If you can afford to go to rehab or you have family that can afford to put you in rehab, how bad could things possibly be? But what will you do if you can't go to rehab next time? Where will you go? You don't believe in God and I'm not here to try to convince you to believe in God. Maybe someone has recommended AA or NA to you before and maybe you have gone to a meeting or two, but the whole God thing just turns you off. So what the fuck will you do? I will tell you what I did before I ever tried AA.

A year before I ever tried an AA meeting, I was filling my schedule with exercise, two depression support meetings a week, and sex with random strangers. Unfortunately, the routine made me fall into a deep depression as usual. I begged my psychiatrist for help. As a last resort, he recommended that I look into ECT or electroconvulsive therapy. Electro shock! I looked into it and made some calls. A month later, my psychiatrist approved an ECT session. I went in for my first treatment. It wasn't what I expected at all. On each side of my temples, a doctor held black handles which were attached to long cords. I could feel the electrical pulses in my head. It almost felt like a vibrating massage in my brain. Afterward, it felt as if a layer of relaxation was coating my brain. I moved a bit slower and my reaction to the environment around me was slowed down tremendously. I felt a deep numbness. My sexual appetite was immediately gone. I lost interest in everything. I had absolutely no desire to eat or talk to people. I felt as if I had literally become soulless. This lasted for a few days. Yet for a month after that, I still had no interest in anything. I didn't *feel* anything. I could not feel happiness or sadness or anything in between. Regardless of the lethargy, I went in for another treatment a few months later, but that would be the last time I would go in for an ECT treatment. I wish I had a more interesting story about getting electroshock therapy, but I don't. It was a gray and strange time, but I am glad that I tried it. A few months after my last ECT treatment, I just didn't want to go on anymore. I was tired of the life I was living. With all the medications that were supposed to help me but didn't, the financial poverty, and the shitty sex life, I was tired of eking out an existence. Everything appeared flat and dull and I was not being challenged, but every time I tried to take on more responsibility, I would have to stop after a few days because my mind couldn't take it. I would have panic attacks or get dizzy. I had become accustomed to going at full speed with life, but my mind wouldn't let me anymore. I just didn't see what the point of life was if you could not meet your expectations.

I became more and more depressed. I would not be able to sleep for a few days at a time and I had to go to the hospital for exhaustion and suicidal ideation. The doctor told me that I needed to get some sleep. He gave me three nights' worth of Ambien and I went on my way. I walked a couple of blocks to a new long-term stay facility for people with mental illness. Someone like myself that was at the end of his rope. I walked right in and told the front desk that I needed help. They sat down with me for thirty minutes and asked me a few questions. At the end of the conversation, they told me that I wasn't sick enough to qualify for their services. Defeated, I took a cab home. At home, I had a month's worth of Xanax and a bunch of other random medications that I never took. I planned on going home, taking all of it, and just going to sleep. When I arrived home, it was about ten a.m. My grandmother already had breakfast waiting for me. We never spoke about my trip to the hospital, but not because my grandmother didn't care. She knew I would talk about it when I was ready. After eating a few pieces of bacon, I went and lay down on the floor in my room. I stared at my ceiling fan and hypnotically watched the blade go round and round and round. I stared at the fan for a good hour. I was going to kill myself. I was going to take every pill that I had hidden in my room and go to sleep forever. I knew I was going to. Suddenly, while staring at the ceiling fan, my cellphone rang. It was my friend Jason. At the time, Jason was one of the few people that I still picked up the phone for. Jason is the first person I met when I went to my first depression support group meeting. Jason helped me through my worst times. He had lived through it all and he had been sober for fifteen years when I first met him. I picked up the phone and Jason had a feeling that I was going through some stuff. When Jason had a feeling about something, he was usually right. I didn't tell him that I was about to kill myself. I knew he could tell by the low tone of my voice. He talked calmly and slowly to me. I told him that I couldn't live the life I was living anymore, but I didn't know what to do. Jason told me that he was going to an AA meeting at noon the next day and asked if I would come with him because he needed help with some writing ideas. He was always writing something, and on occasion, I would give him ideas. I agreed to meet him at the noon AA meeting. So, now that I had an obligation, I didn't take all those pills. Something that simple gave me a reason to go on, at least for another day.

When I walked through the door of the AA meeting, it was full of men in their mid to late sixties, some men younger but mostly older men. It was a very loud group of guys. Everyone seemed to get along and there were outbursts of laughter. It was a bit jarring. I hadn't laughed in a while and I had been suicidal for four years straight. I sat down next to Jason.

Immediately, a man introduced himself to me, "Hi, my name is Robbie." Robbie shook my hand. Robbie was in his late sixties as well, but he was very happy and vibrant. I liked him right away. I didn't like anybody anymore, but I liked Robbie. I introduced myself. The meeting soon started. They went through the basic spiel that all AA meetings go through no matter where in the world you are. They asked if there were any newcomers or anyone new to the meeting. Robbie looked at me with a smile and motioned for me to raise my hand.

I said, "My name is Marques and I am an alcoholic and this is my first time here." Everybody welcomed me. It *was* my first meeting and I *was* an alcoholic. That was all true and I could at least tell the truth while I was visiting. After all, I was just meeting up with Jason. The meeting went on for an hour. Towards the end of it, one of the guys asked if I would like to share. I said, "Sure." I was used to sharing at my depression support group meetings every week, so I didn't think sharing at an AA meeting would be any different. I introduced myself again and repeated that I was an alcoholic. I told them that I had not had a drink in almost ten years and that I was still miserable. I told them that I was suicidal. I told them that I wanted to live, but I didn't want to live the life that I currently had. While I spoke, I suddenly had a major panic attack. It was as if telling that level of truth was creating some kind of chemical reaction in my body. I spoke for about five minutes. I didn't think I was ever going to return to that meeting, but it felt so good to let off some steam.

After the meeting, Robbie came up to me and asked if we could meet for coffee sometime. Immediately, I said yes. I didn't know why, but I really wanted to talk with Robbie more. I also realized that my suicidal thoughts were gone. Like I said before, I wanted to kill myself for four years. Every day for four years, I had truly wanted to end it all. I never had a break from that feeling, not until I went to that first AA meeting. I told Robbie that I would meet him the next day and he asked if I could meet him at the noon meeting the next day. I said yes. After talking to Robbie, I went over to Jason's place and passed around some writing ideas for a couple of hours and then I went home feeling like life might actually be possible after all. I was curious to see what tomorrow would bring for the first time in a long time. The next day, I met Robbie at the AA meeting and sat next to him. We shook hands. I had no intention in participating in the meeting on any level other than just sitting next to Robbie and waiting for the meeting to end. I immediately liked the stories that the people told. I could really relate to bits and pieces of everyone's shares. Everybody had different backgrounds and came from all over the country but they destroyed their lives at one time or another and then put their lives back together with AA. That meeting made such an impression on me. One of the men called on Robbie and he said that he would like to give his time to me and give me a chance to talk. So I talked. If there is one thing I can do no matter what, it's talk. I told the group of men that I could relate to everything that I was hearing and it actually made me feel better. I wasn't sure if I would keep going to AA meetings, but I was so glad it was there as an option. I told everyone that I had tried so many different things in order to improve my life, but nothing worked. I admitted that I had very little trouble quitting using drugs and drinking, but I had a lot of trouble living life. I felt like life was impossible. After the meeting, Robbie told me that AA is not all about quitting drinking. In the beginning it was, but AA was really about helping you learn to live life on life's terms. When Robbie told me this, my mind was blown. I always thought that AA was for people that could not and would not stop drinking. I always thought people would go to AA meetings and then just go home and drink some more. I didn't know that a lot of people who went to the meetings were able quit drinking for years and years.

After the meeting was over, Robbie and I went to get some food and talk. We talked for an hour or so. He told me about all the amazing possibilities that life could offer me. I could only respond with one word, "How?" He continued to tell me about his childhood, his career in the navy, and about being gay. I remember him asking me if I had a problem with him being gay, and of course I didn't. Robbie was one of the most incredible people I had ever met. I didn't give a shit what he was. I just wanted the life he had. Robbie was and still is such a happy, healthy guy. After that conversation, he became my sponsor. From that day forward, I promised that I would work every day to become the most well-rounded person that I could be. Time will tell if this actually happens.

7. Devil Inside

Getting my body back in order was the easiest part of my disease. The mental illness was a bit trickier. At least you can look at your body and see what needs to be fixed. When it comes to your mind, it almost seems like a crapshoot. You have to be willing to try anything. You have to talk about your feelings, meet doctors, and maybe even, God forbid, try medications. I am not a doctor or salesman, so don't freak out on me, but if you suffer from a serious mental illness, there is a chance that some form of medication will help you. Maybe you only need to take something for a few months or a few years, but it could buy you some time while you learn some life skills and learn how to deal with some deeper issues. Maybe you will find out that you have a genuine chemical imbalance and the medication will help bring some piece of you back into balance. Everybody is different and there are a lot of options. And above all the things that I have listed, I have learned that you have to listen. Listen like your life depends on it. If you are suicidal like I was, your life does depend on it. One thing I can guarantee is that if you feel like shit today and you felt like shit a few years ago, and if you do the same things you have always done, you will always get the same result.

It took me about four years to get my mind back. First was the trial phase of medications. This would take a year and a half. Then it would take about a year for my body to adjust to the medications. Then it would take a couple of more years to really get my groove back. About ten years sober and a few years on meds, and I was finally able to really start my life over. For years, I thought I was destined to be in a kind of invisible prison for the rest of my life. Still, not everything is perfect. I didn't become suddenly close to my family as a result of sobriety. I didn't get the dream job. My fear of commitment and emotionally strong women would remain at an all-time high for many more years. To be completely honest with you, I am still not close to my family today. Too much has happened. I am so different now. My family has, in a sense, remained the same, and I feel millions of miles away from them on every level. Geographically, I have grown out of Portland. Small towns just don't offer me what I want. The culture, the pace, and the opportunities that big cities have don't exist in small towns like Portland, Oregon. Mentally, I can't relate to my family either. We have different value systems. This has proven to be one of the lonelier side effects of the disease and remains to be true for me even in recovery. When you are sick, you feel like nobody understands what you are going through, and when you get better, you feel like nobody could possibly understand the process you went through in order to be healthy or at least healthier than you were in your using days. But this could all be said no matter what you face in life. Single mothers go through their own kind of battle while raising a child on their own. War veterans have their own hell to deal with. We all have to deal with a kind of mourning phase. But if you look at all the examples that I have just listed, the ones that tend to make it through are the ones that have reached out to other people, the ones that tell someone that they are scared and feel like they have lost all hope. Those are the people that have a chance—the single mother, the war vet, and the man or woman that lost the love of their life. There are support groups for all these people. Today, it all seems so simple, but in the beginning, the answers were all invisible to me. I thought I was expressing myself when I was talking to my doctors, but all I was really doing was complaining about how much pain I was in and how my parents fucked me up. All I was focused on was how unfair life is. Everyone would nod and write notes. I would do that for almost four years. I was drowning in resentments. *Why me, why me, why me?* Asking that question over and over again would cost me tens of thousands of dollars. When I started making the transition from seeing doctors and specialists and gradually making it to more AA meetings, my life started to change very quickly. At first, I showed up to noon AA meetings. I would share at meetings once a week and once a week turned into two times a week. I started practicing what AA calls the twelve steps and the twelve traditions of Alcoholics Anonymous. Robbie was my full-time sponsor now and we would meet up every Monday at six p.m. and read the 'Big Book' one chapter at a time. We discussed anything that I might have had a question about. Robbie was high energy and so much fun to spend time with. Plus, his Partner would always make the most elaborate meals for us. The experience was warm and safe. It felt like family.

All those years of practicing sobriety on my own, from November 2001 to May of 2009, I was slowly losing myself in a way that I would not be able to understand for many years. During all those years pursuing a fix to my mental health problems, I was actually sick in a different way. Yes, I had depression and anxiety, but there was something else going on. What I was really suffering from was a rotting soul. My soul was dying. What good is a healthy body and a strong mind if your soul is dying? For me, the human soul is real. For years, I thought the soul was something you talked about while on acid or magic mushrooms. When the high was over, you just didn't talk about the soul anymore (not until the next psychedelic trip). I have always been a firm believer that everything has its time and place. I personally feel that I have in my lifetime experienced all three types of major illnesses that any one human can experience: physical, mental, and spiritual illness. I believe all three are a true phenomenon. I also believe that the disease of drug and alcohol addiction is one of the diseases where you have the horror of experiencing all three types of sickness at the same time. Addiction is a triple threat and I believe this is why it destroys and kills so many people and entire families every year. Those four years spent in and out of hospitals for depression and anxiety, the meds, the random sex, the suicidal thoughts, the electroshock treatments… all of that… why? My soul was sinking.

Again, I didn't believe in anything. I had hate in my heart. I didn't want to hurt anyone. I just wanted what everybody had and I didn't. I wanted someone to talk to. I wanted to live in a house that was comfortable. I wanted everyone around me to not be afraid of everything. I wanted people to listen and talk and participate in one another's lives. I am not a firm believer in good and evil. I am not into anything like 'Old Testament' with the lighting and fire and do-what-I-say-or-I'll-burn-your-house-down kind of shit, but I do believe in *something*. Over the years, I have had some crazy experiences. I have had too many experiences to count. For example, a couple years back, I had a severe migraine and I was having troubles with a woman that I was dating. Finally at three a.m., I just got out of bed, got on my knees, and said, "God, please help me with this pain. I don't know what to do right now, but please take away this pain!" Then I opened the 'Big Book' of AA and just flipped to a random page and started reading. My headache completely went away. Or there was the time where I decided I would stop being stingy with the money I put in the basket during what is called the seventh traditions. This is where you put a couple bucks in the basket to pay for the rent of the room that you use in order to make the meeting happen. For years, I would put a buck or two in the basket, but then I realized that I had the habit of spending money on some of the shittiest and most useless things. But when the time comes to support something that is designed to help me become a whole, healthy person, I just put scraps in the basket in order for the meeting to barely break even. Fuck that. I believe that you get back much more than you give. Over the past few months, I've made sure to take care of the basket when it comes my way and I noticed immediately that my outside financial life has been getting better. At work, my commissions and tips are coming in more rapidly. This book that you are reading is a direct result of my theory that the more you give, the more you get. It has become so true for me. I am by no means a millionaire, but I feel like a million bucks more often than not. But when I don't give back, when I stick to myself a bit too long, when I isolate and do not reach out to anyone anywhere, eventually, I always begin to suffer. Once I begin suffering, it can be difficult to get out of it. If I suffer long enough, I might start to get comfortable with the suffering. And maybe to spice things up, I'll find a couple of friends that are suffering like me, and maybe if I'm really lucky, I might just find an attractive miserable women to spend my time with. Wouldn't that be great? Two unhappy people, watching movies in the dark together. Sign me up. Screw having goals and living up to my potential. Why do that when you could date some girl that is still secretly in love with her ex-boyfriend? Fuck productivity and personal accountability. You have an ex-nineties' goth girl to break up with and then get back together with again and maybe accidentally get pregnant after having unprotected make-up sex with for the seventieth time.

For some odd reason, spiritual health seems to get pushed to the side. I guess spiritual health was never appointed a good-enough marketing team. And sure, yoga is everywhere and meditation retreats are all the rage, but I mean real, deep spiritual health. The kind of spiritual health that when your girlfriend of two years has decided that moving out would be best and spending more time apart would be ideal, you are able to calmly give her what she needs. If you are spiritually connected to yourself, you would see where she is coming from and just agree with her and let everything flow. Let her move out. A month goes by and she starts calling and wanting to spend more time with you again because now she realizes what she had now that you have been gone for a while. Or maybe she meets some guy with a long ponytail and a beard at some hot Buddhist stretching class and she feels that their chakras align perfectly together and that your relationship was just a test for her to see her true self. If you have true balance and self-worth, you would be able to let her go onto her next chapter and not take it personally. If you can truly love someone and then watch them walk off into the sunset with someone else, then you must have found balance within yourself.

It is mid-June 2018, and I have spent the last two years essentially alone. I have had no interest in starting a romantic relationship just for the sake of having a romantic relationship. The very thought of that sounds like a prison to me. I have a lot of momentum in my life right now and a relationship would completely fuck that up. Now, if I were to meet someone very special, that is a whole other story. A special person doesn't slow you down or impede your progress. If you find someone to be special and that person feels the same way about you, I think you join forces. There is no battling for each other's time.

Relationships are more often than not very messy and painful for addicts and codependents. How do you think you would react in situations like the one I just mentioned? How have you behaved in the past? How was your last breakup? Was there a lot of arguing? Maybe some screaming? She calls you an asshole and you call her a bitch? After a breakup, did you start 'partying' more? More booze? More coke? More hangovers at work? I want to make it clear that this is not healthy behavior. If your girlfriend broke up with you last month or you lost a job and now you are in a twenty-eight-day spin-dry rehab, there is definitely a big problem. Healthy people don't go on coke binges after a woman rejects them. A healthy, well-adjusted person finds more constructive ways of dealing with emotional pain. Maybe they talk to someone that they trust about it. Maybe they go to the gym an extra day a week. There are so many healthy ways to lick your emotional wounds. Up until maybe a year ago, I was just another melodramatic over-reactor. For years, my life has always been either amazing or horrible. I think I would prefer that my life be horrible rather than just okay. Having an okay life always seemed like another form of failure. If your life is horrible and there is nowhere else to go but up, at least you have an adventure ahead of you. When things are okay, you are basically just existing. 'Just existing' always seemed like a kind of death to me. You are awake and moving around, but that's it. What else is there? It would take me so many years to understand that it is okay for life to be flat for a while. I would learn to look at the flat times like a time for rest. Life would eventually bring you turbulence again. This is a guarantee. Life will also bring you rewards as well. Use the flat times to rest. Find different ways to educate yourself. This will help you weather life's future storms. New forms of education will help you take better advantage of the rewards that you will eventually receive as well. I feel that the soul also needs to be educated. I feel that this comes from outside of your being. I feel that meaning is attached to faith. When you lose your job or a loved one dies, I feel that faith is far more valuable than lifting weights or doing Pilates. I am a firm believer that all human beings will experience situations that only faith will be able to mend. I believe that every human being will experience things that they just can't explain. This is fine. This is normal. To me, faith simply means that you are comfortable with not having all the answers. To me, faith means that you understand that you don't have complete control. All the car insurances in the world will not protect you from a drunk driver. You can't control the days of other people. I know that you have no control over what I do today and I have no control over what you do. After looking both ways before crossing the street, I have to have faith that nothing will fall out of the sky and crush me to death. If you watch enough news, you know that anything is possible. Things are falling out of the sky all over the world. We know this. We also just accept that wherever we are, there will most likely be electricity. We will be able to recharge our cellphones. We will have heat and water almost always coming out of every faucet that we want to use. Sure, there is so much that has to happen every day in order for all of this to work, but we don't really think about that and say, "Well, it just is." We have faith.

After reaching my physical bottom with drugs and alcohol in 2001, I would reach my mental bottom in 2010. I would have to say that my spiritual bottom happened in 2015. At this point, I had been about thirteen and a half years sober. I had a fine job. I was dating a pretty girl and living in Downtown Portland. But is this all there is? This question is scary for an addict. This question is scary for everyone, but I think this question is hardest for addicts. I also think that this question kills a lot of people with a lot of sober time. Sometimes, yes, *this is always all there is.* Can you handle it? No promotion in the world is going to fill your soul. Cindy Crawford in her prime will not fix you. Pizza at two in the morning will solve nothing. I am still having a personal and private battle with pizza at two a.m. With close to fourteen years sober, I was officially sinking. Again, depression took a hold of me. I was going to at least seven AA meetings a week. I was meditating and praying and talking to my sponsor. I would help other alcoholics when they needed it. But still, I was sinking. Why? Simple. I didn't mean it. I did it for the social position and recognition. "Look at me. I am younger than you and I have more sober time than you! This is fucking easy." This became my attitude for a long time. I began to look down on the people that would come in and out of AA. People that couldn't stay sober were beneath me. I felt like I was some kind of sober Mozart genius. My ego was at an all-time high. Meanwhile, I could barely pay my rent and I would borrow money from my parents and take forever to pay it back. I was an addict and I deserved help. I was given a shitty hand. This was my attitude and this attitude would almost kill me. In the winter of 2015, I started fantasizing about hanging myself. But I knew something was different this time. This wasn't my mental illness. This was due to my refusal to believe in anything outside of myself. I didn't believe in God. I believed that if I worked hard, everything would fall into place. If things didn't fall into place, I would believe that life owed me something. When life didn't give me what I wanted, I would become resentful. My resentment always turned into depression. After months of this, everything just kind of stacked on top of itself and I was underneath it all.

Finally, on a really raining day and after calling out of work for three days straight, I got on my hands and knees and I asked God to teach me to pray. I begged God to take away these horrible feelings. I begged for God to teach me what people could not teach me. I was missing something and I had no idea what it was. At that moment, this horrible weight was lifted out of my body. The horrible visions of hanging myself disappeared. I was able to leave my room. I took a shower and went to the gym and swam laps. I called a friend and told them what happened. I called my sponsor. I am not going to lie to you and say that I have not had a bad day since. I still have my battles with depression. I still eat late at night. I still watch porn on occasion and I have sought out escorts here and there. I am not perfect. I still enjoy the dark side of things on occasion. But killing myself just doesn't seem appealing. For me, God is real. When things get really hard for, I always pray, and so far, hundred percent of the time that bad feeling that I am praying about goes away. Not understanding how or why is part of the game for me. I have learned not to debate this shit with myself or anyone else. I believe that there are just as many types of gods as there are people in the world. I also believe that if you want access to a god and you want help, then something more powerful than you will be there for you. But I also believe that you have to mean it. You can't make a deal with God and you can't connect with something that you don't really believe is real. If you don't believe in God or you have a problem with the idea of God, that's totally cool with me. It may offend other people, but who cares. This is your life and you can technically do and believe whatever you want. But is it working for you? Is your way of doing things working? Yes or no? If you don't know the answer to that question, you might have even deeper problems than you are aware of. Getting better and moving forward will be a lot easier if you know where you stand in the world. For me, I am an addict in recovery. I cannot ever drink or use drugs ever again. I believe in God. When I work with God, my life gets better. I keep my shit straight and when I get confused, I pray. It's that simple. I eat when I am hungry, I sleep when I am tired, and I pray when I am scared. Why should life be harder than that?

8. Next

Spring of 2015: I feel that I have a pretty good map of how the world works now. I have a strong understanding on how to maneuver through the world with a handicap like addiction and alcoholism. I have made peace with the physical, mental, and spiritual sides of the disease. I have come to the conclusion that God, as I understand him, is here to help me. I also believe that God has given us a brain to use and we should use it well. We can make decisions on our own. I love using my mind, but I have to always be aware that, at times, my mind likes to play tricks on me. My brain loves to get into trouble sometimes. The trouble that my brain likes is weird sex, really heavy, expensive French meals, and the most dangerous of all, my brain loves it when I feel sorry for myself. When I feel sorry for myself, I always begin to think I should get more of something that I already have. I have the disease of *more, more, more*. The trick is to keep my mind in check. I have learned that keeping my mind busy is a good thing. I keep my brain busy with reading, small projects, and exercise. The projects do not need to go anywhere. Keeping the brain busy is just good for everyone. Idle hands are the devil's playground. If I am not at work or at an AA meeting, or swimming laps or writing, things could get a little dicey. It always goes back to boredom. If my body and mind are not working, it can be trouble. But if my soul starts to get a little itchy and scratchy, that's when I do really dumb things. I have been known to leave my place at one a.m. and just go to some shady part of town, to try to find a woman that has an hour to spare and wants some company. I rarely have this problem come up, but it does pop its head out once in a dark blue moon. On occasion, I will go to a massage parlor and get a happy ending. To this day, I just have no real interest in maintaining a long-term relationship with a woman. Dedicating myself to one woman just seems like a miserable idea. Spending a large portion of my day with a woman just doesn't seem like a great way to spend my time. But finding a curvy Latina with a pretty face and a big booty to spend an hour or two with does sound quite attractive to me (ideally between the hours of eleven p.m. and one a.m.). Then she somehow just magically disappears. That sounds great. Over the years, so many people have told me that eventually I will find sincere interest in others and I will want to settle down. I have friends with ten or more years of sobriety and they have all partnered off. What's my deal? Again, am I just broken? Outside of my work, which keeps me very busy and social, I prefer to spend my free time alone. I love sleeping in till noon. I like getting a haircut every two weeks. I enjoy my weekly ninety-minute massages. I love my ridiculously expensive meals. And I love sex when I want it.

It is really difficult to find a beautiful woman with the body type that I like that is open to fucking a few times a month with no expectation of more happening on the emotional front. I have also learned that the women that are open to this kind of setup that I want are rarely emotionally stable. For some reason, most of the women that want what I want tend to be mentally ill. What does that say about me? I am extremely picky, and I am just not interested in hooking up with fours and fives. I am willing to pay top dollar for a nine or a ten. Thinking back, in my experience, I have always paid one way or another when dating an extremely beautiful woman. The places they want to go are nicer, they tend to be extremely high maintenance physically and emotionally, and the sex is never that great. The better-looking the woman, the worse the sex. A beautiful woman does not have to try in bed. Why would she? Men have been standing in line and offering her all kinds of shit just for a taste. Why would someone in that position ever need to be good in bed? Being good in bed takes energy. Why would you exert energy if you don't have to? And sure, I know that there are beautiful women out there that love sex, but what kind of lottery do you have to win in order to find that one in a million specimen? Does this theory make me a bad person? I'm just telling it how I see it. I think we have all been brainwashed into believing what sex is supposed to be. I think people are telling us what we are supposed to be attracted to, how we are supposed to fuck, and everything in between. Nobody tells me what I should be into, if I should pay or not, and why it is good or bad. So many of my female 'friends' have told me that I shouldn't have to pay. I always tell them that I don't have to pay. I choose to pay. I tell them that I am paying for peace of mind. Has a woman that you broke up with ever come to your work just to make a scene and embarrass you? It's happened to me, and it sucked. Has a woman kept calling and texting you or sent you photos of her new guy a couple of months after you broke up with her? That also happened to me and it sucked too.

I moved in with a woman because the sex was great once. After eight months, I became very bored. What a surprise, right? Well, one day, I came home and all my shit was on the front lawn. Granted, I was emailing back and forth with a new female interest, which was a shady thing to do, but fuck, I was homeless for a minute. Every man would agree with me and every woman would say I deserved it. I want nothing to do with the kind of person that thinks it's no big deal to just kick someone out on the streets. Sure, kick him on the couch and give him a couple of weeks to find a place. But unless he has been physically abusing you, just relax a bit. For me, women are simply just more of a liability and less of an asset. It's all too risky to invest that much money, time, and effort into anyone. Unless you are a wealthy man and you are comfortable with possibly losing half of everything that you have one day, just don't get married. How exactly does it benefit you to get married? If divorce rates are at sixty percent, why would you chance it? What business could you possibly want to open or invest in when you are facing a sixty-percent failure rate? Women are the only one. Why? It's simple, because men are simple. Are you willing to ruin your entire life for pussy? Am I the only one that finds this to be ridiculous? Don't get me wrong—I love pussy too. I just don't want to buy it a house, a beach house, a boat, and have kids with it. Pussy is more of an activity that I enjoy, like swimming, eating a nice meal, or a weekend getaway. This is the category that I put pussy in. This mindset has saved my life many times. I have no children or child-support bills. I do not owe alimony. My debt is very small. I can sleep in on my days off. I can sleep with whoever I want. I can do pretty much whatever I want without having to defend whatever it is that I want to do.

After giving this list of amazing side effects of bachelorhood, some woman always asks this one stupid question, "But don't you get lonely?" Of course I get lonely! But no matter what position in life someone is in, everyone experiences loneliness. There is a difference between loneliness and a vapid level of codependency. Am I saying that everyone that is married is codependent? No, I am not saying that. I will say that I think eighty-five percent of the married people today suffer from an insipid level of codependence. And of course, everyone is going to freak out over this comment. I get it. I am poo-pooing on everything that you stand for. I am shitting on your entire existence. I'd be pissed too. I am judging you and I think you are an idiot. Sorry, but let's just skip the bullshit and agree to disagree. And don't worry. Next month, I will probably meet that one woman that will change my entire universe and frame of thinking. What will I be then? I will be just another person that has become a vapidly codependent person. I think codependency in small doses is basic human nature. I think there are different degrees of codependency. If you are with someone and you want to get out but just can't, that's not good. Get out. If your partner is abusing you in any way and you stay with them, what the hell for? I get it;

it's not as simple as just leaving. You have kids with them or a house investment or a million other things, but get the fuck out. Just cut your ties. A million dollars isn't a lot of fun to spend if you are dead. And sure, not everyone is in a life-or-death situation, but what about being true to yourself? What about having self-respect? Why are you so scared to be alone? Why do you hate yourself so much? These are the things you should be working on, not a marriage that has been a big pile of shit for the past four years. None of us is getting any younger. Just *do* you. Live your fucking life. Who taught you that living your life to the fullest was such a sin? Who told you that being happy was selfish? Fuck those people. If your parents taught you this shit, they can go fuck themselves too. A lot of parents have been telling their kids so many lies. I'm sure that some parents have no idea that they have been passing down a lot of lies and some parents actually are aware of it, but it's just easier to tell their kids lies than to do some actual work on themselves and help their kids become functioning human beings. Fuck lazy people. Have you ever seen a six-year-old just glued to a cellphone watching some random Disney film while her neurotic bat-shit crazy mother is on her cellphone talking shit about the baby daddy? Sure, we have all seen this. It's the new normal. These poor kids are the product of shitty, codependent parents. These kids represent generations of shitty parents doing a shitty job raising their kids. But who am I to judge, right? I don't have kids. I can't even make a relationship last longer than eight months, so who the fuck do I think I am? I will tell you. I'm just a shitty human being just like the rest of you, but I consciously made a decision not to fuck up some helpless being just because I have nothing better to do. This all sounds pretty rough, right? Well, what can I say? I'm just a big dickhead with a heart of gold, I guess.

I am not just bashing on people having children for the sake of it. My point is: take care of what you have. If you have kids and you are struggling with something to the point that you are in a rehab facility or you keep having to move back home, just stop for a moment and focus. Think about everything you have in your life. Think about the people in your life. Who are the people that want the best for you? Who are the people that you know are no good for you? From personal experience, I would recommend getting rid of the bad right away. Don't even call them to let them know you have to part ways. Just cut them out. Now think of the people that you have a positive history with. Who are the people that have called you to see if you are okay? Who are the people that have told you that you have a problem? These are usually the people that care about you. Try keeping these people around. Now, are there any people in your life that you are not sure about? Do you have people that might be in the gray zone of your social circle? What do you think you should do about these people? Answer: nothing. Just let these people stay in the gray. See if they reach out to you. If they do, then you know where you stand with them. If you have children, take care of them. Stop the bullshit for you, but get your shit together for them. But remember, if you ever say that you need to quit using and drinking for your kinds, you are fucked. If you don't start the day getting better for yourself first, nothing will ever really change. Good intentions just don't go very far with addiction. The disease of addiction eats good intentions for breakfast. People with good intentions die from addiction every day. And addicts kill people with good intentions every day as well. I hope I have made myself clear. If not, I will say it again. Get sober for *you*. Everything else falls into place. You want to keep your kids? You will keep your kids. You want to live in a safer neighborhood? Stay sober, work your ass off, and you will move to a safer neighborhood. The world will open up to you if you stay sober. If you don't believe me, let me ask you this one question. Do you have proof? Do you have proof that all of the things that you believe are possible or impossible to be true? Where did you get the answers? From people? What people? Books? Which books? Why do you believe what you believe? You don't you believe in God? Why? Were you gang-raped by a bunch of priests? Probably not? But why then? Did you grow up in an extremely strict and religious household? Were you told 'no' a lot? Now this would make more sense. But maybe there is more. Who hurt you? Who hurt you and how does it relate to God? Was it Dad? Was it Uncle Jake? If you can't even talk about it, I guarantee you that you will stay sick. If drugs are the problem, you will keep relapsing. If food is the issue, you will keep eating. Whatever you are dealing with, it will stay with you until you uncover the root of the problem. Face it, talk to people about it, and take direction on what to do about it. If this sounds too hard for you, then you may be in a lot of trouble. You can disagree, but I do not gain or lose anything if you stay sick or not. I do prefer that a person be healthy over sick any day of the week, but if you want to say, "Fuck you, hell man, I don't know you," then fuck you too. But if you want to stand up and do something about what's going on, there are thousands of men and women just like me that will help you. I will always reach my hand out to a drowning man, but I will never let him pull me down with him. Addiction is a crazy disease and staying sober is just as crazy. I am a firm believer that when it comes to addiction, there are specific moments in time where I don't have to outrun the bear; I just have to outrun you. More often than not, I will always be there to help though. So where are you with all this? Where is your head at? If you want to keep going, I have a lot more to come. I am just getting started really. There is a whole universe outside the whole my-name-is-Bob-and-I-am-addict-and-I-need-help. Stopping is the easiest part of changing your life. The wave of black water that is going to rush at you is the hard part. The ghosts in the closet, looking at your part in the mess, the apologies, the true loneliness, finding out just how small you really are, and learning to be okay with it… these are just a few things that will come your way. I have been there. So many people have. I am going to talk about it and I am going to tell you how I got out and I hope you are ready to listen. After that, it's up to you what you do next.

9. People

I think I have made it clear that I believe addiction is a disease centered in the mind. One of my biggest struggles that I believe to be directly attached to my disease is people. My relationship with the people in the world is overall challenging. I don't like being told what to do. Who does? But some people are just better at taking direction than others. At times, I will experience physical pain when someone tells me what to do. My mind will start to swirl with resentments beginning to build, depending on who is telling me what I should do. It's been this way since I was a child. It's not good and it has never served me well.

As a child and all the way through my twenties, I loved having all the attention on me. The approval of others was my life source. If I was scolded by a loved one or rejected by anyone on any level, I would be crushed. At school, I had to be in charge of all the games and activities. I was the organizer and the cheerleader. If someone was being picked on, I would stick up for him or her. I was never picked on as a child and hated to see someone bullied. But if someone had a beef with me and I did not like them, I would do my best to make them feel uncomfortable. In arguments, I would give horrible verbal lashings. I can remember a handful of arguments that I would have with schoolmates over the years. I have said some horrible things to people over my lifetime. I loved to debate and I was bloodthirsty when it came to giving my opinion and being right. I never focused on any one type of person. I would just counterattack when someone pissed me off. I have always been an equal opportunity hunter. Big or small, if you want to talk some shit, we can talk some shit. Needless to say, I had problems with most adults—my stepfather, teachers, and a few bosses here or there. When I first got sober, I worked for a florist for two weeks. I pissed him off so bad that he started crying and attacked me out of the embarrassment that he suffered from my biting tongue. I have this strange ability to find your weakness and use it against you. I will see all your cracks within seconds. Just a couple of days ago, I was locking up my bike outside of a Trader Joe's and this bitchy Asian girl came up to where I was parking and asked me if I would make some room for her. I said yes. Then I began locking up my bike. If you live in San Francisco like I do, you have to really lock up your bike. No pussy footing around. I use a U-lock, a cord, and I lock my seat to my bike. A bit much? No, not in San Francisco. I have lost two bikes because I didn't secure them enough. The bike thieves in San Francisco are little ninjas. They know every trick in the book to steal your bike. The young woman asked me if I locked my bike this way every time. But it's not what she said; it's how she said it. She used that snarky, bitchy, spoiled Bay Area fake-ass valley accent that ninety percent of everybody that lives in San Francisco uses. I said, "Yes, every single fucking time I lock my bike like this. Do you have a problem with that?" She told me that it didn't leave a lot of room for her. There was already a bike on the other side where she wanted to park her bike, so it was going to be tight no matter what. I said, "Look, you have three options right now. You can wait until I lock my bike up and then see if you still have room. Or you can pay me $75.00 for the spot I am about to use or we can fight for it." She called me an asshole. I told her that this is what equality looks like. If she wanted to be treated like an equal, then she was going to have to get used to how men treat one another. I explained to her that men can be aggressive and competitive with one another and that we can be assholes. I told her that she didn't get to cherry-pick how she wanted to be treated in life. Then I walked away and went grocery shopping.

Look, I know what you are thinking. I am an asshole. And I agree. I was a total dick to that girl. I know better and she didn't deserve it. I do not act like that all the time and there is no excuse for it when I do. It's like I need to let off some steam sometimes. I feel like there are two or even three of me sometimes. As I write this, I am listening to Philip Glass. I am calm, open, and collected. But there are times where I can be hypercritical, aggressive, and sharp. Then there is the clown side of me—high energy, people-pleasing, and scattered. I tend to spend my time in one of those three personalities. When I am at work, I am the high-energy tiger. When I am out and about biking around the city and getting shit done, I tend to be the aggressive guy. Late at night, my favorite time of the day, my favorite personality comes out. The old soul comes out. The deeper and more genuine romantic in me comes out. I wish I could be this guy all the time. As I write this, I care about people and I am open to love. I could be vulnerable right now with the right person. I could look into her eyes and tell her the truth and listen to her tell me her truth. I could be in love right now and be fine with it. But I know when I wake up tomorrow that I will have to turn back into the happy, high-energy how-can-I-help-you machine. It is a vicious cycle. I do not know how to be one man. To be perfectly honest with you, I would be lost if one of my personalities were to die tomorrow. Without the aggressive side of me, how would I get through the pressure cooker that life can be? Without the high-energy talk-show host personality, how would I do my job properly? And without the deeper lone wolf side, how would I get through the night alive? I need all three of me to get through all this. Life would eat me alive if I didn't have my small team inside my head. I just think it would be a lot easier if I could take the best attributes of each and just consolidate them into one force. I pray that over time I will achieve this. Some people wish and pray and work hard for their dream girl or the dream job. I simply wish, pray, and work for peace of mind.

10. Life Lessons

St. Patrick's Day, 2018: I have been living in San Francisco for almost two years. My neighborhood is North Beach and I love it. I love everything about San Francisco. Even the things I hate about San Francisco, I still kind of love. My relationship with San Francisco has been so intense. It reminds me of my feelings for Nicole, my ex-fiancé. It was love at first sight. I grew up going to raves in San Francisco in the mid-nineties. Every time I would arrive, my eyes would fill up with tears. I would become overwhelmed and filled with thrilling emotions. It was like sex. Then, when you add some high-quality MDMA and old school house music to the mix, it was pure heaven. God, I love San Francisco! When I was finally able to move to San Francisco permanently, I felt like I won the lottery. Yes, it's expensive as shit and yes, a lot of the people are snobby assholes, but so am I, so fuck them. I didn't move here for them. I moved here to kick some ass. Before San Francisco, I was living in Key West Florida for about a year for work. I hated every minute of it, but I had to do what I had to do in order to gain the skills that I would need in order to move to a city like San Francisco. I am a hotel concierge and I love it. I will never become rich doing what I do, but I wouldn't trade it for anything. I get to be a well-dressed magician for work every day. I get to eat at the best restaurants, experience amazing theater, art, and naughty massages whenever I want. I have dreamed about this since I was five years old. Caviar, rare and expensive cheeses, duck liver pate, and hot Brazilian escorts, these are my four favorite food groups. San Francisco is famous for its neighborhoods and I get to live in one of its best spots and it's only five blocks from my work. I have been planning and scheming and sharpening my knives for years and I finally made it. It has not been easy. I have lived through every form of poverty one can endure in order to get here. It blows me away that some people were actually born and raised in San Francisco. San Francisco is as close to magic as you could ever get. There are only a handful of cities in the world that offer what San Francisco has to offer. Everybody told me that it is too expensive to live in, and I could tell that some people thought that I was crazy for moving to the Bay Area. But I want to let you in on a little secret. The entire time I lived in Portland, I was never able to make a real living. I was always broke and I never felt like I could find a way out. For a long time, I thought it was me. Was I defective? What was wrong with me? I felt like everything I tried would turn to shit. As soon as I moved to San Francisco, my whole world blew open. San Francisco has seen multiple gold rushes and it has seen a lot of hard times as well. The city has burned down and rebuilt itself. Dot Com bubbles have burst. Entire industries have disappeared and it still finds a way to reinvent itself. The only way a place can do this is if it attracts the kind of people that dream big, work hard, fail big, get back up, and kick ass again.

I can relate to this. Most of my life has been me failing and getting back up. I am almost forty years old and I have yet to see major financial success. Well, I have never been really financially successful in legal terms. But in the past two years, I have been able to do something that I believe in and love and get paid really well for. When I left Key West, I was making $14.00 an hour doing the same job that I do in San Francisco. What the fuck is that all about? I was never able to save money before. I could never dine out at any restaurant that I wanted to on any night of the week before. I could never get massages on a weekly basis two years ago. When I was ten-years sober, I could barely pay my rent and eat. There was no exotic travel in my future back then. There was just stress, depression, and constantly asking myself why I keep trying. I am so glad that I stuck with it though. I kept working. I kept going to AA meetings every day. I kept exercising. A small part of me knew that if I kept trying, life would get better. I knew I had to find a way to keep loving what I did. I had to find a way to believe in and love my dream. I would force myself to believe in God. I am not sure why, but something inside me kept pushing me to do all these things. This is also around the time when my stepfather would start believing in me, I think. We would never become best buds but a mutual respect started to develop between us. To this day, we do not talk but we have respect for each other. I don't even think we like each other but if my stepfather were in trouble, I would do anything to help. Back in 2015, something happened. At first I thought I was cursed, but it turned out to be a blessing in disguise. I was still living in Portland and I was working as a concierge for Hilton. Suddenly, my hours were cut. There were weeks where I wasn't even on the schedule. I couldn't afford this and I was scared shitless. My parents offered to help me out a bit. I got a part-time job for a couple of months to get me through what I was hoping would just be a slow period at the hotel. I looked online for full-time concierge position all over the country. Finally, I saw a concierge position opening in Key West. I called them and told them what my situation was and that I just wanted to work and gain more experience. The Waldorf Astoria in Key West offered me a concierge job and they told me that I could stay in employee housing for $300.00 a month. I was sold. I took the job and three weeks later, I was in Key West. This was actually my first true culture shock. I went from a rainy, mid-sized, liberal west coast city and flew all the way to a tiny island that would be ninety percent humidity, only about fourteen thousand people, and the island was two by four miles. Everybody was drunk all the time. Everybody would sleep with one another's girlfriends. The new general manager started two weeks after I did and he fired roughly one third of the entire employee population in less than six weeks. Work was crazy, island life was crazy, and even the weather was out to kill us. The cockroaches were larger than my thumb. Lightning and thunderstorms would knock out the island electricity on a weekly basis. Finding good food was next to impossible. I basically lived on my green veggie shakes and Cuban sandwiches. Employee housing was like living in an episode of MTV's *Real World*. Employee housing was filled with strangers that would drink and use coke every night and everybody would either fight or fuck. At the time, I was thirty-six but most of the people in my building were in their mid-twenties, so I can't blame them for being such psychopaths. In order to stay sane, I went to AA meetings at a place called Anchors Away every day and joined the local gym. I stayed away from the employee housing building as much as possible. I was there to grab a snack or to sleep. I did meet some amazing people in AA, Key West. I would say that out of all the AA meetings I have been to, the best AA I have ever experienced was in Key West. I actually went to an AA meeting in Cuba and I caught an AA meeting in Haiti as well. I love that I can go to an AA meeting anywhere in the world. Without my AA meetings, I would not have found the courage to travel and I would not have been strong enough to survive all the chaos that I experienced over the past few years. I fully understand why people turn to alcohol when they first move somewhere new; you don't know anyone and everything is new and unfamiliar. It's scary being the new kid at any age. I had a handful of panic attacks when I first moved to Key West and the panic attacks came back for a few days when I moved to San Francisco as well. I have had plenty of days when I didn't know how I was going to make it through all this. I never wanted to drink, but it was really hard.

It took me about a year to get comfortable in my new San Francisco skin. Eventually, I would get my groove back again. Right as I was starting to reach that point where you can just go on autopilot for days at a time, something horrible happened. An old building that was connected to my apartment building burned down. My room was just twenty feet from the fire.

I was at work while the North Beach fire was happening. Finally at about eight p.m., some guests came up to my desk and told me that there was a fire next to a park in North Beach. This made me nervous immediately. I Googled North Beach fire and sure enough, the internet was full of images of the building that was on fire and it was right next to my place. I lived five blocks from work, so I just ran to see what was going to happen, and yes, indeed my building was about to burn down. So many people, including myself, just stood on the corner and watched thirty-foot flames devour an old liquor store and three restaurants. Once the fire was put out, everyone in my building was instructed to go to the North Beach Police Precinct. Fifteen of us went and our neighborhood representative told us that the city would arrange housing for us until we could move back into our buildings. We were told it would be a week, maybe two weeks, before we could move back. Of course this would all be too easy. The city placed us in an SRO (*Single Room Occupancy)* building in San Francisco's Tenderloin District. The Tenderloin District is the roughest, most violent area of San Francisco and it has a major drug epidemic on its hands—drugs, prostitution, and more drugs. I had to live on the corner of Turk and Hyde for three months. The first month was really rough. I was triggered like a motherfucker. I was calling every city worker that I could find to rant and rave about how unacceptable it was to put me in a rundown building. The room that I stayed in had no heat. The showers that I had to share had almost no water pressure and it would take at least ten minutes for the water to become hot. For three months, I took almost all my showers at my gym or at work. People would squat in our stairwells. One guy lived in the bathroom closest to my room for two days before being escorted out. It took two days for the police to get the documentation they would need in order to kick out the guy living in our bathroom out. Only in San Francisco! I would see prostitutes beat the shit out of each other for twelve dollars. I witnessed a shooting just three days before I wrote this paragraph that you are reading right now. Some guy in shiny, silver Audi shot off four rounds at a blind eighty-year-old black man in a wheelchair. You can't make this shit up. Well, seeing it in real life is so much more interesting.

The first month of living in the Tenderloin was quite jarring, seeing so many people defecate on the streets right out in the open, walking past people sleeping in the middle of the sidewalk, all the people smoking crack right out in the open, all the drug dealers and streetwalkers, day in and day out. There was no break from it. The pace of it all was relentless. It just didn't stop. By Week Five, I was beginning to crack a bit. Even if you have your shit together, being surrounded by poverty on this level is a bit much for the human spirit to take after a while. All of your senses are drowning in negativity. You smell urine and human shit. You see people beat the shit out of each other. You hear the word 'nigger' every three seconds. Poverty isn't just about not having any money. Poverty is a kind of culture. It has a feeling to it. You can feel something get its hooks into you and just suck all your energy out of you. This is something that someone that grew up in a safe middle-class family will never understand. True poverty can put you under a spell. It can hypnotize you. After three months of living in the Tenderloin, I have acclimated to what goes on around me. I am not fazed by anything that I see anymore. I have made a few friends in the TL. All of them are drug addicts. I smoke cigars with my buddy Jamaul and we listen to heavy blues music at one a.m. We just talk about our day. He sells crack and cheap guns on the streets and I sell San Francisco to tourists. I ask him not to smoke pot and drink while he is dealing on the streets. I tell him it isn't safe. He tells me what all the different street calls 'mean.' Everybody on my block calls me White Spanish. I am known for being sober but if I need anything, everyone is willing to get me whatever I need at any time. How sweet of them! Living in the Tenderloin has helped me to stop hating addicts. Yes, for years I have hated my own kind. I have learned that the only thing I really hate is poverty. I might not trust a lot of people, but I do not hate anyone anymore. This doesn't mean that I will cosign someone's shit. I still refuse to date a smoker and I tend to stay away from people with less than two years of sobriety. The difference is that today I do not look down on anyone. Well, most of the time I do not look down on these people. Recently, a young woman that frequents the AA meeting that I go to told me that I think I am better than everyone. I corrected her and said, "No, you think I am better than you. That has nothing to do with me." She didn't know what else to say, so she walked off and smoked a cigarette with her friends that do not challenge her. These are the people that I like to stay away from. I find that telling the truth is the best repellent for these types of people.

A lot of people do not like my sharp and jagged approach and opinions about addiction and recovery. I talk a lot about taking responsibility. I talk a lot about addiction being a mental illness. I talk about how if you are allergic to everything and you can't stop using drugs and your life is an overall shit show, maybe Mother Nature is trying to tell you that you are not necessary. And if you are not necessary, I don't think the universe wants you to create more versions of you. So many people just seem to not get this. Everyone innately thinks they are so special. I know I do. I think I am so fucking special sometimes. I am an egomaniac with an inferiority complex. Look at me! Stop looking at me! So many people have walked out of AA meetings that I have spoken at over the years. One of my mentors has told me many times that if everyone in the room likes you, you are probably lying. It is good to be well liked, but it is also good to tell the truth and my truth rubs some people the wrong way. Women have accused me of hating all women. I tell those women that just because I do not like them as individuals doesn't mean that I do not like women on the whole. I simply just do not like *you*. That never goes over well.

Men can also be assholes. I go to one of those upscale 'she-she' athletic clubs. I run into so many different kinds of assholes every day. You have your really effeminate straight guys with the heavy lisp that only gay guys had fifteen years ago. Then you have those guys in their fifties that just try too hard. They deepen their voices and they always stand in your way. You've got the socially unaware, loud, dirty NASCAR fans that just never seem to die off. Then you have me. I have a shit ton of tattoos and I am distant, aloof, and bored with everything. Last week, some guy said something stupid to me in the sauna and I just told him I am not interested in talking. I put my wet towel back over my head and went back into 'Marquesland.' A few days before that, I was biking down Market Street, minding my own business. This bike messenger kid kept cutting me off and then I would catch back up with him. The bike messenger asked me if I had a problem. I looked at him and told him to fuck off and then I just stared right through him. I think it's funny how so many skinny, pale, and out-of-shape men that have never been in a fight in their life actually think they are hot shit. But all men have a few things in common and one of them is that if you look a man straight in the eye and let him know that you are willing to fight him, ninety percent of all men will back down. In San Francisco, ninety-nine percent of all men will back down because men in San Francisco are pussies. Sorry, but it's true. If I were living in the south, I would never be as aggressive as I am here in San Francisco. If I lived in Atlanta, I know that a lot of men would be willing to throw down, so I would just pick my battles a bit more cautiously. It is really easy to be a hard ass on the west coast. Portland and Seattle are just as bad as San Francisco. The women are lazy and bitchy and the men are spineless. Of course I am speaking in generalities, but you get my point. Again, I am no better.

So if I hate people so much, why do I work in tourism? Why the fuck do I work in a busy hotel? Simple. I'm fucking crazy. Sure, I do not talk to myself, I don't cut myself or punch myself in the face, but I think there are a million and one ways to be a masochist. For me, I surround myself with people during my work hours, and on my days off, I get tattoos. People and tattoos are both very painful and both are beautiful.

As I get older, I am becoming more and more of a lone wolf. In AA and other twelve-step programs, everyone warns you about isolating. The AA promises, which are given under Step Nine, talk about taking interest in others. But as time goes on, I personally need people less and less. A day has twenty-four hours. I sleep eight to nine hours a day. I work eight hours a day, five days week. I go to four or five AA meetings a week, at an hour a pop. Then I swim three or four days a week and hit the steam and sauna twenty minutes each. There are one hundred and sixty-eight hours in a week and I spend one hundred and twenty-one hours a week doing what I feel I need to do in order to live well. God forbid, I want some alone time. I always feel so bad for all those skinny white girls that I see speed-walking with their yoga pants and matching tank top, rolled up yoga mat over their shoulder, starving, and who haven't been properly laid in four years. Is there a factory making these women somewhere in the Midwest that I don't know about? They are everywhere. They are walking daily planners, just pushing as much shit as they can into their weeks. Do they enjoy anything they do? They are always in a hurry to the next thing they have to do. And why do men find these women so appealing? I just can't get a hard-on for skinny white women that are always in a rush. Fuck that.

I want to take a moment and talk about the type of people I do like. I love people that live a conscious lifestyle, people that enjoy food and reading nonfiction, people that enjoy taking care of themselves, and people that don't smoke. I love people that chew with their mouths closed. I really enjoy passionate, talented people. I love great storytellers. One of my favorite people that I have ever met is a tattoo artist named Ed. What a nice guy! If you are under forty-five years old and you have a tattoo, it's because of Ed. Ed has told me a few amazing stories. Ed is able to tell incredible stories because he has dared to live an amazing life. He has seen the world and yet he is a cool guy. How often do you meet brilliant, grounded, and humble nice guys? I hope one day I become someone like that. I really enjoy people that are honest. One thing I have learned is that so many people are so full of it. People lie about the stupidest shit. You ask a woman how old she is. She tells you she is twenty-six. You find out she is thirty. Why the fuck did you tell me you are twenty-six? I went on a date with a beautiful woman from Venezuela recently. She is forty-one and has two kids. She was only staying in San Francisco for two months when we met. What a beautiful person inside and out! She was clean cut, healthy, honest, and proud her herself, her children, and her life. An honest person has a feeling about them. It's a good feeling. Honest people are just easy to be around. I really appreciate someone that is smooth, gregarious, and transparent. I have known so many people that just had a strange vibe about them. I would ask them simple questions like, "What do you do?" and I can immediately feel a tension begin to grow in their chest. Why? I get it if you are unemployed and you do not want to talk about it, but if I see you driving a new Range Rover and you get weird about answering a simple question like that, there is just something off about you. Or people that make excuses for people they have never met, what the fuck is that? I am telling you a story about an interaction I had with some guy on the street and you feel the need to explain why he might be a total prick. Why? Who gives a shit about his childhood? You know what else I like? Funny people. I love funny people. Could you image being buddies with Bill Burr? Sure, he seems a bit angry and judgmental, but who isn't? The difference between your anger and Bill Burr's anger is that Bill Burr is funny. If you think you are funny, you're not. Funny people just know they are funny.

One strange phenomenon that I have noticed is that my favorite people are all loners as well. My favorite AA people love their alone time just as much as I do, and in their free time, you will find them walking in their neighborhood with headphones on and listening to music. Or they will be at some café by themselves writing a book on their laptop. Most of their favorite activities will be activities that they can do alone or with one other person—tops. My favorite activities, as I have mentioned before, are swimming, eating, getting tattooed, biking around the city, reading, writing, listening to music, and of course spa days. Where on my list would a group of people be necessary? I do love conversation. I love fast, intense, and deep conversation. Let's talk about the transgender community. Or maybe we should talk about Nietzsche or how about masturbation? I don't care what the topic is. Just be fun to talk to. Be quick-witted, a little sarcastic, and smart. Have strong opinions about shit. But I draw the line at your interest in child pornography or your involvement with some hate group like the KKK or Hutu extremists. I am not into that shit. Other than that, it's an open playing field.

If you like to talk and you are always looking for cool new people, hit me up. My contact information will be in this book somewhere. I'm not famous yet, so I will definitely make time to bullshit with you. After all, this book is about connection. Sure, I might talk a lot of shit, but I want you to have a kickass life. The human struggle is real and it sucks at times. So if you think you have nobody to talk to, you officially have one person to reach out to and that's me. No excuses, you *can* make it out of the hell you are in. Forget how you got there. Just get out.

11. Poverty

I want to talk about poverty. What exactly is it? The dictionary tells us that poverty is the state of being inferior in quality or insufficient in amount. Most people think that poverty is just not having any money. When you watch a commercial that asks you to donate money to villages where children have no food or medicine and have flies swarming their faces, yes, that is one kind of poverty. But like the disease of addiction, which is a disease that centers in the mind, poverty too is not just a physical deficiency. True poverty affects the body, mind, and spirit. San Francisco is basically the richest city just after New York City. Moving to San Francisco has taught me what real poverty is. I have met so many people making six figures a year and I would definitely consider them poor. If you are thirty years old, have severe diabetes, obese, your kids hate you, and your wife is leaving you because you drink too much, I am sorry but you are poor. I don't care how much you make. Your ass is broke. When I lived in Key West, a friend of mine and I flew to Jamaica and Haiti. The US does not have the kind of poverty that those islands have, but I saw little kids playing and laughing. I rarely saw overweight people there. Violence is a different story. Poverty and violence go hand-in-hand more often than not and there is a lot of violence on those islands. When I worked in Key West, one of the first things I learned was not to get into any kind of confrontation with the Jamaicans or the Haitians. There is a good chance of getting stabbed. It's just a possible reality that one needs to be aware of while living the island life.

A lot of other factors play a role in poverty. What is the region's politics like? Are there any jobs? What is the weather like? You might ask, "Weather? What the hell does being poor and the weather have to do with anything?" Think about it. If you live in a place that was a factory boomtown back in the 1960s and now all the jobs are gone, plus you have horrible, long, humid summers or long crazy winters, life is just going to suck that much more. Have you ever been to Flint, Michigan, or Stockton, California? Have you ever heard of Detroit? These towns are titans of poverty. Cities rise and fall all the time only to find a way to rise again. Houston and New York were sinking ships at one time and look at them now. The entire state of Texas is printing money. Chicago, what the fuck is going on in Chicago? Gang violence has exploded again and it's regained the title of murder capital of the US. Chicago used to have the busiest airline in the country. Atlanta's airport has stolen that title. Why are so many of America's middleweight cities passing Chicago by? I will tell you. People. People make a city and some cities are filled with winners and others are filled with losers. Yes, I know that is a massive generalization, but if you do your homework, you will understand what I mean. Let's use the example of family. Let's take two families. Let's say that both sets of parents were born and raised in the Minneapolis, Saint Paul area. Both sets of parents are between the ages of forty-two and forty-four and both sets of parents have two children of ages eight and ten. Both sets of parents work. We will call the families Family One and Family Two. The parents in Family One both have four-year degrees. The mother is a teacher making $44,000 a year at a private school and the husband is a moderately successful architect making $72,000 a year. The parents from Family Two have different careers. One parent is a hairstylist making $34,000 a year and the other parent manages a large grocery store making $49,000 a year. The parents from Family One come from college-educated parents and there is no history of substance abuse and smoking is frowned upon. The parents from Family Two both come from families where alcoholism, drug addiction, smoking, and lack of exercise run in the family. One parent from Family Two is a daily smoker and the other parent has gone to rehab two times in the last four years for alcoholism. Not only do the parents from Family One make more money, but they also have fewer bad habits that they spend their money on in a daily basis. Plus, rehab isn't cheap. Now that I have painted a simple picture of both Family One and Two, I think it is safe to say that there are some basic differences. If there was a game called 'who are the better parents,' who do you think would win? If you could choose right now, which parents would you want? Now take Family One and put them in an upper middle-class suburb of Minneapolis like Eden Prairie and then put Family Two in a poor area such as the suburb of Harris. Why did the parents from Families One and Two pick the areas that they live in? Did they have a choice? Did it simply come down to income levels? If Family Two made more money, would they then choose to live in a better neighborhood like Eden Prairie or would they pick the same poor neighborhood they live in and just buy more cigarettes and alcohol with the extra money? Since these families are not real, we will never know the answer to that question, but from personal experience, I would say that Family One and Two are right where they deserve to be. Am I saying that some people deserve to succeed and other people deserve to struggle? Hell no! I am not a malicious person by nature. What I am saying is that all human beings with an IQ over ninety are capable of making choices. These people can choose to get out of bed. These people can choose to drink a glass of water and take a multivitamin first thing in the morning or they can chose to smoke a cigarette and drink a beer. This is a choice. Then that person can jump in the shower and go to work or they can skip the shower and work and just go back to bed. Regardless of what you choose to do, if you do it long enough, your life will definitely have a certain outcome. If your life turns out to be a pile of shit after smoking, drinking, and not working, you can't really blame your parents for it. Let's say you were abused. Let's say your father beat the shit out of you your entire childhood. Does that mean it's okay to treat your mind and body like shit? I did for years and it's just not a good idea to abuse yourself when all you have is you.

Emotional poverty is a whole other ballgame. Why do some people feel good more often than bad and vice versa? Today, more and more children suffering from depression and many ten-year-old boys want to kill themselves, not to mention the twenty-year-olds who one day decide to go out and shoot up a school. My parents gave me all the toys a kid could ever want and still by the time I was ten, I just wanted to die. What the fuck? Society seems to have an obsession with finding out whose fault it is, but in the end, what does that solve? We always find out after the massacre that little Jimmy was depressed and suddenly the parents are surprised that their son was a psychopath and say that they never saw the signs, not even one little sign that their kid was nuts. One parent's denial can in a way aid in the death of a classroom full of children. Again, it's not about blame. It's about being honest with yourself and trying your best to prevent something horrible from happening. So many parents would rather pretend that nothing is wrong because they are afraid of what other people might think. They are afraid that people will see *them* as failures. So, they do nothing. They sit quietly at the dinner table with their fucked up families, hoping that the problem will eventually go away. This was my mother. This was most of my friends' mothers. But why were they so afraid to talk to their kids? My parents never really talked to me. I was aware of this when I was a child, and yes, this lack of connection had a serious effect on my psyche, but what's done is done. It's up to me to dig myself out. An older friend of mine always joked that he might be the reason why his son is fucked up, but it is up to his son to dig himself out. Sadly, in so many ways, that statement is so true. We can't pick the people we come from and we can't control everything that happens to us in our lives. All we can do is try to improve things.

If you don't get along with your parents and nobody is making any real effort to patch things together, then try to find other adults to connect with. Maybe you have friends with amazing parents. Spend as much time as you can with those people. Do you hate your job? Is it a toxic environment? Try job shopping. Go to other companies like yours if you like your industry and ask for informational interviews. Spend time at places that you would like to work. Get to know the people there and get a feel for the culture. If you don't like your girlfriend but you stay with her out of habit, try becoming friends with other women. Don't go into it with the intention of fucking other women while you still have a girlfriend, but just meet other women. Maybe not all women are boring and mediocre in bed like your girlfriend. Maybe you will grow some balls and break up with your mildly shitty partner. Maybe you are the problem. Maybe you are shitty. I think ninety percent of mental poverty stems from a lack of self-esteem and self-awareness. If you knew that you had options in life, maybe you would put up with a lot less bullshit. What if you could just work hard, find a way to like yourself, and get laid on occasion? Maybe you wouldn't think life was such a horrible thing that simply had to be endured. If you want to spend your free time alone and you just don't have any interest in crowds, then fuck it. Just hang by yourself and don't feel any guilt about it. If you want to go to concerts three days a week but you don't know anybody that wants to go to a concert with you, just buy a ticket and go. I guarantee you that you will have a better chance of meeting someone that loves concerts as much as you do, at a concert. I mean… you are at the very place that you want to be and there will be people there. Just say hi. It's that easy. Try going to one concert every week for a month. If you can't find one person to pal around with, I don't know what to tell you. But that's not going to happen. You will be fine. The reason why I say that is because if you have wanted to get out more and meet people but you haven't taken the plunge, the reason for this is always the same for everyone: fear. You are afraid. I get this. I have some fears of my own. If a lack of self-esteem and self-awareness is ninety percent of mental poverty, what is the foundation of low self-esteem and self-awareness? You guessed it. Fear it is. Now we know the root of why you or I or anyone else feels like shit. The common denominator will always be fear. But sometimes this can be confusing because you're not sure what it is exactly that you are afraid of. So try writing your fears down on paper. The first time I ever wrote my fears down on paper, I was thirty years old. Once I looked at all my fears on that piece of paper, something amazing happened. My fears shrank a bit. Having them on paper kind of depersonalized everything for me and separated them from my true being in a way. Granted, new fears always come up, but at the time of my first internal inventory, this was a revelation. I always thought that you would always have the same fears and you would just have to learn how to live with them. I never knew that you could get rid of fear and move forward with your life. Soon after learning this, I also learned that it is okay to fail. I then learned that it is okay to fail a lot. I grew up thinking that failure was the worst thing you could do. Once this thought pattern became a concrete ideology, I just stopped trying. By learning that I could kill my fears and fail without guilt, my life once again just blew right open. I began to try new things all the time: new foods, new cities, new people, and new everything. This would help me find out who I was on many different levels. This knowledge would put my past even further behind me, and my future would become brighter and more vibrant every day.

Eventually, physical and mental poverty would become, for the most part, a thing of the past for me. After years of consciously working to strengthen myself with exercise, great books, sobriety, AA, my newfound belief in a higher power, good people, and of course finding a life purpose, my world began to really take shape. While doing all these things that I just mentioned, I would learn that I was subconsciously working on and mending from a whole other kind of poverty—spiritual poverty. The first time I ever heard the term spiritual poverty, I was thirty-four years old. I had no idea that spiritual poverty was even a thing. How could believing in some kind of God make your life better? Could you actually gain some kind of wealth simply by believing in a power greater than yourself? I have volunteered in one capacity or another since I was twenty-seven years old, but I did it just to stay busy. Sure, it enriched my life a bit and it felt good to give back, but I basically wanted to keep my mind off wanting to kill myself. Today, I feel that once you know fully why you do what you do in life, only then can you unlock the true and whole potential of the tasks that you carry out. If I simply go through the motions of life, I will get the bare minimum of rewards. But if I give everything I have and I love what I do, the rewards are endless. I never would have learned this lesson if I did not reach my spiritual bottom. Those last few years before I started going to AA meetings were terrible. I spent every penny I had in order to figure out what was wrong with me. The whole time I was dying in a way that I had no idea was even possible. My soul was dying. No doctor can cure a sick soul. As ridiculous as it sounds, I am confident that the only thing that can help a spiritually sick person is love. And trust me, I am one of the most jaded people you will ever meet. I am full of sarcasm. I hate the idea of marriage and having a family and all that romantic comedy bullshit, but I do believe that if you are on your deathbed, love will make you feel better. Late at night when I am feeling down, I will watch YouTube videos of men giving their girlfriends puppies for their birthday. The girlfriends' reaction will bring me close to tears every time. I love that sappy shit. I also love the videos where military dads will go to their daughter's school and surprise her. Every time the daughter runs to her daddy, my eyes fill up with tears. That is the kind of love that heals a broken heart. Antidepressants and mood stabilizers cannot revive a sleeping soul. Only real-life experiences such as puppies and the love of a child can do that. And since my apartment building doesn't allow dogs and I don't want kids of my own, I will have to settle for God.

12. Last House on the Block

I have to be honest with you. Alcoholics Anonymous is the last place on Earth that I thought I would end up. The first time I ever heard of AA, I was about nineteen. My biological father went to AA for years. My father got sober on my birthday in 1983. He told me that when I was a baby, he couldn't take it when I cried, so he would drink really heavily. Later in life, my father would tell me that he had PTSD and bipolar disorder. Today, I know that my father was not a bad man. I learned that my father is extremely mentally ill and he lacked the ability to take care of another person. For most of my father's life, he would be too sick to even take care of himself at times. He told me that once he became so drunk, he forgot that I was in the house and he tried killing himself in the garage. He was about to hang himself when he heard me cry. He snapped out of it and realized that he couldn't kill himself and leave me alone in the house. A couple of months later, he left my mother and me because he knew he could never be a good father. He would try to kill himself a couple of more times and finally in 1983, he would go to his first AA meeting. When I was nineteen, my biological father visited me at the café I managed in Portland and asked if I could take my lunch break so he could talk with for a few minutes. I had not seen my father in years and I was a bit apprehensive, but it seemed important, so I agreed to speak with him. We sat down at the Pioneer Square in Downtown Portland. We sat next to each other and we both just looked straight ahead at all the people walking around the square. My father finally said that he had asked to speak with me because I was on a list of people that he wanted to make amends to. I told him I did not know what 'amends' were. He told me that making amends are like telling someone you are sorry. My father then sincerely apologized for never being in my life. He apologized for never paying child support and never being able to help me financially. He handed me two hundred dollars and we continued to talk for twenty more minutes. To be honest with you, I was so stoned during our meeting that I could not really rap my mind around what he was trying to do. I went back to work and he went his way. I did not see him for another seven years after that conversation. I have no idea what my father did with his life during these years. I know very little about him, to be perfectly honest with you. My father is more like a ghost that comes in and out of my life. We would spend some time together when I was about twenty-six. Around the time that I started losing my mind, my father started coming around. He knew I had what he had. I had the dark gene that my father's father gave to him. He knew what it was like to have the world crumble around you. He could also see that my parents reacted the exact same way his parents reacted when my father would have to be hospitalized for his manic-depressive fits. Both our parents would pretend nothing was wrong. Both of our parents ignored the problem. Around the time that I started losing my shit, I was either living on my own or I was back at my grandmother's house. My father was nineteen when he started losing it. He moved out at eighteen, and soon after that, his parents moved to a small town outside of Portland. My parents lived full-time on a ranch in Eastern Oregon. They lived six hours away, so they had no idea what was going on. It was all very convenient. I would tell my mother what was going on, but she always just wished me luck and then hung up the phone. My mother stopped calling when I got sick. Only my grandmother would have the balls to stay in my life. My father's parents pulled the same shit with him.

Over the years, my father would tell me about his experience with Alcoholics Anonymous. He told me that nobody stayed sober and all the men and women took turns dating and fucking one another. He said AA was just like high school. After hearing all of my father's stories, I decided to stay away from AA meetings. I forgot all about Alcoholics Anonymous for many years, although I did learn later that some of what my father said was true. I also discovered that my father, being an alcoholic with PTSD and bipolar disorder, would tend to over exaggerate some of the information that he gave me. But this is typical alcoholic shit. We like to tell tall tales that are based on the truth. I think being slightly full of shit is just a side effect of being a junky.

When I got sober at twenty-two, that was it. I knew I would never drink again. It really wasn't that hard to quit for me. Yes, it sucked, but it wasn't the horror story that I thought it was going to be. This is why for so many years I didn't think I was a real alcoholic. I always thought an alcoholic was somebody that basically drank himself or herself to death. Many men in my family have done this. There was no way any of them could quit. I only drank heavily for seven years, and when I quit, I felt like I had flu for a week, I puked a few times, I would sweat and have diarrhea, but I didn't feel like I was dying. It was like having food poisoning for a week. I never needed to be hospitalized. I never had to be surrounded by doctors for forty-eight hours straight. No, I just quit. How could I be a real alcoholic? To this day, my whole family on my mother's side still thinks I never had a serious problem. Even after telling my family stories about waking up in different states and not remembering how I got there, or having to get my stomach pumped twice in four month when I was twenty or the electroshock therapy sessions, my family just tells me that I was going through a phase. Eventually, I would stop talking to my family about these matters altogether. There is really no point.

After going to meetings for many years, on occasion I wish I didn't have to go to AA meetings. Sure, I don't have to go to AA meetings, but I have tried not going to meetings for a week straight a few times, and by Day Three, I always get a little itchy. I would get short with people. I give a shit a little less. I want to sleep more. I basically become an asshole. I have learned that the world is a better place if I go to AA meetings on a regular basis. It's like the saying, "Happy wife, happy life." In my case, the wife is my brain, body, and soul. As long as I do whatever it takes to be mentally, physically, and spiritually healthy, my life just seems to work better. Going to AA meetings and working the twelve steps and twelve traditions on a regular basis seems to make the world more bearable. If I stray from my program, I start to hate the world a little more and more again. When I am healthy, the only thing that I hate is poverty. Poverty makes people behave like animals. Poverty makes the world a hard place to live. I want the world to be the best place it can be, so if I do my part, like stay sober, I can help the world be one percent better. This is all I can really do. When I am truly sober and not just dry, making the world one percent better is good enough for me.

13. The Good, the Bad, and the...

For years, I have wanted to tell the world about my personal experience in Alcoholics Anonymous. What I am about to say will offend a lot of people. No matter what culture you were or are a part of, telling your truth can be a dangerous thing? People often talk about their experience in the military, scientology, Catholicism, or cult survivors... you name it. When you tell a large audience what it was like for you and when you shed some light on the dirty corners and open closets that are full of skeletons, people are going to get pissed off. Most human beings that belong to and thrive in large organized groups like religion or major corporations tend to be the type of people that do not like to rock the boat. These people are the middle children of the world. They are 'hear no evil, see no evil, and say no evil' kind of people. I would love to say that there is nothing wrong with these kinds of people and I would love to mean it, but I would be lying. People that do not ask questions and always follow the rules no matter what kind of give me the creeps. These kinds of people make guys like Hitler possible. Hitler never would have happened if people had asked more questions. Granted, going into the Hitler story is a much more complicated issue than these people were bad, and shame on you but still, ask more fucking questions. Granted, it is hard to work up the energy when you have been starving for a few years to ask major questions like, "Is this guy going to kill millions of people in the next few years?" When you don't ask questions and you just go along with the crowd, bad things can happen. Things can get so bad that one day, you might find yourself in some fucked up cult out in the desert somewhere and all of sudden you're being ridiculed in front of a hundred people by the group leader, and later that night being sexually molested by the same man that was shaming you in front of your new 'family' wearing white robes.

Before I go any further, I want to make one thing clear. Alcoholics Anonymous is not a cult. But Alcoholics Anonymous was created and is operated by human beings— very sick human beings. The only thing in this world that can somehow fuck up a simple, perfect, and beautiful idea is a human being. Yes, most of the people in Alcoholics Anonymous want to do well and improve themselves, but some of them also get the message twisted and can go off the deep end. I have been to a few meetings that made me wonder if I was somehow taken back in time and transported to that crazy camp in *Wacko* Texas. There are AA meetings all over the world. I personally have been to AA meetings all over the US, Cuba, Haiti, Jamaica, Canada, and Mexico. No two meetings are the same. I have attended some amazing meetings and I have also been to some really shitty unorganized free-for-all meetings. But this is just my opinion based on experience. The worst meetings I have ever been to will be some other guy's favorite spot to go every night of the week. Certain meetings seem to attract certain types of people. Some meetings will attract foofy soccer moms that wear fake fur and spray on too much perfume. Some meetings will attract really old men that chain-smoke and smell like they have been welding all day. Other meetings will attract younger twenty-something hipsters that live off some weird inheritance and tend to relapse every sixty days. AA meetings are like restaurants. There are thousands of them and there will be a few that you love and a few that you hate. Every meeting I have ever been to will have your core members, usually six to eight people that go every day. They will have their inside jokes. They will be a bit clicky, and either they will let you in right away or they won't (kind of like high school). Remember, AA is full of alcoholics and most of them, if not all of them, including myself, have the emotional intelligence of a sixteen-year-old. Most alcoholics are extremely sensitive, untrusting, and at times superficial. But all human beings are guilty of these traits on occasion. If a group of people in AA takes to you really quickly and bombards you with their phone numbers, I think you should be a bit cautious. If you are pretty or handsome, watch out. If you are an attractive woman, some women will be overly nice to you. This is because they want whatever it is that you have. Whatever your X Factor might be, they want it. On the other hand, some women will be total cunts to you and ignore you. Some men are going to be very nice to you as well. Young and old, some men are going to be so polite and understanding and they will ask you to coffee or lunch. If you are not with a group of people, I would recommend that you do not go anywhere alone with a man from AA for a while. Let's face it. You have shitty judgment and really poor taste in men. Give yourself a solid year to figure out who your friends are. If a woman with a lot of sober time comes up to you and tells you that she is going to be your sponsor, again watch out. Some of these women can be very controlling. They tend to be single, bitchy, and unhappy. If you are a guy and newly sober, you have a whole other world of things to look out for. Men, regardless of whether they are sober or not, are going to be men. Men can be very territorial in general and an AA meeting can be seen as a 'territory' for a lot of men in AA. Some will be very standoffish. They will want to see where you fit in the social hierarchy of the group. Some men will want to be your best buddy right away. Watch out for these guys. They tend to be codependent and they also want whatever kind of cool factor they might think you have. If you are an attractive, well-put-together man, a few gay men will come out of the woodwork and possibly try to see what you are all about. In the beginning, a lot of different people will be hungry for your attention for several different reasons. This isn't the way things will be hundred percent of the time, but more often than not, a lot of people will experience some of the things I have mentioned. I have experienced a lot of these things myself.

I personally am a straight white man. I am smart, capable, and well-spoken, and for the most part, I have my shit together. Some people love this about me and some people don't. You can't make everybody happy. There is a good chance that you will get your share of haters. I know I have over time. There are some other things I have observed in countless AA meetings over the years, such as almost all meetings have that creepy guy in the back that has really poor boundaries. A new girl will come to the meeting for the first time. She will be sweet, a little scared, and she will show up a few days in a row and *poof*, she will disappear. Where did she go? The creepy guy in the back kept trying to talk to her after the meeting and he would look at her in a strange way. He made her feel uncomfortable and she stopped coming to the meeting. Another thing that happens is a younger guy will wake up one day and he will have a fire under his ass and decide he's going to get sober and he's going to be the new spokesman for AA. He's going to go to the eight-thirty p.m. meeting every night of the week and he will make suggestions on what needs to be changed. He's also going to start correcting people when they read something wrong. He's going to have it all figured out. Within a couple of months, he will meet a pretty girl. It will get serious and we will never see him again. I've also seen that most meetings have the resident cougar. There will be a woman in her mid-fifties that wears leopard-print tights, matching jacket, huge leather purse, is overly tanned with tones of perfume, chain-smoker, and loud. Personally, I love these women. I am always friends with these women. They are funny, the conversation is great, and I all around just love their presence. Another stereotype that I see at a lot of AA meetings is the middle-aged guy that has a nice car and always dates a younger woman that has just gotten sober. These guys are total predators in their own special way. He will have eight years' sobriety and she will have of twenty-six days. Another one is the young pretty girl in AA. The pretty girl never has anything to say. She just sits there. She is well dressed and has great posture, but she is just empty inside. She is always on her cell-phone and always leaves fifteen minutes early because she has something better to do. You will see her for another month and then she's gone. You will then see her four months later, not looking as good as the last time you saw her, but she will repeat the same bullshit as last time. For years, I wished that I could meet a gorgeous woman in AA. She would have five years of sobriety, she would be funny, sexy, and in decent shape, she would like me, and we would fall in love. It's ten years later and still this has never happened. But fuck it. What? Am I going to stop going to meetings just because I don't meet that special someone?

I know that my main purpose, if not my only purpose, for going to AA meetings is to stay sober and help other alcoholics stay sober, but I have to admit that I wish a few things were different. I wish more people could stay sober. It is disheartening to see so many people go in and out of the rooms. Over the years, I have found that Alcoholics Anonymous is a numbers' game. Only ten percent of all addicts will ever try a twelve-step program as a means to get sober and stay sober. Out of the ten percent of the people that do try a twelve-step program, only ten percent of those people will still be sober a year later. Sadly, only ten percent of that ten percent will be sober ten years later. The number-one cause of death for the majority of all of these people will be alcohol-related. Every AA meeting regardless of its geographic location has the potential to be packed full of people at any given time of the day. Most of the meetings I go to average fifteen people. Sure, every major city has a few really big meetings. I have been to meetings where two hundred people will show up. These meetings tend to feel like Amway seminars. Everybody gets dressed up like it's prom. All the clicks from all the different meetings around the city will get together. I chaperoned a high school dance once and it felt just like one of these big meetings. I find the whole scene to be really cheesy. Granted, the most attractive women will be there, which is nice, but the guys with the used 2010 BMWs will be there as well, all in the name of a higher power, of course. For whatever reason, I find wearing your best Sunday suit to hear people talk about sleeping in a ditch fifteen years ago to be a bit retarded.

I know you have been waiting for me to bring up thirteen stepping. Or maybe you have never heard of the thirteenth step. The thirteenth step is simple. The thirteenth step is when two people in AA start fucking. It tends to be frowned upon when someone with some time starts hooking up with a newcomer. A newcomer, of course, is someone with under a year of sobriety. Someone new to sobriety and recovery is going to be very vulnerable. From what I have observed, all newcomers are emotionally retarded and having sex with an emotionally retarded person is just wrong. In my opinion, it makes you a predator if you do this. I can honestly say that I have successfully never done this. I have come close but, thank God, it has never happened. I have found that the best policy is to treat newcomer women like they have the plague. Why? Let's put it into perspective. You meet a thirty-year-old woman. She has been sober for a month, but she started drinking heavily when she was sixteen. I believe in the phenomenon of arrested emotional development. Arrested emotional development basically means you are stuck with the behavior of an adolescent, commonly brought on by some form of trauma. Usually sexual abuse or severe physical abuse will trigger something like this. Have you ever talked to a grown woman that uses a baby voice when she speaks to you? It's fucking weird. Have you ever seen a woman in her mid-fifties dress and act like she is twenty-one? Doesn't this strike you as odd on any level? These are many forms of arrested emotional development. The healthier you get, the more these kinds of people will make you feel very uncomfortable. Why? Because spending your time with adults that operate like they are twelve is a very strange experience. So that thirty-year-old woman you meet that started to drink and party hard at sixteen and has been sober for a month is technically only seventeen years old on an emotional level. Let's say you are also thirty and let's say that you have seven years of sobriety under your belt. Why do you want to be with a seventeen-year-old girl? What do you have in common? Have you noticed that when you talk to her, she never makes eye contact with you? Have you noticed she is constantly checking her cellphone even while you are in the middle of a conversation? She doesn't know that checking her cellphone while you are talking to her is rude and you let her because you want to fuck her. Am I right? You might even catch her in a lie. You might notice that she lies all the time. Why do you put up with this? Maybe because you suffer from some form of arrested development as well. If this is the case, please do the world a favor and stay single for a while longer. Please do not get married or have children right away. I guarantee you that you will just continue the cycle that you grew up in. And why are so many addicts in such a hurry to meet some chick or some dude, get married, and make babies? There is a whole world out there. Try going to Europe. Go backpacking in Australia. Try starting a business. Try something new. There is plenty of time to meet someone and reproduce.

I never understood why even in 2018, people see the ultimate form of success to be man + woman = baby. I find it hard to believe that so many people just lack the curiosity to actually explore the world they live in. Actually, I think most people are very curious. So what's the problem? I will tell you. It all goes back to what I wrote earlier. Fear. People just lack the balls to try. It is much easier to meet someone that you find attractive enough, get married, and make a couple of babies. These are all safe options. People would rather go into their eyeballs with debt, become new parents, and go through the stress of not sleeping for five years rather than take a moment and find out who they really are. People are terrified of their own thoughts. I know I am. They are horrified to find out who they really are, so they seek out distraction. What's more distracting than a four-year-old and two-year-old child running around the house screaming? When you have children, you never have the time to think about anything except the children. How convenient for you! You are going through the motions in an okay marriage, you have two kids, and you struggle financially. Or maybe you don't. Maybe everything is great. When the day is over, you eat a dinner out of a box, you watch your three favorite TV shows, and go to bed. After five years of marriage, you are having sex once a month because, well, you see each other every day and they will be there tomorrow. Now, you might think I am being a bit harsh and judgmental, and technically, you are right. I am being both harsh and judgmental. You might think that some people enjoy living the kind of life that I just described. And sure, people might enjoy this. If they didn't, they wouldn't do it. Or would they? But it doesn't mean they should do it. Living a so-so life is not what humans were meant to do. Humans have the biggest brains with the highest IQ of any animal. We can build amazing things. We have been able to fly to the moon for a while now. There is a whole world out there. If you are not even the slightest bit impressed by the world you live in, then you might as well be the beginning of the zombie apocalypse. But again, people are curious and they are impressed by the world around them. They just don't do anything about it. I was just like this. My life never really started until recently, to be honest with you. And I am not writing this as a way to say 'fuck you' to anybody. I am writing this because I want everyone to live the life they want. If you can't live the life you want, at least try. That's why I am writing this. Look, I live in a studio apartment in San Francisco. It's nothing to brag about. I am still learning how to build the frame of the life I want.

I feel like my growth process in recovery is almost identical to the growth process of the bamboo seed. Some bamboo will take twenty years to grow out of the ground. For those first twenty years, the bamboo seed is growing a huge root system underneath the ground. Then, one day, the bamboo will shoot out of the ground and the sky's the limit. The dragon bamboo has been known to grow up to thirteen hundred feet. I can relate to the dragon bamboo. Today is June 27, 2018. I am just over sixteen and a half years sober. I know that I have grown a little every day since my first day of sobriety, but the last four years have been crazy. I have experienced so many different forms of advancement in my life. My mental health, my career, and my soul have reached a level that I never thought to be possible. My reason for telling you this is because I would never have been able to achieve any of what I have done without Alcoholics Anonymous. Yes, I did just talk a lot of shit about AA, but AA is just a microcosm for the rest of the world. There are a lot of assholes in the world. There will be assholes at your job, at school, and in your family; everywhere you go, there will be assholes. Over the years, I have learned that you learn the most from assholes. Thank God for assholes. The world is full of traffic. People are just another kind of traffic and there are going to be days where you just can't take it. On those days, what do you do? What tools do you have to overcome the really bad days? Medication can only do so much. Your girlfriend or boyfriend can only do so much. Money can't buy you out of everything that life throws at you. So what do you do? Have you found the answer already? If you have, please let me in on your secret. We all want that secret fix. But I have a feeling you haven't found the answers. If you had, you wouldn't be reading this book. For all I know, you are in some tiny cell somewhere and you simply have nothing better to do for the next eight to ten months.

So what have we learned about Alcoholics Anonymous? It's a little fucked up—a lot of insecurities and messy boundaries, but overall people mean well. I also think that Alcoholics Anonymous can help people learn how to take responsibility for themselves. Personally, I have learned the concept of patience and how to use patience as a tool in my daily life. I have learned that I am worthy of living a good life by working the program of Alcoholics Anonymous. I have learned how to help people and not expect anything in return. Plus, the whole concept of a higher power has really grown on me over the years. For some reason, praying to a higher power helps me. Now that I think of it, I have never heard anyone say that praying made him or her feel bad or worse than they already did. That would be an odd thing to happen to someone. So maybe a part of me wants to convert you. I think when someone finds something that improves their life, they simply want to share it. A part of me really hopes that you open yourself up to the possibility of a higher power. I come from a place where I tried everything to be happy and to have a purpose. Maybe you do not want to be happy or have a purpose in life. If that is the case, then we are at a stalemate. I simply do not know what to do with people that do not instinctively want to improve. But if you do want to improve yourself and your life, now that is something I can relate to.

A lot of people believe that Alcoholics Anonymous and the Big Book of Alcoholics Anonymous are divinely inspired. I personally agree with this theory wholeheartedly. Human beings are so flawed, even the smartest ones. But an alcoholic is the most flawed human being you will ever meet. How could a group of drunks come up with something as amazing as Alcoholics Anonymous on their own? It seems impossible to me. A handful of guys were hopelessly addicted to drugs and alcohol their entire adult lives. They get sober around the same time and then just write one of the most important books ever written and then find a way to come up with some rules to live by, and ultimately somehow people from all over the world start doing the same thing. Something far greater than a group of miserable, shitty drunks had to have helped with this. Before Alcoholics Anonymous and groups like it, the worst drunks around the world were being locked up in insane asylums, being put on heavy tranquilizers, and sprayed with fire hoses when they acted out. Nobody would even hand these poor guys a towel. They were left to air-dry naked in their cold cement rooms, isolated from the rest of the world. Maybe God just couldn't stomach seeing human beings treated like animals. Actually, healthy human beings wouldn't even treat an animal the way people were treating alcoholics a hundred years ago. Alcoholics were the lowest of the low. Some people still think we are. If I was a parent and my child was hit and killed by a drunk driver, I am sure I would agree. Alcoholics committed some of the worst crimes in history. Ted Bundy, John Wayne Gacy, Jeffrey Dahmer, and Aileen Wuornos are some of the most famous serial killers and they all had a history of alcohol abuse. It kind of creeps me out that my junky brain operates a bit likes a serial killer's brain. Rather than being addicted to killing people, I was addicted to booze. I never hurt anyone physically while under the influence. I am one of the lucky ones. On the other hand, I did break my mother's heart by rejecting her and never coming back. Sure, over the years we have created some kind of relationship, but we both know deep inside that emotionally I never came back home. She knows that I do not associate her with the warm feelings of home. Even with many years of sobriety, I still have some ice in my veins when it comes to my mother. I wish the ice would melt, but it just hasn't yet. I do however believe that I have a better chance of things getting better between my mother and me if I keep working my AA program. If things stay the same, I can live with that.

One thing that I have heard over the years in AA meetings is that a lot of people think that AA just doesn't work for them. I have also noticed that all of the people that have tried AA and claim it doesn't work all say the same thing. They will all say that they went to AA meetings for a few months, eventually stopped going to meetings, stopped talking to their sponsor, and eventually started drinking again. They all say this. They all isolate themselves from people that want to see them get healthy and stay sober and they go back to hanging out with their friends that drink and hang around the same family members that put them down, and everything just, well, stays the same. Then they blame AA for not working. I really wish people would stop blaming other people and institutions for their fuckups. I hear so many people cry about what their parents did to them or their ex-boyfriend or wife. Basically, what happens is that some drunk didn't get what they wanted, so they started drinking again? That's four-year-old bullshit. In Alcoholics Anonymous, we say that some people are naturally incapable of being honest with themselves. I agree with this statement. But there are options. In the case of severe alcoholics, Alcoholics Anonymous seems to be one of the best, if not *the* best option. It's not the only option. There are non-twelve-step rehabs that you can try. I have heard that scientology has a program to help addicts get sober. You can keep going to the hospital for medically induced detox treatments. I am not sure how much all this costs, but it is available. I also know that AA is free. Sure, there is that basket they pass around, but other than that, it's basically free. Actually, no, the Big Book is about $10.00. You can get it on Amazon for as low as $5.99. That's a lot cheaper than going to some rehab in Scottsdale, Arizona. Twenty-eight days and $49,000 later, maybe you will be cured. Or maybe they just had an amazing salad bar and as much yoga as you can handle. If you can afford it, why not check it out, right? Personally, I have never been to rehab. I was always a bit jealous of those that got to go. Maybe I just have a bit of resentment and that's why I talk so much shit about rehab. Or maybe I know that AA really works and I'd rather save my money for my back tattoo and a trip to Singapore. We all have to spend our money on something. I guess going to rehab isn't any sillier than me spending $10,000 on a geisha girl back piece. Actually, they are equally ridiculous. So I'll shut up.

14. Mr. Softy

I want to talk about one of the fucked up side effects of my disease. Not everybody has the same side effects but I read a lot of books about addiction, the mind, and the body. I've also talked to other addicts that have had some of the side effects that I have had for years. One of the side effects that I have been dealing with for most of my life is sexual dysfunction. Back in my drinking days, I would have a hard time keeping it up during sex. Or I would blow my load way too fast. I could never pace myself. I just wanted to climax as soon as possible. I just wanted to get straight to the good part. It drove my girlfriends nuts. I have to admit it to the world and myself that I am a very selfish lover. I can be very intense and passionate, but overall it's all about me. After I climax, all I want is a sandwich and then I want to go to bed. If I really like you, I will want to cuddle but only after I have my sandwich. I have always been this way. There was this brief time in my life where I was pretty good in bed. It was between the age of twenty-five and twenty-nine. I can honestly say that I totally 'rocked' in bed back then. But in my drinking days, sixty-five percent of the time I was just too loaded to be any good. Then once I started going to AA meetings, for some reason my desire to get laid kind of died off. I would say my libido cut in half when I turned thirty. I just stopped caring. I lost interest in chasing women. For one thing, I grew tired of the games that most women play. Today, I understand the necessity of the games women play. I understand why they play hard-to-get. A woman gets pregnant, the man doesn't want a child, and he takes off. That is a horrifying future for any woman to bear. Women do have it harder than men in this world in some ways. Sure, women get free drinks and a lot of attention, but they also have to deal with a lot of bullshit too—all the judgment from other women, the high risk of rape once you let your guard down even a little bit, gaining weight, losing weight, the shitty monthly cycle, and the list goes on. I genuinely feel bad for women. The older I get, the lesser I want anything to do with most women. And no, I don't hate women. I don't fear women. I used to fear women, but today I simply feel kind of sorry for a lot of women and it's hard for me to spend a lot of time with people that I pity. I observe people and I have noticed over the years how unhappy so many women have become. I watch how the world treats women, and it sucks. If you are a woman, most women don't like you, most men don't like you, and every magazine and commercial is telling you that you are fat and the only thing that will fix your problem is some expensive product. I can see how a lot of women might try to find the richest guy they can, forget about love, and make his life as miserable possible. Misery loves company, right? It's like some kind of subconscious revenge on mankind.

I think for many years I was angry with and afraid of women. I grew up with my mother telling me never to trust women. I remember being five years old and my mother would tell me that all girls lie and that they just want to get pregnant and trap a man. Why the fuck would a mother tell their five-year-old son that shit? That's fucked up. When my mother wasn't looking, I would look in her purse not to steal anything but just to see what was so important. Why did she always need that handbag with her wherever she went? That ugly brown leather purse was so mysterious to me. Every time my mother caught me digging in her purse, she would slap my hand and tell me to never look in a woman's purse. I would try looking a few more times and I would get caught. The last time I ever looked in my mom's purse or any woman's purse, I was seven years old. It was just too risky. I've carried that fear with me for years. I have also experienced my mother's severe mood swings. I would ask my mother what was wrong with her and she would tell me she was on her period. My mother's mood swings were frightening, to be honest with you. The whole mood of the house would change for a week. The air would be heavier and I would learn to just stay away from my mother. The next week would be a little better and the next week after that a little better. It was like that every month. Being aware of my mother's mood swings would play a major role in my life. My mother's dark moods have definitely helped cosign the way I learned to react to the world around me. Over time, I too would become very moody. It was as if I was having sympathy mood swings. By the time I was ten years old, I started experiencing depression at the same time that mother would go through her own depression cycle for the month. For a week, she would be cheerful, giving, and fun to be around, but the other three weeks out of the month were a total crapshoot. You just didn't know what you were going to get. Only now at thirty-nine years old have I finally been able to break away from my mother's mental death grip. I left home at fifteen, and for years I could not shake my mother's insanity. No matter how far I would move away, my mother's guilt trips would still have her hooks dug deep into my sides. Sigmund Freud's entire career was based on fucked up relationships between mothers and their sons. If Mr. Freud were alive today, he would simply look at me and say, "Told you so."

I wonder how many books have been written by men that have talked about how they finally stood up to their mother and finally told them to fuck off one day. There is a really great line in the movie *Fight Club* where Brad Pitt tells Edward Norton how the last thing this next generation of men needs in their life is another woman. We were all raised by unhappy, overbearing single mothers and these mothers were determined to turn their poor sons into the men they thought their ex-husbands should have been. They should be honest, faithful, and they should never question her. So America's mothers have found a way out. They decided to raise their boys to be weak beta males that would spend seventy-five percent of their daily energy apologizing to all the women that would enter into their lives. I ended up doing the same thing for most of my life. Until I was about thirty-six, I put certain women on pedestals and did my best to stay in good graces with them. Once I moved to Key West, I just snapped out of it. When a woman would be rude to me, I would just walk away. If I asked a woman a direct question and she tried talking around the question, I just left the conversation. I walked out of many dates because of a woman's poor behavior. They never seemed to know what the problem was. None of them knew what they did wrong.

Why? *Beta males*. Beta male dads raising beta male sons to have no self-confidence and self-worth. Beta male dads kiss their wives' and daughters' asses just so they don't have to sleep on the couch they paid for in the house they bought. For years, I would ask myself ridiculous questions. What if I am not tall enough? What if I do not have enough money? What if my dick is too small? These thoughts do not help any man's erection. It's actually scientifically proven that self-doubt is one of the top boner killers. Not only does a fear of women affect your sexual appetite but letting other men bully you is another self-esteem killer. Grown men letting other grown men fuck with their heads seems very odd to me. I remember being in the tenth grade and this skater kid called me a faggot in my English class. My classmates and my teacher heard him call me a faggot, but nobody ever did anything about it. My fucking teacher just let it go. Today, I would backhand that fucking prick for trying to shame me like that. Today, I do not take shit from anyone. Just the other day, a couple of kids were skating on the sidewalk. One of them swerved into me, so I grabbed onto his backpack and ranked him off his board. The other kid started talking shit to me, so I just took his board out of his hand and I threw both skateboards into traffic. A truck ran over both skateboards, destroying them. I asked them what they were going to do about it. They just walked away. As an adult, I have learned that the majority of human beings are cowards. There are a lot of ways for a person to be a coward. Men will hang out in groups and talk shit to some random guy walking down the street. The group of guys will call the guy walking down the street a little bitch; they will taunt the poor guy and humiliate him. Why do people do this? Women will date men that make good money but are doormats and never stand up for themselves. These women are cowards and I think they must be afraid of men. I think in order to grow past all this shit, you have to just snap. You have to just say, "Fuck it! No more!" And from that day forward, you demand that people have respect for you and you demand that you have respect for yourself. I think the best way to maintain a massive erection is to have the ultimate amount of respect for yourself and not take shit from any man or woman. I think you have to earn your dick's respect. I have always treated my dick like it had a mind of its own. I believe that if a man wants his dick to work for him, then he has to behave in a way that his dick will become his teammate and help him kick some ass. With that said, good luck.

15. Without a Net

I see you are still reading this. I want to ask you a couple of questions. Do you have a tangled relationship with anyone in your family? Your mother? Your father? Who are you closest to in your family? Who do you like the least? Who is your best friend and why? How did you meet? Does your best friend have any friends that you can't stand? Do you have any friends that you could just do without? Why don't you get rid of them? Why don't you make new friends? Do you want new friends? After answering these quick questions, where do you stand with the people who are closest to you? How do you feel about your co-workers and how do they feel about you? Do you feel like a shallow person because you do not think one of your friends is good enough to be in your life?

For me, it is not about good or bad. All people will do good and bad things throughout their lives. For me, relationships are based on the exchange of time, energy, and resources. For example, you meet a friend for lunch and decide to pick up the tab and the next time you go to lunch with that friend, he will pick up the tab. But if you have a friend that you go to lunch with and you have picked up the tap the last five times in a row, it might be time to evaluate that relationship. After lunch while you are walking out of the restaurant together, try asking your friend if everything is okay. Ask him if work is going okay. If he wonders why you want to know, just kindly respond with the fact that you have been paying for all the lunches lately. Make sure he is okay. If everything is fine and you go to lunch a week later and you pay the full bill, I'm sorry, Charlie, but it's time to find a new buddy. I would consider this to be a healthy process of elimination. Make sure that your next friend understands the concept of give-and-take.

I know that I already wrote a quick chapter titled *People*, but I want to dig a little deeper. *People* focuses on ways that I have maneuvered in a world that is full of human beings. In this chapter, *Without a Net*, I want to focus more on understanding why it is that we keep certain people in our lives and get rid of others and how we pick and choose our future people. Is it all just out of habit? Or perhaps we keep choosing to hang out with the same losers because of a sense of familiarity. To be honest with you, I am going through two different phases in my life simultaneously. There is one thing I have become quite good at. I have become proficient at getting rid of people that are just not good for me. I do not get rid of people out of revenge, malice, or jealousy. What I look at is how a certain person makes me feel. I used to have a friend in my life for quite a while. We stayed friends for almost fifteen years. When I quit drinking, her partying ways unfortunately continued to progress throughout the years. All of her weird wannabe rocker boyfriends, the coke, drinking too much, and the bulimia that she thought she was hiding were just too much. She was the only person in my life that I let slip by. I knew what she was doing, but I played stupid to it all. She was like my little sister for many years. Although I stopped hanging out with her as much, I did stay in contact. She just wasn't growing as a person. She was always talking about how much she had grown since the last time I saw her, but it was such bullshit. She always had a new guy living with her, but he looked and acted just like the last nine boyfriends she had living with her before. She'd get into a fight with her boyfriend and he'd slap the shit out of her. She'd take a cab to my place at one a.m. and she would tell me all the horrible things that had been going on for the past six months and then go back to him the next day. But the funny thing is that I would have called her a few months before these devastating nights would happen, and when we spoke, everything was fine. She was having the best time of her life with boyfriend number 39. Was she lying to me then or she was lying to me the night that she had to escape to my place? Was he abusive to her this whole time? Did he ever *really* abuse her? Were these bad relationship stories a cry for help or was she just trying to get my attention?

Eventually, I started to pity this friend. I pitied her but also grew tired of all of it. I had to realize that this particular friend was not bringing any value to my life. I know this sounds brutal, but some people are just so self-destructive that they are able to pull other people around them down with the ship. Some people take on the role of the soul-sucking vampire that drains all the energy out of your body while you listen to them drone on for the next two hours about all the bullshit and how it is someone else's fault. She is thirty-six years old and she is telling the same stupid story that she was telling me when she was nineteen. Nothing has changed. Well, her boobs are not as plumb and as perfect as they once were. The circles under her eyes are deeper than ever, her teeth are a bit stained, and her hips have become narrow. The worst thing that can happen to a woman is to become old. I remember meeting this friend at a rundown dive bar in South East Portland. Right when I saw her, I knew I couldn't do it anymore. I couldn't listen to her bullshit anymore. But I would. I would listen one more time for old times' sake. I sat there and listened to her shit all over—friends, her job, her coworkers, and her boss. For four years, she'd been telling the same story about some beauty salon she was working for and how she was always being treated poorly and how if she didn't get this next raise, she was going to leave. It was four years of this shit. Then she would tell me how her boyfriend wasn't fucking her as much. I just don't think any man can passionately fuck his girlfriend after listening to her rant and rave for an hour about how much her life sucks. Jesus Christ, grow up or shut the fuck up!

My relationship to this woman is what I consider a bad habit. You stay friends out of muscle memory. You talk but she doesn't listen. She is just waiting for her turn to talk and then you listen to her blabber on for a bit longer and then you chime in. This isn't a friendship. This is bullshit. Cutting this friend out of my life back in 2016 was the beginning of a new era for me. When I ended my friendship with this woman, it was as if my training wheels had been taken off. I realized that I would need to be more aware of my friendships. Who am I spending time with? Are they rude to the waiter when we are getting dinner? Do I have a friend that always wants to start shit with strangers at a movie theater? Do I have a friend that I know is having an emotional affair with a woman that is not his wife? Not anymore. At one point in time, I have had friends like these but I just don't put up with this kind of shit. I don't have friends that lie to their wives and send naked videos of their cocks to trampy twenty-six-year-old blond girls. If you want to fuck other women, then have the balls to divorce your wife and then go fuck stupid blond girls. Oh, but you have kids and you can't just leave your wife. Well, you are a dumbfuck, aren't you? I don't have friends that are dumbfucks. Sorry, just not my scene.

I also want to make one thing clear. I hold myself to the same standards that I hold my friends to. Like I have mentioned earlier, I come from a family that is addicted to many different things. A friend of mine says that alcohol comes in three forms—solids, liquids, and gasses. I have a family made up of sever alcoholics. I have family members that are in denial and compulsive liars. I have a family that chooses to keep their heads in the sand and wait till it's too late. I want to be one of those live-and-let-live guys, but I find the only way I can achieve this is by not spending time with a lot of these people. For now, I cannot really talk to my mother. My half-brother and I are just so different that we do not really have much interest in knowing each other. My stepfather will always be that workaholic, crazy inventor, so he just doesn't have the time. It took me almost forty years, but I am slowly becoming okay with being a quasi-orphan. Most of this is my choice. I still have days where I wish I could have come from a functioning family, but I am over it. What is a healthy functioning family anyway? What does that family look like? I probably wouldn't fit in to that family either. Right now, what I have is my health, my sobriety, my passions, knowledge, and my skillset. I think I will just keep sharpening my knives so when the day comes, I can help return all the favors that I have been given. I can't waste my time hoping that a family that I have not been a part of since 1995 will one day want to get together and fix what went wrong. I have to be grateful for today and pray that I can kick some more ass tomorrow.

16. Loneliness

The only person I ever loved unconditionally was and is my grandmother. She is the only person I have thought of every day since I can remember. All of my best and simplest memories that I store in my piggybank mind have something to do with her. The first time I made pancakes was with my grandmother. When I was four years old and I taught myself to ride my bike without training wheels, I remember glancing over at the kitchen window and my grandmother was watching me. When I was twenty-seven and I was hallucinating and thought a man was living in my closet, I called my grandmother at one in the morning. My grandmother answered the phone and she helped bring me back to reality. She didn't call me weird or crazy, and I knew she wouldn't. That's why I called her. Even now as I write this, I had to take a break from writing so I could cry. Maybe I am crying because two weeks ago, my antidepressant was cut in half or maybe it's because I miss my grandmother. I have not seen her in nine months and before that, it had been two years. I am not the kind of person that gets homesick and I am not all mushy with my family. I can't remember what a lot of them even look like anymore, but my relationship and feelings toward my grandmother are sacred to me. My love for her is the only normal part of my life. I feel human when I think about my grandmother. I just don't have deep feelings for people outside of this. I find some people to be interesting, even fascinating, but I do not have feelings for them. I have always seen people as extras in the movie that is my life. My closest friends and acquaintances play supporting roles, but if things get too complicated, they can be replaced. I think my friend Peter out in Portland is the closest thing to an emotional connection with another human being that I have outside of my grandmother at this point in my life. I mean sure, if my biological father, mother, stepfather, brother, or any other family member were to suddenly die, I would cry and it would be hard, but my grandmother is another story. When my grandmother passes, I will probably lose my shit for a while. I could see myself checking into a hospital for a bit just to make sure I didn't hurt myself in any way. If my grandmother were to pass today, it would break me. As far as human connection is concerned, my grandmother is everything to me. I could go on and on, but you get what I am saying.

One of the few things I hate to admit even to this day is the fact that I get lonely. I am sure I have talked about this earlier, but loneliness is a topic that is really important to me. I remember being fifteen, I had just moved into my grandparents' house and I was lying on my twin-bed mattress. I lay on my back for hours just staring at the ceiling. That was when it finally hit me that I was kind of an orphan. I was a stray cat. I belonged nowhere. It was such an empty feeling and yet I chose it. I knew that I made the choice. It seemed normal to me. I remember crying and going through past memories. I remember thinking of all the times that my mother would drop me off at relatives' homes for a couple of weeks here or a couple of weeks there. I was always being left somewhere. I always felt like my mother was trying to get rid of me. It was just a natural and instinctual feeling. I never trusted her. I still do not trust her today. I remember having these thoughts when I was four years old. For part of one summer, I would be dropped off at my great-grandparents' house out in the middle of the Washington State Desert. Another summer and I would be dropped off with my grandparents on my father's side out in the Oregon State Desert. Or I would be dropped off at my mother's father's house in a shitty coastal town in Washington State. All of these people were either crazy or sever alcoholics. My mother knew this, but she left me anyway. I would tell her I didn't want to go, but she would force me to stay. I always felt like an outsider. I was an outsider. For years, I never knew why my mother was always dropping me off here and there, but eventually I figured it out. I reminded my mother of my biological father. I reminded her of the bad times. I looked a lot like my father; I talked and laughed like my father. I would become mentally ill like my father. My mother didn't know what to do with a mentally ill husband and she certainly didn't know what to do with a mentally ill son. Sure, I would never become as fucked up as my father, but I definitely had some variation of what my father had.

For some reason, no matter how fucking nutty I would get, my grandmother could just take it. Most of the time, I would just be depressed and lounge in bed and then go out late at night (nothing too crazy). I oscillated between being lazy or hyperactive. I was never violent, I never stole anything, and I was not verbally abusive. Those were the kinds of things that my grandmother would never put up with. I just slept, did drugs, and went out dancing five nights a week. The thing that drove my grandmother nuts about me was my obsession with money and my hatred towards poor people. I know she took that personally because she grew up very poor and would only briefly get out of that poverty just to be brought back to it in her mid-fifties because my grandfather was incapable of working. Why? Depression. My grandmother's second husband was also an alcoholic, and in the late seventies, she threatened to leave him. So in 1977, my grandfather quit drinking. By 1988, my grandparents would lose everything because my grandfather would become so depressed that he just could not work anymore. He was a moderately high-functioning drunk and had made some good money in the real estate game. But once he quit drinking, he started making poor decisions with his money. He bought cars and tractors that he didn't need, and before he knew it, the bills started staking up. My grandparents eventually had to live in my aunt's garage for a year. My family resented my grandfather for this. I could feel the hatred my family had for him. Everybody looked at him like he was a total fuckup. In a lot of ways he was, but I felt sorry for him. I knew he was not a very smart man from a young age. I knew early on that he just didn't have what it takes. He was an abusive drunk that lived in a lot of fear. But what abusive drunk isn't living in a lot of fear, right? When my grandfather died in 2014, I knew that a lot of people were relieved. I have not heard anyone even mention his name since he passed. It was as if he was never there and I knew that was the way my family would treat it. I think my grandfather was an incredibly lonely man. I used to lie on the couch and watch him chain-smoke and stare at the wall. He would sip his coffee and just stare at the fucking wall. Once I took mushrooms and watched him. I remember thinking I could hear his thoughts. I remember thinking I could see what he was thinking about. I would close my eyes and I would see him on a ship in the Korean War. He was in his early twenties, standing at attention and waiting for his orders. His hair was black and his eyebrows were thick. He was, in this picture, the man that my grandmother thought she was marrying. I came to realize that by staring at the wall, my grandfather was reminiscing about his glory days and just waiting to go back to them. He was also legally deaf. Over the years of using power tools without ear protection, he had lost about eighty percent of his hearing. Having a conversation would be close to impossible. I can only imagine how isolating this would be for him. Over time, people just gave up trying to talk to him. He couldn't hear anything you would say and people hated having to yell inside of a house. It was just uncomfortable. Plus, since nobody really liked him, they were even less likely to put out any effort to talk to him. Jesus, how shitty is that! My grandfather was and is the epitome of a dry drunk. Watching him all those years, I never could have imagined that I too would have my turn at losing my mind in a dry drunk stuper. Today, I know that if I decided to never go to my first AA meeting, I would have eventually ended up sitting in a chair, staring at a wall. The end of the road for a dry drunk is just that. The end before the end is just you, a chair, a wall, and your thoughts. You are at the mercy of your thoughts and feelings and you lack the capacity to do anything about it. All of your chances are gone and all that is left is the time that you have between the present moment and the moment of your permanent end. That is true loneliness and I have scratched the surface of it. If I play my cards right, I will never have to go there, but if I get lazy and think I am too good for this shit, then there are plenty of chairs indoors and out with my name on it. I have a progressive mental illness, and if I choose to stop working at what helps me live and thrive, then I am fucked. So far, I am one of the lucky ones. I have seen what happens to people if they choose not to stop drinking and I have seen what happens to people that decide to stop drinking but do not find humility and gratitude. Both die horrible deaths. My grandmother's first husband died in a hospital bed with a coffee cup full of whiskey next to him, and her second husband died in a hospice center where no one would go to visit him. I wonder how different the lives of these two men could have been if they only had the courage to tell someone that they had a problem and that they needed help.

17. My Side of the Street

"Cleanliness is next to godliness." I think this phrase means a lot of things to a lot of people. For me, it means to take a shower, brush and floss your teeth, and comb your hair. It means cover your mouth when you cough. Chew with your mouth closed. Maybe iron your dress shirt and pants and wear the same-colored socks. Never disrespect your grandmother. While working my sober program, I also learned another phrase: "Keep your side of the street clean." This is basically just another way to say the first phrase that I mentioned. Jordan Peterson mentions cleaning your room and sorting yourself out in his book *12 Rules for Life*. For some reason, keeping your shit together is important. Smart human beings all over the world will agree on this. The military requires you to clean your room, make your bed, and polish your shoes every day. If you fail at doing these simple tasks, you literally get screamed at. There must be a good reason for this. For whatever reason, the military believes that keeping everything clean and tight will save your life. Like the military, Alcoholics Anonymous believes that keeping your little tiny world in order will also save your life. It's the small simple things that are the hardest to do. Yet it can also be these monotonous, repetitious tasks that break most people.

I want to use an example of why it is important to keep your side of the street in order. Let's say you are at work and you get into an argument with a coworker. Who cares what the argument is about? But the argument creates friction between you and the coworker. Every time you see each other, you act as if you do not see him. Or maybe when you glance over to this coworker, he is glaring at you. These negative encounters make the resentment that you already have toward your coworker even worse. This can go on for months. Resentments can become so intense that things can turn violent. This is very common in the workplace because so many people lack the ability to communicate their feelings in a rational way. Again, it all goes back to fear. But what if you get in an argument with a coworker and the very next day, you go to that coworker and apologize for the things you said. Don't worry about who was in the wrong. Just apologize. What do you think will happen? I am willing to bet that your coworker will simply return the favor. He or she might in return apologize to you. The worst thing that can happen is that the person tells you to fuck off. But I guarantee you that once you apologize to that coworker, you will feel better no matter what their response will be. No matter what negative feelings you had yesterday, those feelings will go away quickly if not minutes after you apologize. There is no science behind any of this, so it cannot be proven. It goes back to that flimsy yet horrifying concept of faith. You may have noticed that I talk about fear and faith quite a bit. In my experience, all the bad things that I have been through in life are always attached to fear. But with all the good things that I have experienced in life, faith has been a part of it in one way or another hundred percent of the time. I think you can track the quality of your life by how much fear or faith you are living in. First, let me use myself as an example to explain what I mean by this. For my entire life, I have obsessively worried about being poor and becoming homeless. I have worried about going insane like my father did. I have always worried about getting fired from my jobs. My most powerful thoughts have always been my most negative thoughts. It has also been my experience that whatever it is that I focus on, I usually get. Between the age of sixteen and twenty-four, I was homeless twice. I have been fired from two jobs and quit at least ten jobs before my employers had the chance to fire me. By the age of twenty-seven, I had all but completely lost my mind and was put on multiple psych drugs in order to make it possible for me to function on a day-to-day basis. Every single one of my deepest, darkest fears has come true all before the age of thirty. I did not learn how to even scratch the surface of changing the direction of my thoughts or my life until I was thirty-five years old. Yes, I did get sober at twenty-two, and yes, I did start going to AA meetings when I was thirty, but it would still take another five years of daily mental practice to change the way I thought and the decisions that I would make on a daily basis.

For a long time, I could not figure out how to have positive thoughts. I mean I really tried. Finally, my sponsor suggested that I try praying for positive thoughts. He didn't say that if I didn't find God, I was fucked. He didn't say that praying would work; he merely suggested that I try. So I tried it. I can honestly say that every time I have prayed, whatever it was that was bothering me at the time calmed down a bit if not completely. Maybe the problem didn't totally go away, but my depression, anxiety, or anger would reduce dramatically. And yes, the feelings may return the next day, but you always have the option to pray again. Maybe the problem will become smaller over time and eventually disappear. You might be thinking that I am full of shit, but I have nothing to gain or lose if you do or do not believe me. If what I'm saying is all bullshit, then believe me I would have killed myself years ago. Now, I want to isolate the things I was thinking about. What was making me so upset? Most of the time when I get upset, I am usually thinking about what other people are doing wrong. What I just said is the key. The reason behind most of my depression, anxiety, and anger is people not doing what I want them to do. If I like a girl and she is not interested in me, my feelings get hurt. If I apply for a job that I really want and they say no, my feelings get hurt. When I call my mother and she seems completely disinterested in talking to me, my feelings get hurt. Trust me, I know that if you read all this out loud, I sound like a total bitch and that I should just get over myself and move on. But this is the ridiculous mental world of an addict. It's all about me, me, me, and feelings. Feelings, feelings and more feelings. If you were to write down how you were wronged by another person on paper and how it made you feel, then read it out loud to yourself a week later. You would probably laugh at yourself and feel a bit embarrassed at the same time. Why? Because the thing that had you feeling so shitty for a week was borderline retarded to begin with. Someone bumps into you on the bus and gives you a dirty look. How many thousands of people stew over something like this every day? Ninety-nine point ninety-nine percent of the time, the things that are pissing you off or have you all bent out of shape have nothing to do with you. I think that most people with a nonalcoholic brain simply get over shit faster than someone with an addict brain.

There are some simple things that I need to do in order to function in the world. There are simple but sometimes annoying things that I don't always want to do, but if I do not do them long enough, I will start to unravel and come apart at the seams. The first thing that I do when I wake up is pray. Actually, the first thing I do when I wake up is say, "Fuck!" Then I pray. Well, I pray three out of seven days a week right when I wake up. On the days that I forget to pray, I will most likely go into the walk-in freezer at the hotel I work at and meditate or say the serenity prayer. Every time I do this, I feel better. *Every time?* Every damn time! If I go a couple of days without praying or meditating, I definitely feel it. I get lightheaded and start bitching. If I take a few minutes to breathe and silently thank God for everything that I have, everything around me settles down. I will find a quiet corner somewhere, close my eyes, take a few deep breaths, and think about all the good things that I have in my life. I am thankful for my little studio in San Francisco. I am thankful for my bike that helps me get around town quickly. I am thankful for my job. I am thankful for my grandmother. I am thankful for my sobriety and AA. I am thankful for my health. I am thankful that I get to be an above-average-looking single guy with no major physical disfigurements today because that could all change tomorrow. My list can be as long or as short as I want it to be. After thirty seconds of doing this, I feel better. This is all very easy to do. I have also noticed that if I follow my internal gratitude list with small acts of kindness towards my coworkers, friends, and strangers, my day becomes even better. On the days that I wake up and feel shitty and I decide to do nothing about it, I tend to feel shitty until I actually decide to pray, meditate, or make up a quick mental gratitude list. This is just me. I have trained myself to be this way. Or maybe this is actually how a lot of human beings are wired. Maybe helping others really makes us all feel better.

When I come home from a long crazy day and I walk through my front door and see that my bed is made, this image puts me at ease. If I come from a long insane day and the first thing I see is my messy bed, the first thing I think is that I have to make my bed. A messy bed may only affect me a little bit but that little bit could be what sends me over the edge one day and I decide to fuck everything off and go to the bar. What if a clean or messy bed is that one percent difference that could save or destroy your life? People relapse over stupid reasons every day. I ran out of toothpaste! Fuck it. I want a drink. Why won't my girl text me back? Fuck it. I want a drink. I missed *Game of Thrones*! I need a drink! If you have been trying to quit drinking or using drugs and you recently relapsed, what did you relapse over? Was it a gradual thing for you or did something just slam into your face one day? Do you know why you relapsed? When I drank, I drank when good or bad things happened. I drank every night. If my mother and I got into a fight over the phone, I would drink. If I asked a girl out and she said yes, I would drink. I drank from ten p.m. to three a.m. every night. I had no interest in drinking during the day. I had no interest in doing anything during the day. All I did was hit the gym before work, go to work, and then drink after work with my friends at bars. If I ever went to a family function or a daytime barbecue, I never drank. I knew that if I were to start drinking at a daytime event, I would not be able to stop. I always preferred to drink in the city and no more than a mile from my place. If I did drink at a family event, there was a good chance I would get into an argument with someone and I didn't want to chance it. And sure, some people drink all day and night, but I was specifically a night drinker. I went to nightclubs or whorehouses or chic bars. I could never relate to the kind of people that would go tubing in the local river and just float around and casually drink beer for eight hours. I preferred to sleep until two in the afternoon, lounge until four, go to work, and then hit the bars. I preferred a smaller, more contained life. In some ways, I still do. Even with more than a decade of being sober, I still love to sleep in or just relax. On my days off, I might not leave my place until six in the evening. I will drink a veggie protein shake and slowly make my way to the pool and swim my laps. Then I'll lounge in the sauna and steam room. I will then hit an AA meeting at ten p.m. I might not say a word to anyone until I get to the meeting. Once in a blue moon, I will go to a cigar bar and smoke a cigar. I enjoy my little world that I have created. Every time I spend the day with a small group of people, I come back home feeling completely exhausted. If I go to a birthday party or some big event, I make sure that I have the next day off because I know I will need all of that day to rest. I always feel completely drained after spending a lot of time with a group of people. Sometimes, an intense one-on-one conversation will put me out for a few hours and I will need a nap. I have been this way my entire life. Yet I hide this from anyone that has ever been close to me.

Over the years, I have learned that I really need to pace myself when it comes to people. I have learned that I need to stay away from certain personality types. If I get the feeling that I am spending time with someone that is competing for attention, I will cut my time with him or her short. Or if I meet up with someone and they just complain the whole time, I will pretend that I received an emergency text or phone call and skip out. I have learned so many little tricks on how to vacate a social situation that makes me feel uncomfortable. I have also known since I was about ten that I have certain psychic abilities. I can actually feel what people are thinking. I can feel another person's trauma. I find people that need a lot of attention to be exhausting. After talking to a man or woman long enough, I can sense what kind of abuse they must have endured during their childhood. I have noticed so many interesting personality types that are directly attached to the kind of abuse or trauma they went through during their lifetime. Over the past few years, I have wondered about a few types of people. Why are so many men and women that were sexually abused as young children so hypersexual as adults? I have met so many women that were sexually abused as young girls that became extremely sexually active adults and take great risks and put themselves in danger for attention. I have met a lot of men, usually men that identify as homosexual, that were sexually abused as children and became extremely sexually active. I have been told so many stories by addict, gay male friends concerning this topic. The vast majority of my gale male friends that were molested at a young age always tell me stories of crazy group sex parties and sex that involves pain and submission role playing. Why is this? I don't get it. All I have are the stories that I have been told. The other thing I have noticed is that so many women that I have met that were raped by one or more individuals in their college years became much more conservative. A lot of the women that I have talked to say that they hate being touched in any way or they do not have any interest in sex. What is it about being sexually abused as a child versus being abused as an adult? Why is the brain telling you to behave one way or another? Luckily, I was never physically abused in any way. If I were, I would definitely talk about it with a therapist, my friends, and in AA. Or maybe I wouldn't. Isolation was how my parents reprimanded me. If I did anything wrong, no matter what it was, I was sent up to my room for days. If I got a bad report card, I would be sent to my room. If I did anything wrong at all, it was always, "Go to your room. Go to your room and don't come down till I say you can." Three to five days would be the normal punishment. It was fucking miserable, to be perfectly honest with you. I was sent to my room for four weeks without coming down except to go to school, meal times, and to use the restroom. This time in my life would prove to be one of the darkest, saddest, and loneliest times of my life. The only thing most prison inmates are remotely afraid of aside from prison rape is solitary confinement. I think this says a lot about the human condition. Healthy humans crave interaction with other human beings. Why would you cut someone off from other people for extended periods of time? Why would you cut a child off from social interaction for long periods of time? I get having your kid sit in the corner for thirty minutes, but why three to five days at a time? Only a mentally ill person would do that to their child. Once I realized that my parents were not exactly correct in the head, I was able to really let this go. I would not become aware of this until I hit my mid-thirties. My entire life I thought that the way I was punished was normal and I certainly never considered it abuse.

My best friend who was severely abused by his father as a child was the one that brought up how fucked up my childhood was. Peter always told me that he would have gone insane if he had been locked away like I was as a kid. I was in complete denial of the fact that I was abused as a child. Deep in the back of my mind, I always knew that my mother and stepfather were a bit off, but my friend Peter was the first person to use the term 'mentally ill' when describing my parents. One day, I was talking to Peter when I was in the middle of a depression and he basically shook me by the shoulders and yelled at me. He said, "Dude, your parents are just fucked up! Normal parents don't force their kids to stay in their room for a week at a time while they sit downstairs with your younger brother and laugh at what's on TV. That's mental illness, Marques." That conversation woke me up a bit. For the first few months, I was in a kind of shock. It was hard to admit that I came from an abusive family. I never knew that there were so many different kinds of ways to abuse people. I always thought if you weren't beaten up or raped as a child, you had no excuses for anything. I think that is just a lie that sick adults tell children so they do not feel guilty for the shit they put their children through. On top of that, it is really hard to say out loud that your parents are mentally ill. Admitting something like this frees you from more bondage that you have lived with your entire life. Living a good life means that at one point in time, you had to mop up the murder scene that you came from. You have to clean the floors and the walls of your mind. You have to open the windows and let some fresh air in. Maybe an entire remodel of how your mind works is in order. In order to live a great life, the ugly stuff needs to get taken care of.

18. Afraid of the Dark

I have always had an overactive imagination. My imagination combined with a one-track mind and the need to have what I want immediately has proven to be dangerous at times. When I was three years old, I climbed my grandfather's ladder and snuck up to the roof of the house. My family was in the middle of our big annual Fourth of July barbeque. My mother noticed that I had been gone for a while and that was rarely good. My uncle just happened to look up and see me on the roof wearing nothing but my underwear and my grandmother's cowboy hat. I remember my mother screaming and yelling at me to get down. I remember my grandmother telling my mother to stop screaming. My uncle climbed up the ladder and I started running around in circles on the roof thinking we were playing a game. I remember laughing and wanting to jump off the roof. I had no concept of pain at this point in my life. Right before I jumped off the roof, my uncle grabbed me and carried me down the ladder.

When I was seven, my Stepfather Phil told me that I could not be Dracula for Halloween. He told me that I had to pick a different costume idea because I had already been Dracula for three Halloweens in a row. I freaked out and ran to my room. I grabbed a clothes hanger and broke one of my bedroom windows out of anger. A few minutes later, I went back downstairs and poured gasoline on the Halloween display that my family made and burned it down. Every year, we would take five or six bales of hay, a bunch of corn stocks, and about fifteen carved pumpkins and put it in our front yard. At night, we would light candles and the scene looked amazing. For some reason, when Phil told me I could not be Dracula for Halloween, I just snapped. I had never been that angry before. I did not know what to do with the anger, to be honest with you. I wasn't used to being told no, and for some reason when he told me no, my brain went into meltdown mode. The only thing that made sense was to burn down the whole fucking thing. I wasn't trying to get back at my stepfather. I wasn't trying to hurt anyone. I just wanted the feelings that I had to go away. Creating something bigger than my feelings was the only thing that made sense to me at the time. Once the bales of hay began to burn, a sense of calm came over me. After a few minutes, I snapped out of the trance I was in, ran into the house, filled up a bucket of water, and threw the water on the flames. I ran back into the house a few more times, and eventually the fire went out. My mind went into panic mode. For the first time in my life, I experienced true guilt and shame. It was overwhelming. I just wanted to disappear. I ran into the house and told my mother that I really messed up. I took her to the front yard and showed her what I did. My mother had her own version of a meltdown. This would be the first time I would be sent to my room for a few days. I remember the look my stepfather gave me. That was the moment that I knew he did not like me. I don't think he had ever experienced anything like what I did that night. Phil was and is very close with his family and he worships his father. He would never have done anything like what I had done that night. A true psychopath could only have carried out the scene that I just described to you. Someone with a normal brain would never do what I did. I will always remember that Halloween night as the beginning of the end of my family, or at least the beginning of the end of my relationship with Phil. From that moment on, it was me versus my stepfather. The negativity between he and I would only get worse over time. It was a slow burn that would eventually explode and then fade into nothing. Halloween 1986 to Spring Break 1994 would prove to be some of the most tumultuous years for my family. I feel bad for everyone involved. I feel bad for my mother because she had to be caught in the middle of the war that my stepfather and I would wage on each other. I feel bad for my younger half-brother because all he wanted was to play outside and be happy.

My brother was always very simple. I hated my brother and I let him know every chance that I got. I feel bad for my stepfather because I think he just wanted to work hard and provide for his family. Phil was in over his head when he tried being a stepfather. Marrying a woman with a child must be incredibly difficult. Marrying a woman with a child that was born with an alcoholic brain is simply next to impossible. From the very beginning, I wanted my stepfather out of the picture. I also feel bad for myself. Maybe I shouldn't, but I do. I just feel like I was misplaced. I feel like adopting me out would have been the best idea. My mother was only twenty-two when she had me. She wasn't ready to be an adult yet, and she certainly wasn't ready to be a mother. My mother has told me on many occasions that she never wanted to get married and she never wanted children. I always thought that was fucked up because she got married twice and had a child with both of the men that she married. I always wished that she would have put me up for adoption and given me to a functioning family that had the resources to take care of me. If my mother would have adopted me out, she could have gone to college and maybe lived the life she actually wanted. I have always known that she was never happy and I knew that she settled for the life that she lives today. I always thought that was so sad.

After the Halloween fire that I caused, I began to have trouble sleeping. For weeks, I couldn't stop thinking about that night. I would listen to my small FM radio until midnight and finally fall asleep. I remember listening to a lot of *Pink Floyd, The Doors,* and *Jimi Hendrix.* On occasion, my stepfather would walk by my door and tell me to turn off the radio and go to sleep. This would make me want to listen to my music even more. I would turn the radio down and just keep listening. Once my guilt over the fire faded away, I began to focus on wanting to leave home. I fantasized about hitchhiking to New York or Los Angeles, but I fancied myself more of a New York kind of boy. I was so attracted to the tall buildings and people walking on the sidewalks. I wanted to wear a long black trench coat and sunglasses. I wanted to smoke cigarettes and drink whiskey. I wanted to be cool. I never fantasized about having a family and living in a big house with a yard. I wanted to live in a loft in Manhattan miles away from where I was. I wanted to be as far away as possible from everything I knew. This feeling would never go away. Today, I am basically living my dream. I live in the best neighborhood in San Francisco, doing what I love to do, and yet I still have days where I wake up and just want to be anywhere but where I am at the moment. Today, as a matter of fact, I woke up and had to pray for ten minutes just to get out of bed. God, please help me get out of bed. Please help me walk to the shower. I have to say this prayer out loud all the time. A part of me still believes that I will never be happy until I have that loft in Midtown Manhattan. Once I get the loft, I will need two pugs, a boy and a girl named Hansel and Gretel. Then I will be happy. Actually in order for me to be truly happy, my loft will need to be located above a nice French Bistro, and it would be nice if there was a raw juice shop next to the French Bistro. Next to the raw juice bar, there better be an art gallery or I will be pissed. And if there wasn't a high-end cigar shop close by, I don't know what I would do! Granted, I only smoke three cigars a year, but still, I don't know if I could live in a loft that wasn't close to a cigar shop. This list could go on forever. I could be miserable anywhere. I could live in a French whorehouse and get pissed off because there were no Brazilian escorts to play with. I would write an angry letter, go on a hunger strike, and everyone would look at me like I was an idiot. They would be right.

Fighting sleep to get back at my stepfather and fantasizing about my big escape from the little farm town I lived in started to consume every part of my being. What I soon learned to be called 'insomnia' would really kick in when I was fifteen. It actually took me years to figure out that my leaving home so young would cause a lot of trauma. To make a long story short, leaving home really fucked up my head. On one hand, I didn't have to deal with all the rules and the suffocating tension that consumed my parents' house, but on the other hand, I was dropped into a world of the lower working class. There would be no new clothes anytime I asked, no more trips to the beach house, and even the endless supply of food would be gone. My whole life changed overnight. My cushy upper-middle-class lifestyle vanished in a flash. Drugs were expensive and I didn't have any money. Even the inside of my grandparents' refrigerator was sad. Whenever you opened the fridge, all you would see was a jar of pickles, leftover spaghetti, mayonnaise, some butter, some milk, and maybe some juice. Aside from the refrigerator, there was a small bread drawer with a couple of loaves of the cheapest bread you could buy and a small dry pantry with as much Campbell's tomato soup that you could ever want. It was like I was transported back to the Great Depression. Going from riches to rags was actually the hardest thing I had ever experienced at that time. Being poor really did a number on my head. I don't think anybody likes being poor. Personally, I think it sucks. Poor people rarely go on summer trips to Europe. Poor people never talk about going to the ballgame with their dad. I have never heard a poor person say, "Well, what we didn't have in money, we made up for it in love." I have never met a really poor family that was open and loving. I think that saying is such bullshit. The poorest families I have ever met all had a few key things in common. Aside from not having any money, I have noticed that the poorest families all had a lot of drug and alcohol abuse happening. There were never any college graduates and many of the family members never graduated from high school. Another thing I have noticed about the poorest people I have met is that most of them smoke, have really poor diets, and never exercise. They consume lots of sugar like soda and candy, a lot of boxed food and imitation cheese, and a lot of potato chips. I have also noticed that the poorest people I have met have a very weak grasp of the English language. Sadly, the poorest people that I know are members of my own family. I have always had a lot of shame around this. I never talk about my family to my friends. I never date a woman long enough for her to meet my family. I think I mentioned earlier that one of the main reasons for my never marrying is because I do not want my fiancé to meet my family. If I were to ever meet the love of my life, I would be very happy to introduce my soon-to-be wife to my grandmother, but I just do not want to have to take my girl to meet the parents. I dread the day I ever have to do this. Now, I know I sound like an elitist piece of shit. Trust me, if I didn't know all the details and back-story of my life, I would think the same thing. But all the poverty and alcoholic druggy bullshit that comes with my family, it's just not worth the trouble. I truly don't think I can get over this, and because of that I may just die alone. I know that is all a bit melodramatic, but what woman is going to marry me without meeting my family? I mean, she is going to want to see where I come from, and I just don't want anyone to see that part of me. You would literally have to put a gun to my head and tell me that you were going to blow my head off if I didn't let you meet my family. That's the only way it would happen. I have thought long and hard about my attitude about my family and gone back and forth with what it all means. Do I have these feelings because I am a bad person? Is it my disease that curses me with these feelings? Again, am I just a selfish piece of shit? Being around my family just makes me feel physically uncomfortable followed by severe depression. Why? I was really hoping that over time the longer I stayed clean and worked my sober program, I would be able to just let my family be who they are without judgment. I find that the only way I can let my family be who they are without judgment is to just stay away. Once-a-year visits— tops—are about what I can muster these days. Having these thoughts and feelings keep me up at night. Not feeling a connection to one's family is actually quite disturbing. It's very isolating and lonely. I have met so many people in my AA meetings that have much lower bottoms than I could ever dream of having, but over time a lot of them reconnected with their families. Why not me?

My thoughts about my family are only one of the issues that plague me. Becoming poor again is always on my mind. Being homeless with nowhere to turn often feels like a real possibility for me. If I have one bad month, I could lose everything. I live paycheck to paycheck. I always have. There is no other income coming in and I was not blessed with some random money tree in my backyard. There is no trust fund or credit card that seems to never run out. Whatever I make is what I have and so many things are on my mind all the time. My self-esteem is directly attached to my income. That's all I care about, to be honest. My paycheck and my monthly commissions are everything to me. Without those, I am nothing. I couldn't care less if an attractive woman is attracted to me or not. Hell, I will just buy one for a couple of hours if I really want one. And how do I do that? You guessed it: money. We need money to do anything. We have all heard it before, but love definitely does not pay the bills. No, my skills and hard work pay the bills.

Something else that gets my mind racing is thinking about when my grandmother eventually passes away. Aside from sincerely missing her, I will have nowhere to go if my life falls apart. Again, another selfish thought! I am obsessively afraid of not getting what I want and losing what I have. I have this recurring thought that when my grandmother passes, I will lose my mind, my job, and my apartment. I will be homeless because I will have no one to call and ask for help. Why? Because I didn't give a fuck about anybody but myself. Nobody wants to help a person like that, and I don't blame them. I am completely aware of the fact that I do not deserve anything. I know that relationships grow and thrive because people want to be a part of each other's lives. All *I* want is to have my rent paid, swim my laps, get a massage once a week, and eat at amazing restaurants. I don't really need relationships other than for resources. I wish I wasn't like that, but it just seems to be who I am. I love having a lot of acquaintances. It's nice to go outside and go to a café and talk with my regular waitress or go to my bike shop and chat with the local mechanic. I love stopping by and talking with my tattoo artist for ten minutes about politics. I love people in really small doses, but I personally do not need much more than that. At night, I will think about this and it will all come crashing down on me. Am I am a superficial sociopath that gives and takes freely without any true emotion behind any of it? My doctors say no, but sometimes I wonder. I love giving to people because I love how it makes *me* feel. When someone thanks me profusely for helping him or her, it makes me very uncomfortable. It makes me feel uncomfortable because their feelings make me uncomfortable. A part of me gives so much because I think it will save me a spot in a better place after I die. Some people call it heaven. I think that the more you give, the better seat you have in heaven, kind of like a VIP pass. I hate waiting in line for anything and I don't like mediocrity. I consciously chose a career in the service industry because if you serve others, maybe you will have the best afterlife. I have chosen a career where all I do is make other people's lives better. I feel that because of the decisions I made in the past, I will need to pay a kind of penance for the rest of my days. Yes, I only used drugs and drank daily for seven years, and yes, I was a drug dealer for a very short span of time but I put certain people in a lot of danger on more than one occasion. For the most part, I have forgiven myself for this, but I do not feel that I will ever be completely off the hook for what I have done. I think that rapists, child molesters, and murders should be put to death. I think that poor people that have children should be sterilized and forced to adopt their children out to people that can afford to raise them, and I think that drug dealers should have to serve a life of servitude. I was a drug dealer, so based on my belief system, my future is simple. Yes, I know, life isn't fair.

Having these simple yet very harsh thoughts about life leaves very little room for error. If everything I really like is bad for me, like drugs, alcohol, fatty French food, and prostitutes with big asses, what is left? I seem to spend a lot of my mental energy trying to stay away from all the things I love. So instead, I drink veggie protein shakes and take niacin, magnesium, and multivitamins. Yes, I do splurge with massages, hot escorts, and three-Michelin-star restaurants, but the tug of war between the good and bad is exhausting and it's always there. Am I a bad person for paying for sex? Yes? No? Why? Because it's illegal? So the law dictates whether I am good or not. If I pay for sex, get caught for it, and go to jail, should I really be sitting next to a guy that shot his uncle in the chest? Paying for sex is as bad as killing someone? What the fuck! I think about this shit all the time at one in the morning. My mother will ask me why I think about this stuff. She will tell me to just stop thinking about it. Stop thinking about it? Why didn't I think of that? Just fucking stop. Okay, done. I'm cured! Thanks, Mom. No, it's not that easy. Remember, alcoholism is a disease that centers in the mind. If you go to an AA meeting, you will hear someone say that it is an allergy of the body and an obsession of the mind. Once you take care of the allergy of the body, meaning you stop drinking, then you have to deal with the obsession of the mind. What they don't tell you is that an alcoholic doesn't just obsess over alcohol. An alcoholic obsesses over everything. A lot of alcoholics obsess over money, sex, food, work, you name it, and an alcoholic obsesses over it all.

How does one merely stop thinking about something? How do you tell your brain that it's time to take a break? Personally, I have tried a lot of things to get my brain to shut off. Unfortunately, the only things that have ever been able to turn my brain off were alcohol, drugs, prostitutes, food, and sleep. See how an alcoholic is fucked? You're damned if you do and you're damned if you don't. When I was nineteen, I started taking Tylenol PM. I took Tylenol every night until I was twenty-four. I told a doctor this and he told me that I should switch to Benadryl. Okay, so then I took Benadryl until I was twenty-seven. The last time I took Benadryl was the night I woke up experiencing a panic attack in October of 2006. It was about four a.m. and the world was spinning. I walked to the emergency room, which was about four blocks away and the doctor gave me a sedative. Soon after that, different doctors would try different medications on me. I have covered all this earlier in the book, so I will save you the recap.

From 2006 to 2009, I was cursed with a debilitating level of insomnia. I would go two, three, and sometimes four nights without any sleep. If I ever made it to five nights without sleep, I would always take an ambulance to the ER. I did this once a month for fourteen months. Finally one early morning, I met a nurse practitioner that saved my life. I can't remember her name and I wish I could because I have wanted to thank her for years. I remember telling her what I had been going through and she told me that she knew of an amazing psychiatrist. She gave me his business card and told me that she would call him and have him reach out to me. As I write this, I am so grateful that I would meet this doctor. This psychiatrist did reach out to me the next day and he fit me in to see him that very same day. I saw this doctor once a week for six months. I am confident that without that chance meeting at 4:30 in the morning with that special nurse, I honestly would not have made it much longer. I have met so many nurses and doctors in the past and very few of them made any real impact in my life. It's not their fault. It's just the nature of the beast that is mental illness. Without those two specific health care professionals, I would have stayed doomed until I finally pulled the trigger. Thank God for nurses and doctors. So many of us would be fucked without them.

To this day, I still suffer from chronic insomnia. I still take a special prescribed medication, and when the time comes that I no longer need it, I will be truly free. I am one of those dual-diagnosis addicts. I have met hundreds of alcoholics that simply got better once they quit drinking and using drugs. Their depression and anxiety went away. The mood swings, the violent thoughts, it all just went away. Ninety-nine percent of these addicts I am talking about claim that once they found a higher power, started working the twelve-steps of Alcoholics Anonymous program, and did everything else that is mentioned in an AA meeting, they were basically cured one day at a time. I am so happy for those people. But there are some addicts like me that also work a twelve-step program, pray, meditate, help other addicts, get sober, and still need some outside help. Some of us need a doctor of some sort on the side. Some of us go to therapy. Some of us are put on mood stabilizers and antidepressants, and if we don't take them, we spin out of control in a way that only a few of us will ever know. Yes, I am one of *those* addicts. If you are one of these addicts as well and you decide to work a twelve-step program, you will eventually run into alcoholics that do not believe in doctors and medication. They will share in a group setting on how they do not believe that a person that takes medication is truly sober because if they believed in God or were working a stronger program, they would not need medications or doctors.

I will let you in on a little secret when it comes to these kinds of people. These people are assholes. These are the type of people that probably have some kind of mental illness outside of being an addict and they are too proud to admit it or too stupid to look into it. A lot of these people also tend to relapse. Any person in a twelve-step meeting that openly condemns another addict for doing something that they don't do is one of the sickest people in the room, so fuck them. If a doctor is prescribing you medication, and it helps you and you think that you need the medication, chances are you need the medication. Maybe you won't need it forever. But maybe you will, and that's okay too. I am not trying to sell anyone on taking medication. A lot of medications have shitty side effects like chronic drowsiness and weight gain, and I have had to deal with my share of side effects over the years. So if you don't absolutely need meds, I personally would stay away from them, but like I said, I am one of those people that need meds. I am however against bullying, and if someone doesn't take medication or gets off their medication without their doctor knowing about it because they are afraid of what people might think, I say fuck that. Fuck what other people do. Do what's best for you. This is another one of those topics where I always tell people that if someone is fucking with them about taking medication, please tell me and I will personally wreck that fucking asshole. A few years ago, a kid in his twenties told me that his sponsor fired him because he was on antidepressants. Later that same week, I yelled at that kid's sponsor in front of the other thirty people that were in the AA meeting with us. I waited until someone called on me to share and I stood up and walked over to that fat coward and shamed him in front of everyone. I probably shouldn't have called him a cunt because there were women in the room but I was very upset. I will literally fight for anyone that is being bullied like that.

I want to be very open and transparent about my shitty relationship with sleep. I am almost forty years old and I still have a fear of the dark. I hate being alone with my thoughts while the lights are off. It is truly the worst feeling in the world for me. When I turn the lights off to go to bed, I always wish I had someone next to me. I wish she would run her fingers through my hair and tell me everything will be okay. I wish she would do this until I fall asleep. One of the few child memories that I have of my mother is when I was upset and I would lie on the couch with my head in her lap, and she would just run her fingers through my hair. I would cry and she would tell me that everything was going to be fine. I would fall asleep and a couple of hours later, I would wake up and my mother would still be there. She would be watching a movie and I would keep my eyes closed and feel safe. A part of me will always want that. I think the hole that I have inside of me that I have always tried to fill with drugs, alcohol, food, money, and sex will always be there until I find someone that I can trust completely. Again, it always goes back to fear and faith, in this case—faith in love. I might struggle with insomnia until I can find it within myself to love and let someone love me. I think all the things that I obsess about are all just distractions. If I consume myself with worries, then I will never have to look at the basic root of my problem. I am fully aware that I do not think that I am worthy of any kind of love. I know that I don't think I deserve it. That is a very hard thing to live with, as some of you may already know. It is painful. Nobody wants to admit to anyone that they don't think they deserve a good life. At times, this thought will only last for a couple of minutes. But I have discovered that this fleeting thought is actually what it's all about. That fleeting thought is why I drank and used drugs. It's why I pay for sex. It's why I overeat. It's why I sleep for twelve hours at a time on my days off. If I can't have love, then I will seek out simple pleasures in order to distract myself from what's really going on. I will focus on moving up in the world. I will focus on solving your problems. What else am I going to do? I certainly can't solve my own problems. I used to have a lot of problems, but today I only have one. My only problem today is that I believe that I do not deserve to be loved. Perhaps with more work and deeper faith, I will someday overcome this setback.

19. $300 an Hour

The first time I ever paid for sex, I was twenty-three years old. I was in Las Vegas for nine days for a few fashion shows that were happening. I was staying at the Hilton. Before my trip to Las Vegas, I deposited a check for about twelve grand. At this point in my life, I was starting to feel the loneliness that seems to plague all alcoholics whether they are sober or not. I was only a year sober and, to be honest with you, I had no real social skills to speak of. I don't think I really had any interest in people, so social skills weren't necessary at the time. The only person I really talked to was my grandmother. In my mind, my grandmother was all I needed.

I remember looking at the clock next to my hotel bed on my first night and it was eleven p.m. My skin was crawling with boredom. I hated the other models that I was traveling with, and I just had no interest in walking the strip. I have always hated Las Vegas. To this day, I still see it as a really trashy place. The only reason I ever went to Vegas was for the Neon Sign Museum and the escorts. Vegas has the hottest escorts I have ever seen. I have been with escorts all over the US, and Vegas is tops. Whatever you are into, you can get it in Las Vegas. Hot blonds, hot brunettes, thick women, skinny women, and sexy cougars, black, Colombian, Brazilian, Russian, Asian, you can get it all. My first time getting an escort was a pretty smooth and easy transaction. I was walking to my hotel and I saw a couple fliers on the ground. I knew that I really wanted an escort, but I had no interest in the younger, glitzy, white blond girls that all men seem to want. I really wanted a hot mid-to-late-forties thick cougar. I had no idea how to find what I wanted, so I just went to one of the valet guys at my hotel and asked. Back when I did a lot of drugs, I would often ask a valet employee where to get what I wanted. If you are ever in a major city like New York, Chicago, Los Angeles, Miami, San Francisco, and of course, Las Vegas, if you ever need anything like drugs, sex, or a hitman for some asshole that keeps bugging you, always go to the hotel valet. If you travel a lot and you are a seedy creepy bastard, then you need to become best friends with the valet employees. Whenever they give you any kind of information, always slip them a twenty. If they really come through for you, give them fifty bucks. Yes, I know the main reason why I am writing this book is because I am promoting sober living but if you are reading this and not interested in sobriety, well, then I just gave you some great advice on how to be the best degenerate that you can be. If you are going to be anything, always be the best version you can be.

Back to my first escort… I went to the Hilton valet and asked if he knew where I could get different escorts. I told him exactly what I wanted. I wanted a hot, thick cougar. The valet didn't know right off the bat, but he had a couple of numbers of guys that could help. I went up to my room and called one of the numbers that were given to me. 'Ricky' was an energetic man. Ricky was very helpful and I would keep Ricky in my back pocket for years. I told Ricky that I wanted a hot curvy woman in her mid-to-late forties. I wanted a woman with darker features, maybe Latina. I like big breasts, a really big ass, and a slender waist. Ricky told me that I wanted 'Maria.' Ricky told me that Maria would be perfect for me. He told me that she was forty-seven years old, about five foot two, 140 lbs., and it was all in her tits and ass. I couldn't wait! Two hours later, there was a very quiet knock at my door. I opened the door and there she was—Maria. We looked at each other and we both smiled. I was immediately under her spell. She looked at me and said, "This mami is going to take good care of you." After that, I do not remember any other words being exchanged. She walked to the bed and slipped out of her candy-red, skin-tight dress. She slipped out of her black pushup bra and left her matching black thong on. She immediately sprawled out on the king-size bed. I walked over to her and she rubbed her right hand over my cock. I was so hard that it hurt. I took off my clothes and sprawled out next to her. We both laughed and then she just did her thing. Sex after Maria would change my life. Sex with that woman was like the first time I smoked heroin or the first time I did some really high-quality MDMA. The first time was definitely the best time and I would chase that experience for years—the tone of Maria's voice, the way she moved her hips and ass, and the way she grabbed her breasts. She was commanding yet feminine. Everything she did was perfect. Even after cumming, I stayed hard. I would rest for fifteen minutes and we would go again. I would come again and then stay hard until our third, fourth, and fifth time together. Those wonderful ninety minutes with Maria cost me $1,200.00 dollars. It was worth every penny, but there was one major side effect. Fucking Maria would ruin me for other women for a long time. No other escort would come close. I have been with two and three escorts at the same time and nothing has ever compared to that time with her. Maria could do one thing that no other woman has ever been able to do for me. She made me think that she loved me and without using any words, she convinced me that I loved her. Trust me, I know this sounds ridiculous. I would do anything for her. I would kill to have another woman look into my eyes the way Maria looked into my eyes while she fucked me. Maria was a true professional. She was like an assassin. She had a job to do and she executed the task perfectly. The next day, I woke up relaxed. All of my muscles were relaxed. My mind was at ease. I can only count on one hand how many times I have felt completely mentally and physically relaxed in my life. All the other experiences I have had with all the other escorts have been purely animal experiences. None of the other women had the smarts to get into my head and do anything they wanted to it. All the other escorts that I have been with thought that fucking me was good enough. Most of the women that I have been with, escort or not, behaved this way. They all think I am lucky to just be with them. Silly creatures. Maria was actually the most I would ever spend on a woman for sex. My comfort zone has always been $300 an hour. The only thing I miss about modeling is being able to afford escorts whenever I wanted. Granted, seventy percent of the time I have felt a bit cheated after it was over, but as long as I got off, I was good with the whole thing. Every once in a while, a woman would come along that would blow my mind. After four or five years of casually seeing escorts, I began to notice that something odd was happening to me. My interest in normal everyday women had for the most part disappeared. A normal woman gives a very average blowjob. And sure, every woman thinks she gives great blowjobs, but what they don't understand is that the men they are fucking are just happy that they are fucking at all. Fucking is like pizza for men. We like it hot, cold, room temperature. A young man will fuck pretty much anything, so when we get a woman that is even slightly above average-looking, we freak out. Most men marry the first above-average woman that they get to fuck. In the back of a man's mind, he is thinking, 'Well, this is probably the best I will ever get, so I might as well marry her.' What a schlep! Ninety-nine percent of all men do not have the balls to go for a woman that they are really attracted to. Most men are cowards and pussies. Just look around and watch couples walk with each other. Nine out of ten times you will see the woman walking ahead of the man and he will follow with his hands in his pockets, looking at the ground. That man is dead inside. Why? Because he decided to stay with a woman that he got drunk with and fucked five years ago. She was only supposed to be a one-night stand but they ran into each other at the grocery store and they hooked up again. They have been together ever since. This sadly is like most relationships today.

Fuck that! If you want to raise your self-esteem, try saving your money and get the hottest escort you can find. Yes, you paid for her but you fucked her and your dick doesn't know the difference. Your dick will want that Grade-A pussy again and it will convince you to do anything to get it. If you have to, get more escorts. Train your brain and your dick to work together. Your dick needs to convince your brain that you deserve a ten every time. Fuck all these lazy fives and sixes. Maybe if men would stop sleeping with mediocre-looking women, they would get off their asses and hit the gym. I believe that men are to blame for all the below-average women running around the place. Women would try harder if men just got some balls and told them to fuck off until they get their shit together. And the same goes for women. Why are so many women dating all these pussy-ass men? Every once in a while I will see a pretty good-looking woman with a skinny, pale beta boy. Why? Do you even give a shit? Do you even like getting dicked or do you just want a golden retriever that brings in a paycheck? At the end of the day, my theory that everyone always gets what he or she deserves is true yet again. When I see an obese woman with purple hair holding hands with a skinny, six-foot-four twink wearing a Metallica T-shirt, I just nod my head in disappointment. There is a good chance those two people will procreate. What chance does their child have? It seems like the smartest, fastest, and strongest human beings are having less and less children while the fattest, dumbest, and poorest humans are cranking out babies left and right. It's really sad.

So where do I go from here? Do I stop seeing professionals for sex? Do I find a white woman born and raised in the suburbs that somehow has self-respect? Or do I drop everything and move to Venezuela for a year and marry a drop-dead gorgeous local and bring her back to the States. I will be honest with you. I am not quite ready to quit my escort habit. I am still having too much fun. White women from the burbs, sorry but I just can't do it. I just can't take the whole middle-class white girl fake vocal fry accent they use. This type of woman will either drive me insane or kill my soul. Venezuela however is an option that I might be willing to try. I have been around long enough to know that no matter where a woman is from, she is going to be irrational and moody, but if I do decide to settle down, I will definitely need to be attracted to her. There is no place on Earth where people are always happy, well educated, attractive, and polite. These kinds of people are scattered all over the planet. You just have to find one that you are attracted to and you can stand the sound of their voice. You may never find this person and I think this scares a lot of people. This is one reason why I am so pro-prostitution. I mean sex will always be very important to most of us. But if you don't like someone and all you want to do is fuck them for a while, just do that. Don't try to convince yourself that you have feelings for them when you really don't. Just let sex be sex. I don't go to a restaurant, have a great meal, and try to kidnap the chef and make him stay with me forever. Most chefs are complete assholes. Why would you ever want to live with a chef? Let him do what he does, which is cook great food, and leave the rest out. I think all of life is like this. So just pay someone what they are worth and move on, whether it is a plumber or a mechanic or a chef or an escort. Don't make it out to be more than it is. And maybe you think I am completely wrong. Maybe you want true love. Well, I have news for you. True love is the hardest thing to find. Finding your dream job and making a million dollars is easier to do than finding true love. How close are you to becoming a millionaire? That's what I thought. So if you don't even know what you could be the best at, why do you think finding the love of your life will be any easier? Most people don't have the guts for true love. I know I don't. For most people, true love is even scarier than the biggest fear they are conscious of. You think your fear of heights is the worst thing ever? Love is even scarier. So if you refuse to go bungee jumping, you will definitely never find true love. Pussies do not deserve true love. Pussies deserve the fives and sixes that the world has to offer.

20. My Bicycle

On my fourth birthday, my mother got me a bright red bicycle with no training wheels, just a kickass bike. Before this bicycle, I played on those old-school 1980s plastic three-wheelers. My grandmother had an old rusty trike that I would cruise around on. When I saw the bike my mom got me, I freaked out. I was determined to learn to ride that thing before the day was over. I would get on that bike at eleven a.m. I would run with the bike next to me, hop on, and start pedaling. I fell off, immediately cutting my hands and knees. I got back up and started running with the bike only to fall again. I'd do this over and over again for a couple of hours. Eventually, my grandmother made me stop. She told me I could practice more after lunch and a nap. I ran into the house and ate the tuna fish sandwich and soup that my grandmother made me as fast as I could. I went into the nap room and just stared at the ceiling for an hour. My grandmother knocked on the door to let me know I could get back up. I ran back outside and got back on that damn bike. Another two hours would go by. I would fall off that bike at least fifty times. My hands, knees, shins, and ankles were all cut up and bloody. My right hip was killing me from falling on it so many times. I will never forget the first time I was able to start pedaling and just keep pedaling and not fall off. I cranked on the pedal brakes, hopped off the bike, and ran into the house, yelling for my grandmother to come outside and watch me ride my bike. At first, my grandmother didn't believe that I learned to ride my bike all by myself. I grabbed my bike and begged her to watch me. I ran with my bike, hopped on, and just started pedaling. I rode my bike up the driveway, slowly turned around, and rode back to my grandmother. I remember the shocked look on her face. We were both so excited. The next day, I rode my bike across the street where a softball field was located. My grandparents lived across the street from a huge park with softball diamonds and gravel roads for bikes. The 1980s were awesome because kids could still go outside all day and play, ride bikes, and get dirty without any fear of being kidnapped or raped by some freak. Parents would let their kids go nuts all day. You could walk around your neighborhood, look for other kids to play with, and the kids would actually just play. Nothing weird was going on, just kids having fun.

That first bicycle would play a major role throughout my life. I am thirty-nine and I ride a bike every day. When I was in the fifth grade, I would ride my bike five miles to the nearest store, buy a bunch of football cards, ride my bike five more miles back home, and figure out how much I thought each card was worth. Then I would sell the cards to students at my grade school for a really high markup. I would make fifty bucks on a five-dollar deck of football cards. My mother never asked me where I was going or how long I'd be gone. I just went.

When I was fifteen, I would ride my bike around my grandmother's neighborhood and just look for kids to smoke pot with. I would have my Walkman in my back pocket and listen to old house mix tapes. Being stoned and listening to deep house while riding my bike in 1994 was the shit. I loved it. Half of the reason why I left my parents' house was so I could do these things without any stress of my parents finding out. The sense of freedom was such an amazing feeling. It was a very simple but brief time. Once I got into the harder drugs, the love for my bike started to fade away and I would spend most of my time in random basements and abandoned warehouses where raves were thrown. Most of the time outside of those two activities I basically spent sleeping. By the time I was seventeen, all the 'innocents' would be gone. The simple pleasures meant nothing. I did not ride a bike again until I was twenty-three. Once I got sober and started working out, I wanted to find a way to do cardio outside of the treadmill. When I wasn't living with my grandmother, I always lived in NW Portland. Portland is probably the best city to ride a bike in. With all the bike paths and bridges, all the other cyclists, it felt like what I thought living in Europe would be like. I loved riding my bike to the gym, cranking out a good workout, and then biking to a café to watch people walk by. Then I would bike around a little more, maybe cross over to the eastside and check out a park and take a quick nap. Then I would bike home. All of my worries would fade away when I rode my ten-speed. I rode my bike for the same reasons that I drank and smoked pot. It was a great way to escape. The only downside to riding a bike was knowing that eventually you would get hit by a car. Maybe not to today and maybe not tomorrow, but you knew it would eventually happen. My time would come in June of 2003. I mentioned before that I was on my way to fitness model photo shoot. Well, that day would be my time. An SUV demolished me and my life changed dramatically. Even though I was wearing a helmet, and thank God I was, the trauma to my head was probably the cause of the vertigo that I would experience for four years. When my vertigo started, three doctors asked me if I had suffered any trauma to the head recently. I told them about my bike accident and they all agreed that being hit by the SUV was probably what triggered the vertigo and the horrible migraines that I was getting. The doctors told me that the vertigo and migraines might only last a week or two or it could last a few months. They told me that some people experienced these side effects, but it was very rare. Well, lucky me, because I was one of those rare cases. Landing on my head would cause me to have hallucinations, crazy vertigo, and on a daily basis I would feel as if a truck was trying to come out of my skull. It was a horrifying experience and it almost drove me to suicide many times. I am probably still experiencing side effects to this day but simply not aware of it because I am used to it all.

I then decided to stay away from bikes for about four years. I developed a kind of phobia of riding. Finally, at around the age of twenty-eight, I would eventually get another bike. I knew I wasn't going to get a car anytime soon. I never really had any interest in cars. To be honest with you, the thought of driving freaks me out. It always has. When I was three, my mother got into a car accident. There was heavy snow on the road and my mother slid into a deep ditch. I remember her screaming and losing her shit. When I was nineteen, a bunch of my friends and I piled into my friend Chelsea's car. Chelsea let me drive. We were all high on ecstasy. I decided to turn off the headlights and drive as fast as I could up a windy road. I took a sharp right and just stopped the car. We all got out and we all looked down. The front tires of the car were only a few inches from the edge of a two-hundred-foot drop-off. That would be the last time I would drive a car. And yes, never say never. I may decide to take the plunge and learn to drive a car, but it isn't a priority for me right now. Until that day comes, I am hundred percent car-free and my bike will remain a major part of my life. Over the years, only a handful of things have been able to pull me out of my deep depressions and soul-crushing anxiety—swimming laps, Frank the pug, talking to my grandmother, and my bike. If it ain't broke, don't fix it.

21. Romance

Human beings have needs. We can agree on this, right? Human beings need certain things to physically survive. This is a no brainer. But human beings also need certain things to feel alive inside as well. Maybe not all human beings but let's just say for the sake of argument, ninety-nine percent of all human beings have a few needs that make life worth living. What are they? What are the things that everyone wants? Love, sex, and romance. You will not die if you do not have love, sex, and romance in your life, but you might feel like you will if you don't ever get it. Let's also make it clear that love, sex, and romance are not the same thing. If you didn't know that, now you do. What is love? The dictionary says that love is an intense feeling or deep affection. If you do not get enough food, air, or water, you will die. This is a fact. From personal experience, I know I can go weeks without an intense feeling or deep affection. I would prefer to have those things, but it will not kill me. I am by no means saying that you should go without love and I am not anti-love. I am just trying to put this into perspective. I have been in love once in my life. I have already told that sad story, but what I got out of that experience is that it wasn't love that hurt me. It was the person I chose to love. And the person that hurt me didn't mean to hurt me. She wasn't an evil person. She was twenty-two years old and she was too young to commit the rest of her life to one person. I wasn't even twenty-one at the time, so I definitely had no business trying to tie the knot. For a decade, I swore off love altogether. I just fucked and had a handful of girlfriends that I never had any plans staying with long-term. That shit is on me.

Sex, another activity that is held in high regard with most people on the planet is a whole other world. Sex, fucking, getting around, catching a fling, these are all fun things to do that a lot of people lose their shit over. I have seen men fight each other almost to death over some club skank at two in the morning. Hell, I have gotten into some intense yelling matches with dudes over women that I had no interest in an hour before the near-death match took place. Men seem to go crazy over sex. Add a little alcohol and cocaine, and shit is going to get nuts. I am sure a lot of women love sex too but not like men do. Most of the sex addicts that I have met are women but the one thing I learned about female sex addicts is that they are not actually addicted to the sex itself. They are addicted to the power it gives them. They are addicted to the emotions connected to sex. Most straight female sex addicts that I have met actually seemed to hate men. I have been to a ton of sex addicts' anonymous meetings and there were a few reoccurring stories. The majority of male sex addicts were sexually abused by a male figure in their life when they were younger, usually their father or grandfather or an older neighbor. With women, there were a lot more stories. There was sexual abuse they endured as little girls by men ranging from their stepfather to an older cousin to a next-door neighbor. There seemed to be a much more broad range of ways women were abused. Then there are the stories of women being raped in their post-teen years: high school, college, first male roommate, or best male friend that they had since the third grade. It always seemed like women had so many more ways of being mistreated. I am not a doctor of any kind, but I am a good listener and keen observer of behavior. There are a lot of men that are fucked up when it comes to sex, but there are simply a lot more women that are fucked in the head when it comes to sex. Knowing this changes how I view sex, especially casual sex. I have never met an emotionally stable woman that is willing to have casual sex. Every woman that I have had casual sex with would end up being mentally ill or emotionally unstable in one way or another. I have met a lot of loose women in my life and the top three illnesses that these women had were alcoholism, bipolar disorder, and borderline personality disorder. Once you have a clear knowledge of this kind of information, it really changes how you look at casual sex as a viable option. And being a self-proclaimed male slut myself, I have been with all kinds of women from all over the world. In my experience, most of the women that I have met with the most emotional problems were white. I don't know why this is but white women just seem to have the most problems. They either have the lowest self-esteem or the highest to the point of seeming completely narcissistic. They will either fall in love with you overnight or they will be completely emotionally unavailable. There will never be anything in between. Most of the depressed Goth chicks I met in my teen years were all white chicks. The Emo fashion trend started in the suburbs of Orlando, Florida. For me, sex and white women do not mix. Four women have tried ruining my life after I broke up with them and they were all white. Granted, the most violent woman I ever dated was born and raised in Brazil. She was scary and my one exception. I have never had any problems with black women, Middle-Eastern women,

Asian women, or any other race, to be honest. I have even had a couple of weird experiences with escorts and both were white. Those girls were nuts.

But with all this put on the table, sex is the greatest adventure of all time. It's amazing, awesome, and great all at the same time. That feeling you get when you meet someone that you are attracted to and they smile at you and you know that it's on, you feel like the king of the world. For a matter of moments, you are the strongest, fastest, and sexiest human on the planet. You are Bradley Cooper in the movie *Limitless*. Of course this feeling fades away and you become, well, *you* again. But don't worry; the great feeling will come back again, until one day when it just stops. Maybe you get too old or you just don't care anymore. Personally, I am reaching an age where I could take it or leave it. Half of my brain knows that hunting for casual sex has too many risks. The other half of my brain keeps telling me to keep getting out there and hit that shit.

What about romance? Romance is either a noun or a verb. Let's go with romance as a verb. Romance means to court or woo. The one thing all my relationships had in common whether the relationship lasted twelve hours or twelve months was the romance. I have always loved the process of seeing an attractive woman from across the room, going up to her and breaking the ice, and complimenting her on her beautiful skin or how great her hair looks. She smiles and we talk. Sometimes we would make plans to meet again in a more private setting or we would just end the conversation after a few minutes to never see each other again. Approaching a woman for the first time still holds excitement for me. I still get anxious and I can feel my body temperature rise. I still have a mini panic attack as I move into her personal space. Sometimes, I am pursuing that feeling I get and sometimes I am actually pursuing her. I can tell the difference as to whether a woman is really classy versus really hot. When I think a woman has class, I am wondering what she is like as a person. She intrigues me and I want to get to know her. When I think a girl is hot, I basically just want to fuck. Classy women tend to be the full package: body, brains, and personality. A hot chick tends to have the body only and little else to offer. They never have much to say. They will tell you it's because they are shy, but the truth is they have low self-esteem and they just are not that bright, but of course you can never say that because you want to sleep with her. Whether the woman is classy or hot, one thing remains the same: romance. I pretend I am interested in them regardless if I am or not. I buy them a drink. If someone walks by with roses, I might buy one. I will ask questions and I will listen. I will make them laugh. I am sure some of them find me genuinely funny and others are just being nice and doing the 'first-date fake laugh.' I am fully aware that I am not the only man that plays this game when it comes to dating. I know that a lot of women are putting on a show as well. Sure, I am smart, funny, and charming at times, but I know I am not God's gift to anyone. This is another reason why dating becomes so much harder as you get older. A lot of people like myself enjoy being single, but on occasion we just want some attention and quasi-forced magic. At the end of the day, that's all that romance is. Romance is nothing more than two people getting together and putting on a show for each other. It's like a play. No matter what your interest in the other person is, you still want that element of fantasy and open possibility. Every time a woman asks me what I am looking for, I tell her straight up that I just want a fuck buddy I get shut down. If I tell her I am open to see what happens, that gives both of us that space to believe whatever we want to believe. If you just want to hook up a few times, you have that possibility. If she needs to believe that it could be something more so she doesn't feel like such a slut, that's good too. I think a lot of women just want a casual fuck buddy, but they know that there is a double standard in the world of hooking up. Men can get away with just saying, "Hell, I just want to fuck today." If a woman says this, other women will think she's cheap, even though they want the same thing, and some men will think there is something mentally wrong with them. Unfortunately, women have to pretend and believe their own bullshit a bit more than men have to. I have mentioned it before and I'll mention it again. Men have it so much easier than women.

The reason why I am talking about love and sex and everything in between is because if you are at the onset of getting sober, I would stay the hell away from all this. Whatever it is that you are into, just take a break. If you try getting into something serious with someone, I guarantee you that it will cut you wide open. Getting emotionally involved with someone and bringing sex into it will fuck you up even more. If you are worried about relapsing, I promise you that sex is going to crush you. You are going to get into a bunch of drama and you are going to drink again. In the first fight you get into, you are going to shoot, snort, or drink something. Why? Because you are emotionally retarded and you do not have the life skills to navigate and bounce back from the pain that you will eventually go through. You couldn't handle it when you were using, so how would you be able to handle it sober? The one thing that you used to feel better is gone now. Think about it. I know I am just wasting air and energy by telling people not to get into a relationship when they are new to sobriety, but I would be remiss if I did not say something. Someone will ask you, "Why did you relapse?" and you will tell them, "Because I met a hot girl and she broke up with me two weeks later." Listen pal, only *you* are responsible for your sobriety, so don't go blaming it on the hot chick who messed with your head!

22. Truth or Dare

When I was a little kid, my grandmother watched a handful of kids my age that lived in her neighborhood. There was Sarah, Haley, Anita, Brooke, Sarah's younger sister, and David, Anita's older brother. There were a couple of younger kids, but I can't remember their names. I was closest to Sarah and Brooke because their mom and dad were best friends with my aunt. I had a major crush on Haley. Haley was smart, pretty, and polite, and her hair smelled good. I will never forget that clean peach-smelling hair. We were all between the ages of four and five. David was a couple of years older and ignored all of us, but I had the time of my life. We would play cops and robbers and we would build forts together. My grandfather had a large pool table and we used to hide underneath the table and pretend we lived in a cave. We would fall asleep under the table together. I always made sure that I was right next to Haley. The girls would all fall asleep and I would stay up and protect them from the lions and tigers that we pretended were in the room. I liked to lie next to Haley and smell her hair. I guess that sounds a bit creepy when I read over that last sentence, but at the age of four, everything is completely innocent. I was never one of those kids that touched people while they slept. I have always had healthy boundaries when it came to another person's body. I am proud to say that I have never been accused of date rape. I guess one out of three men today will be accused of date rape by the time they reach twenty-five. That's fucked up.

Sarah, Brooke, and I would spend a lot of time together in our early years. Sarah and Brooke were total tomboys back in the day, but they would grow up to look like models. We spent multiple days at one another's houses during school breaks. When I was thirteen, my stepfather told me that Sarah could no longer stay overnight. I was heartbroken. Sarah was one of my best friends and one of the only ways for us to spend any time together was if one of us spent the night. I remember riding my bike to my grandmother's house, running into the house, and starting to cry. I told my grandmother that Phil would not let me be friends with Sarah anymore. I refused to go home, but eventually my mother came and got me. Looking back, I totally get why my stepfather was not comfortable having a girl stay overnight. I would assume that my stepfather was afraid that we would start touching each other, but to be perfectly honest with you, that never crossed my mind. Sarah was one of those girls that I treated like all my other buddies. Maybe my stepfather never had female friends that he was just pals with. Plus, Phil always thought I was gay, so why would he care if I was sleeping next to a girl? Gay boys don't like girls like that. My stepfather is kind of an odd guy. He might have thought that if I spent too much time with girls, I might actually turn gay. He was a strict Roman Catholic will little life experience outside of work and school. At least that's all he ever talked about. He never explained why he made the decisions that he did. I don't think he knew how. God, I make my stepfather out to be such a dick. When I was a kid, I did think he was a total dick, but now I just think he is a bit awkward. He simply is not good with people. No matter what Phil does, he will always be the smartest, most honest, and hardest working person around. But when it comes down to sitting in a room and chatting, it can be a painful experience for him. I know I keep digging myself a deeper hole trying to explain what kind of guy my stepfather was without sounding like I hate the guy, but these are the memories that I have of him.

So, to make a long story short, my friendship with Sarah and Brooke would be cut off. We started getting older and our interests became different. I started doing drugs and spending all my time in the city and Sarah went her own way. I am not sure what that way was, but Sarah became a very successful woman. She struck gold in the real estate business. Brooke got her master's degree and went into bank management. When I was younger, I was so jealous that they were able to make something of their lives and I could not make more than fourteen dollars an hour until I turned thirty-seven. For the life of me, I could not figure out how they did it. Granted, I could not figure out much through my entire twenties and the first half of my thirties. The difference between my stepfather, Sarah, Brooke, and my own level of success was based on how hard we worked. My stepfather, Sarah, and Brooke worked their asses off in their unique individual ways while I always slept in until two p.m. on my days off, chased pussy, and felt sorry for myself. It all goes back to my theory that we get what we deserve. My life turned to shit for a long time because I just didn't apply myself. Phil, Sarah, and Brooke all hustled their asses off. Sarah and Brooke didn't have it easy. Their parents divorced when they were young and I grew up with far more advantages than both of them. I think that growing up with fewer advantages can really help to set someone's life on fire. If you want the Ferrari and the mansion, you have to work your ass off. If you grow up with a silver spoon, maybe you just do not see the urgency in things. Maybe you just assume the good life will always be there. None of this is true for everybody. I know a lot of people that grew up with all the advantages that I had and they took advantage of everything good around them. I also know a lot of people that grew up poor and stayed poor because for whatever reason they accepted it and didn't think they deserved better.

I started getting really interested in girls when I was in the eighth grade. I was in private school at the time. My Girlfriend Naree was an accomplished violinist. She was the cutest girl in my class, so I had to have her. But the girl that really got my blood boiling was Jennifer. She was a senior and she had the thickest thighs, biggest tits, and the biggest ass on campus and she was always single. Jennifer seemed to really like me, but she always told me I was too young. Finally, a couple of months before school was out, there was a Saturday concert. My Girlfriend Naree and a bunch of other musically gifted kids would perform. I met up with a handful of other schoolmates from different grades in the music hall where the concert took place. We decided to sneak out during the fifteen-minute break. We walked over to the running track and decided to play a game of truth or dare. Jennifer suggested that we go to the woods behind the school for privacy. Personally, I was very excited. There were eight of us. Five were the hottest girls in the school and out of the three boys, one of them was gay. So that left my buddy Joe and I for the kissing dares. Let's face it. the only reason why teenagers play truth or dare is to watch each other kiss. Jennifer was a bossy young woman, so she took the lead. She dared one of the other girls to kiss one of the other girls. Of course they made out for a solid minute. If you know anything about rich Catholic school girls, you would know that they love making out with other rich Catholic school girls. Once those naughty girls finished with each other, they dared Jennifer to make out with me. Fuck yes! As soon as she looked at me and smiled, I had an erection. It was amazing how fast it happened. We walked a few yards away behind one of the larger trees in the area. I had never French-kissed a girl before and I knew this was my big moment. Jennifer asked me if I was ready. I was so excited that I almost passed out. Jennifer grabbed me and just shoved her thick, wet tongue down my mouth. It wasn't the sexiest kiss by any means, but it was definitely happening. Jennifer took my left hand and put it under her shirt and on her breast. She took my right hand and guided it up her Catholic schoolgirl skirt and taught me how to rub my finger over her clit. Within seconds, I felt this pool of hot liquid come out of her and rush over my hand. My eyes popped out of my head and she just smiled at me. I was speechless. It felt like I was leaving my body. Her lips became fuller and redder. Her eyes changed color and she started moaning. Her eyes rolled back into her head a bit. More hot liquid came out and rushed over my hand again. What the fuck was this woman doing to me? I was so confused and she was so into it. She pulled my hand out from her pussy. My hand was drenched in something that I had never touched before. I experienced something that was a bit out of my comfort zone. I was just a farm boy that wanted to learn to French-kiss. Jennifer was a city girl that had already been doing coke for a year. I felt like I was going up against Mike Tyson for my first fight. When Jennifer and I walked back to the rest of our group, she was so nonchalant and calm and I probably looked like I just got out of the cockpit of an F15 fighter jet. There is no other way to describe my experience other than calling it shocking. I was in fucking shock. This happened in 1993. I can only imagine what kids are doing now. Needless to say, I would never be the same again. From that day forward, I would also prefer older Phat Ass White Girls (PAWGs). Jennifer programed my brain and body not to accept anything else. I have tried dating thin women in the past, but it just doesn't do anything for me.

For most of us, truth or dare plays a small and brief role in our lives. I played truth or dare six times. Each time was awesome. Each time I would get dared to go into a closet and kiss some girl. Every time I would, but none of those other times could compare to my F15 fighter jet kiss with Jennifer. The other girls were just your basic girls that would probably grow up to be basic women and marry basic men and have your everyday basic children. I ran into Jennifer when I was about twenty-five. She wasn't as hot anymore, but she was still just as scandalous. We ran into each other at a dance party in Downtown Portland at the Chrystal Ballroom. She was with another girl. Her friend had that skinny, bitchy cocktail waitress or hairstylist vibe about her. I couldn't stand her, but I endured her bullshit in order to hang out with Jennifer one more time. The three of us got drunk and we did some ecstasy together. We went back to her car and had a threesome in the covered parking garage. It was the most complicated sex I had ever had. Taking turns on each other in the backseat, one girl would climb over the other or crawl to the front seat to take a break or just get out of the way for a few minutes. I told Jennifer that I was going to cum and she just laughed and said, "Truth or dare, Marques." Now that was a great night. *Oh, and I was sober too.*

23. Angels

Have you ever been really down on your luck for a long period of time? Maybe you were unemployed for ten months, your significant other left you, and your dog died all in one year. It's just you and your thoughts, that crazy brain of yours just trying to make sense of it all and nothing is clicking. All you seem to hear is the word no. One day, it's two in the afternoon and you are lying in bed watching a bad eighties movie and your phone rings. A friend of yours that you lent a thousand dollars to wants to stop by and pay you back. It's been three years and you wrote that thousand dollars off a long time ago. Right after you hang up the phone, someone else calls you. You do not recognize the phone number but you answer it anyway. It's a company that you applied to five weeks ago. You had two interviews with them and you thought you had it in the bag but you never heard back from them. Those sluts, they offer you the job. Holy shit! Fifteen minutes ago, you couldn't even muster up the energy to jerk off and now you are up a grand and you start work on Monday. What the fuck? Most of us have been through hard times that last longer than we are comfortable with and most of us have been saved at the very last minute. I know I have. I can't count how many times I have gotten that call right before I was about to take my last breath before drowning in my own despair.

When I was twenty-seven, I almost hung myself. I remember I had been extremely depressed for about two months. I had flu and I was hallucinating that I was hanging myself with a rope tied to my closet's doorknob. I saw myself choke to death. My eyes rolled up into my head and my skin changed color. It was very cold and I had a slight smirk on my lips. I had a look on my face as if I had cheated life. I was finally in a happy place. I had no worries, no feelings, nothing… and that's all I wanted. I wanted nothing. Actually, I just wanted the pain to go away and it was gone. I had finally gotten what I always wanted. I remember looking at my dead self as if I was looking at a beautiful painting. I was mesmerized. The next thing I know, I was rudely awakened by my cellphone. I did not answer it. My phone went off again and again and each time a voicemail was left. I finally picked up my phone to check my messages. It was a good friend of mine from my AA home group. He said that he wasn't feeling so good and that he was worried that he was going to hurt himself. I called him back and told him I would be right over. He lived on the eastside of Portland and it would be an easy thirty-minute bus ride. When I got there, he was in a sleeping bag surrounded by pillows and couch cushions. He had basically cocooned himself in his apartment. His apartment smelled like musty death. He looked horrible. I remember laughing inside because just an hour earlier, I was contemplating suicide and now I was in my buddy's living room and trying to help him snap out of some kind of psychosis. He told me he hadn't left his living room for nine days. All he had been consuming was white bread, dark chocolate, and really strong marijuana. There were a few jars full of piss by his front door and I could tell he hadn't showered in days. At least I was still showering and I wasn't locking my piss away in mason jars. I could however relate to the look on his face. He was torn between wanting to live and ending it all. The pain was too much and he was doing the only thing he knew how to do, which was hide.

I tried talking to my friend to make him laugh. I went into his bathroom and looked over his cabinets. I asked him if he had been taking his medications. He had been off them for two months. I asked him if he could get up. He got up. I asked him if he could take a shower. He got into the shower. He had a bunch of clean towels and clothes to wear because he was not showering or changing his clothes. I got him some clothes. He got out of the shower and put on some clean clothes. I combed his hair for him. I remember thinking to myself, 'I am actually combing a grown man's hair right now.' I made him a sandwich and I told him a story. I knew that he wasn't used to his blood circulating, so he was probably dizzy. I have been through what he was going through a few times. Staying in bed for days at a time and moving very little fucks up your body. Your body gets used to running at a snail's pace because it's not using any energy. Once you get up and start moving again, you feel like you are in a weird dream state and it can be unnerving. Once I got him laughing and moving around, I conned him into going to an AA meeting with me. I told him that I really needed one and I didn't want to go alone. I told him that I almost hung myself earlier that day and I really needed to get to a meeting. He immediately agreed to go. I think knowing that I almost killed myself that day made him feel like less of a freak. He had proof that he wasn't the only one going through what he was going through. It was something we were going through together now. After that day, I would see him at my home group a couple of times a week for a month and then he decided to move back home with his parents to get his mind right. I knew he was on the right track. I did the very same thing he did when I got sober. I could totally relate to his thought process and I wanted to support him as much as possible. I told him that moving home could be the best thing for him. His parents offered to help him and I told him to take it. I told him to get away from his girl and his friends and get away from his fucked up bartending job. "Just retire from your life, man." When I said that, it was as if he snapped out of the spell he was under. I could tell that he never knew that he could simply quit his current life and start over. A week later, he moved out of Portland. Good for him.

I remember being about four years old. I was visiting my grandparents on my father's side during summer vacation. They lived in a small town called The Dalles just outside of Portland, Oregon. My uncle took me to a river that had a nice area to swim. Everyone that lived around town would go there, float around, and drink beer. It was like a scene out of the old eighties' Mountain Dew commercial. There was a steep ledge where water flowed, making it a natural slide. We would take turns walking up this hill and sliding down this rock ledge into the swimming hole. I probably went up and down that slide fifty times that day. On my last time going down, I ran a bit too fast and I slipped. Right as I was about to slide off the edge and fall thirty feet onto some large boulders, a man appeared out of nowhere, grabbed my arm, and pulled me up, saving me from what could have been the end of my life. This guy simply pulled me up with one arm, asked me if I was okay, and just walked away. I remember he was very lean and tan, with blond curly hair, mustache, and jean cut off shorts. He looked like Matthew McConaughey's character in the film *Dazed and Confused.* "Alright, alright, alright." At the age of four, I did not have a very strong concept of death but I knew that guy saved my ass.

In 2015, I took a job at the Hilton in Downtown Portland as a concierge. It took me eleven years and four interviews to get that job. After my month of training, the major holidays would be over and the city of Portland would go through its low tourism season. Immediately, my hours were cut. One week, I would have three days. The next week, I might only get two days. There were a few weeks where I wasn't even on the schedule. I refused to take this lying down. I would talk with all my managers—general manager and HR department. I told them that I agreed to take this as a full-time job. Working two or three days a week or not at all was not what I signed up for. I asked them if they knew that they would be cutting hours and if they did, why they didn't discuss this information with me while we were in the interview process. Everyone just looked at me like a deer in headlights. To this day, no matter what happens, I love being a concierge but I have learned a few things about hotels. One thing I have learned is that most, if not all, hotels are poorly run businesses. It is now mid-July 2018, and I have worked at five hotels. I have worked all over the country with people from all over the world. The one thing that all hotels have in common is that they are all run so poorly, with paychecks not being delivered on time, really low pay, managers sleeping together, lots of druggies and burnouts, and even more bullshit. I think I get even more agitated with all this shit because I am sober. I can see a bit more clearly what is happening from day to day than most of my drowsy, hung-over coworkers. Here I go being judgmental again, but if you have ever been a waiter or a front-desk agent at a hotel or managed a tour bus ticket office, you know what I am talking about. And if it's so bad, why do so many of us stay? Why do I stay? If I am so smart, why don't I just go do something else? I'll tell you why. It's about the moments that you get to experience at these places that you will not experience at a bank or a law office or some major tech company in San Jose. Fewer and fewer places let you work and live in the gray of society. The nine-to-five workday just doesn't fit me. It never has.

Some of my friends asked me why I didn't leave Hilton. Why not go back to The Chamber of Commerce or try taking an assistant job at City Hall? I had the contacts and I had options. I talked to my Hilton's HR manager about this at the time. I told her that I was really disappointed about taking a leap of faith in order to work at that hotel and finally do the job that I had been wanting to do for years. It finally happened and now you are benching me? I didn't get it. Actually, I got it. Hotels, like all other businesses, need to be profitable and they have to cut costs wherever they can when things slow down. My HR manager told me that she would think of something and get back to me in a week. Soon after that talk, I started seeing job posts for concierge positions in Key West. I started calling Key West's Waldorf Astoria HR Department. I told them my story and that I would do anything to get over to Key West and learn. I also found out later that my HR manager in Portland called the Key West property and put in a good word for me. Soon after that, I found myself on a plane taking that horrible flight from Portland to Dallas, Texas to Tampa, Florida, and then to Key West. I knew my honest and passionate conversations with both HR managers were what sent me to Key West. I had no idea what to expect, but I knew I had to go.

I think if you want to be really good at something, you have to put everything you have into it. You have to take risks. You might have to go somewhere that you never saw yourself going. I was always a city guy. I never saw myself living on a tiny island on the edge of the Bermuda Triangle. I had never seen six-foot long lizards and cockroaches larger than my thumbs before, but I was about to. I never had to share a room with a middle-aged Haitian man that went to bed drunk every night and snored so loud that I would have to throw something at him in order to stop his snoring. I had no idea that the thunder and lightning storms and all the jungle rain would shut down the entire island for hours at a time on a fairly regular basis. I had never been screamed at by a six-foot-four-inch tall general manager that flew in two weeks after I did with over twenty years of five-star Southeast Asian hotel experience under his belt. I would learn real quickly that in Southeast Asia, if you look at your superior the wrong way, you could get fired. I saw my Key West GM fire four women because they were too overweight. You can do that in Southeast Asia but not in the States. This general manager didn't give a shit about any of that. He always said that he was brought to the Casa Marina to trim the fat and that was exactly what he was going to do. After about a year of this, I knew that my Kew West adventure would be over soon. But even through all the madness, I still felt a lot of gratitude for the people that helped bring me over to this crazy place. No matter what happened, it was an experience that I would be able to take with me no matter where I went. Experience I was never going to get in Portland. My career was actually moving forward. In Key West, I would learn that the world does not care what you have planned. Things rarely go exactly the way you want them to, but if you can find a way to live with that, you will go as far as you want to go in life. Just be grateful that you are in a position to be a part of all the activity and motion that it takes to reach your goals. On top of all that, never forget the key people who assisted you along the way, the angels that come along once in a blue moon. You will run into them while jogging to your favorite café. You will be working at a job you think is okay and you will help someone that takes interest in what you do, and a month later, you are working with them at some creative marketing firm. Or maybe you are finally working in the oil industry overnight because you just happened to have a pack of matches on you and the man that asked you for your matches so that he could light his hundred-dollar cigar started talking to you and he started talking about oil and not being able to find good help anymore. The owner of the company liked you immediately and he offered you a job, making five times of what you were making at the job you just quit so you could work in oil. This could be the beginning of a beautiful new chapter in your life, or the oil rig you work on could explode and you sustain some horrible injuries, taking you off the job that you just started. Once you take that opportunity, anything can happen after that. You just have to take that risk. Thousands of people will take the exact same risk you are taking. Some of them will become a great success and others will lose everything. Why? Who knows? Maybe one morning, your car broke down and that started a downward spiral for you. Maybe someone you loved died and you didn't take the news very well. Maybe you started drinking every day and night to numb the pain. Life is not fair. All you have is your respond to what life gives you. For every action, there is a reaction. How will you react? One day, you will receive some horrible news. What will your next move be? Will you get off the phone, walk to the nearest quiet space, sit down, and just breathe for a few minutes? Will you go to someone that you trust and tell him or her what you are going through and how you feel about it? Or will you cut your work shift early, drive to the liquor store, go home, and drink a fifth of vodka and smoke a pack of cigarettes? What do you think you would do if you found out that someone you loved died just now? Is there a normal way to behave after being given the worst news of your life? No, there isn't. All you have is what you choose to do. Sometimes, doing nothing is the best thing to do. Just collapse on the floor and cry. Try feeling those feelings and just let them flow through you. If you can't handle it, call someone. Call anyone. Who is the first person that comes to mind? Who would you call?

I would call Peter. The first person that comes to mind for me when the shit hits the fan is my buddy Peter, Peter with face tattoos—Gangster Pete. If Peter didn't answer the phone, then I would call my grandmother. If my grandmother didn't answer the phone, I would take a shower and go to an AA meeting at the Dry Dock. I would see the guy the works the front desk of the Dry Dock. I would walk into the east room and I would see a few recognizable faces. I would push my chair against the wall and lean my head back, close my eyes, and just breathe. I will cry. I would choose do this and I would not drink. I would not kill myself. I would be miserable until I'm not anymore. I will feel a little better after the meeting. The horrible feelings will most likely come back, so I will go to another meeting the next day. I will talk with Peter because Peter always calls me back. Peter and I will talk through my shit and I will be able to go to sleep that night. I will make it through whatever catastrophe I am going through. I always do. I have AA, God, my friend Peter, my grandmother, my bicycle, my swimming pool, and I have AA meetings. I can make it through anything.

24. Daily Reminder

I get asked all the time why I still go to AA meetings. I usually tell people that if I don't go, I'll probably lose my shit and burn whatever city I live in at the time down to the ground. A lot of people tell me this doesn't sound like alcoholism. I always ask those people what they think alcoholism is. They never know the answer to that question. The truth is that nobody knows what alcoholism is. Most doctors have no idea what it is. Shit, most doctors still refer to the four-food group pyramid that was established in the 1930s when asked what kinds of foods someone should eat. How would some guy named Brad know just how deep and dark the disease of addiction is? Women giving up their kids for crack or some random straight guy blowing another guy for ten bucks worth of meth. Whatever it is that is making those people do that crazy shit, it is much deeper than the superficial term that most people use. The word that most people use to describe an addict is selfish. On a lot of levels, all those people would be right. I have never met a junky that wasn't selfish. Even with years of sobriety, I am to this day a very self-focused person. Hell, I love the sound of my own voice. But I do not think that the word selfish describes what addiction is completely. I would compare the disease of addiction to be more closely related to a spiritual or even demonic possession. The description of a demonic possession is very similar to the description or symptoms of an alcoholic. These symptoms often include erased memories or personalities, convulsions (i.e. epileptic_seizures or 'fits'), and fainting as if one were dying. A spiritual possession simply defined is the seizure of a human being by the divine or by an external being. It refers to the ways in which a person is changed in terms of both identity and bodily manifestations through the presence within him or her of a spirit entity or power.

If you are a true addict, this will make complete sense to you. Addiction goes so far beyond selfishness and poor decision-making. When you are in your disease, it is almost as if something else is making your decisions for you. You can see yourself doing something and all you can do is just go with it. The ability to choose right from wrong is completely thrown out the window. You are at the mercy of time. If you can make it through your current binge without killing yourself or someone else, all you can do is try your best not to use again. Your disease is the Hulk and when you are sober, you are Bruce Banner. When you watch the movies, you always prefer the Hulk. The Hulk is more entertaining to watch. Bruce is just a guy. This is how a lot of addicts view themselves and assume the world views them as well. Everybody wants the Hulk. You being an addict with low self-esteem just want to make people happy. You want to be loved, so you give the world the Hulk. When you are the Hulk, everything is amazing until it's not anymore. When the world tells you to stop being the Hulk and that they miss Bruce, it's too late. The Hulk owns you and you haven't been Bruce in a really long time. What if you can't find Bruce? What if you forgot how to be Bruce? What if nobody loves the new Bruce? You would rather die than not be loved. How can you make this work? Fuck! Just kill me! At least when I was bad, people paid attention to me. Sure, they hated me, but at least I knew that I was still alive. What if I can't learn to be good? Or what if I learn and I forget how to stay good? How the fuck is someone supposed to be good every day? That sounds so dull. I can't live the rest of my life being bored. Jesus, now can you just kill me? This is the mind of an addict, people! So many people decide to just say 'fuck you' to sobriety because they would rather die drunk than bored. Can you blame them?

But what if you are in that ten percent of the addict population in this country? What if you genuinely want to be clean and sober? What if you are willing to do anything? What the fuck do you do? Throughout this book, I talk about how I stay sober. All I know is how *I* did it. I will tell you that one of the trickiest things for me is how I forget things all the time. I forget how bad things were when I was younger and in my disease. I have been sober for over fifteen years now and things have been getting better and better for me. The better things get, the less I remember. This past couple of years have been the hardest in some sense. I am making more money than ever and I can do all the things that I enjoy more often. I have skipped meetings to meet up with an attractive woman and have sex. I have skipped meetings and gotten a massage or a tattoo instead. I have become a bit more sarcastic with people because I am tired of hearing their bullshit. I have friends back in Portland that are complaining about the same things they were complaining about three years ago. I just don't want to hear it anymore. I'm fucking busy. Another bad habit that I have in sobriety is that I go to the same meeting at the same time every night. I see the same people and hear the same stories every night. I go to this meeting because I like most of the people that go and because it is conveniently located by my apartment. The problem with this is that familiarity can breed contempt. I get tired of hearing some of the other regulars' stories. I get tired of watching the same people relapse every forty days. My laziness tends to get the better of me. When I do decide to check out a new meeting, more often than not, I enjoy the meeting. Seeing new faces and hearing new stories is like a breath of fresh air. Every time I go to a new meeting, I always think to myself, 'I have got to go to more meetings like this.' Even my bike ride home feels good. But for some reason, I always go back to my old routine. Old habits die hard. All those old clichés are true. I know that if I were to just go to one different meeting a week, that would solve a lot of my sober program issues. I think humans need variety in order to maintain their psychological health. Doing the same things over and over again will drive you nuts.

After swimming laps for a few months, I might get bored, so I will have to try another activity like Bikram yoga or rowing. Just last night, I went to the gym after work and I hit the weights hard for the first time in a couple of months. It was such an amazing feeling. I felt my chest and arms and I thought to myself, 'God, I have to do this more often.' My mind and my body clicked and my entire being remembered why I love to exercise. It feels good, I love the results, and it's so much easier to get laid when you feel and look good. So many people will think this is a superficial frame of mind, but actually those people are the shallow fuckers. Putting in a hard day's work and then putting in more work after your day job is anything but shallow. Giving something everything you've got is hard to do. If it was easy, everybody would look amazing. The entire world would essentially be like Los Angeles in the 1980s but with the brain of someone in San Francisco. This doesn't just go for physical exercise but working hard to improve any part of your life is extremely difficult. Sure, most of the tasks are relatively simple, but taking the time to actually do it seems to be the hardest part. Ninety percent of success is showing up, but only ten percent of human beings seem to actually do it. Why? Is it as simple as laziness? Do people just give up for the same reason so many people think that addicts relapse? I don't think so. I think human beings are more complicated than that. I think most of us have a brain that likes to simplify and streamline our lives. Our brains want us to erase or forget something that we do not normally do in order to make room and save mental energy for something that we do often. *Familiarity is safer* because you know what to expect. If you never read or work out but you keep a mini fridge in your room in order to save yourself time in order to play more video games, then that is what your brain wants to help you do. I know I am supposed to say that this doesn't make you a bad person, but in a way I disagree. I think that lazy people are dangerous people.

Every criminal that ever existed, with the few exceptions of course, have all been given multiple chances. Whether the criminal was, a car thief or a rapist or a bank robber, they have all been given more than one chance throughout their lives to change and make better choices. Why couldn't they stop the bullshit and take a different path?

So many people are born into a world where they have been abused and kicked around by everybody in their life. These people were not given a fair chance. They are angry and they want a piece of the good life. I do not think that the majority of these people were born bad. I am sure that some people were born with a screw loose but not exactly bad. I think that some of the worst psychopaths that this world has ever seen were born with a brain that operates differently than a person with a healthy brain. Name any famous serial killer and I bet all of them were born with something wrong with their brains. I don't know if any of them could have changed for the good. But I do think that a lot of people that commit crimes of any kind can change. Maybe not on their own but if they are lucky enough to surround themselves with the right people, and even more importantly adopt the right mindset, they might be able to improve their life. But how does one that has committed crimes or used drugs most of their lives change even after they quit doing the things that not only hurt themselves but hurt people that they were closest to? It would take me years of staying clean and sober before my life would begin to take off in the direction that I wanted it to. One of the main ingredients to my positive changes has been the people I have met along the way. We also have to keep in mind that not everyone goes about improving their life in the same fashion as everyone else. Some people might see a therapist while others join a soccer team as a means of getting exercise while meeting new people at the same time. Some people might join scientology and others might get heavily involved in a local church. It has been my experience over the years that I need to have an activity that keeps me busy spiritually, mentally, and physically. I go to AA meetings for my spiritual growth, I read and write quite a bit right now as a way to work out my brain, and I like to hit the gym as a way to challenge my body. It has proven to be very difficult for me to balance all three out. Sometimes, I need to go to a couple of more meetings a week while other weeks I might need to rest a bit more so I might take a day off from AA and exercise. I might just go home right after work, lounge, and listen to some mellow music. On other weeks, my body might need a bit more attention. Sometimes, I can feel my body just craving a challenge. On those days, I try to hit the weights hard. Half the battle for me is just listening to what my body is doing. I try to feel out what my mind and body are trying to tell me. Maybe it wants to be creative today. Maybe it wants to work hard.

Maybe it wants to read. Maybe my mind and body are craving sex or food. Vice is a whole element that my being craves. What kind of vice is acceptable? Of course I stay away from alcohol and drugs, but food and sex are the two that I seem to enjoy most these days. I try to use my best judgment when it comes to food and sex. I have been pretty good about the sex thing. I am not using anyone for sex. I am not misleading anyone in order to have what I want. The food thing is a bit more complicated. My relationship with food is quiet, a bit volatile, and with a hint of romance. I have a deeper connection to food than I do with any person right now. I eat almost all my meals alone. I do this so I can eat as fast or as slow as I want, kind of like masturbating to porn. Only a man knows exactly how he likes it at any given moment. I still love eating late at night and I still love heavy cheese dishes. What I have learned to do is before I can have a nice cheese plate, I have to ride my bike around the city for at least thirty minutes. Once I have biked around town, I will go to one of my favorite restaurants that has amazing cheese plates. Once I have thoroughly enjoyed my delicious cheese plate, I will hit the gym and swim some laps. If I do not follow these simple steps, I will most likely fall into a brief depression. It will last a few days, so it is just easier to follow my cheese plate versus gym program.

Speaking of depression, I would like to tell another little story. For the past ten years, I have been on an antidepressant. I have mentioned this earlier. At the beginning of this summer, the summer of 2018, my doctor started weaning me off. As of today, July 27, 2018, I have been off my medication for a month. Emotionally, I have felt fine but for the first week, I could not stop sweating. Heavy sweating and sporadic erections have been the side effects of getting off my antidepressant. Since I moved to San Francisco, so many things have clicked for me—more money, more self-esteem, and more responsibility. This is a Capricorn's dream. I have tried getting off my antidepressant three times over the past ten years. Each time was a very uncomfortable experience. I thought I would have to be on medication forever. I still have one medication that I need to get off, but I am in no hurry. I am hundred percent certain that the only reason why I was able to get off my antidepressant is because of Alcoholics Anonymous. If I am meant to get off my other medication, I am sure that time will come. I have faith that if I keep doing all the little things that I have always done, my life will continue to improve. I believe that if I am meant to have a life partner, I will meet her. I will look up and she will be standing right in front of me, smiling. If I am meant to have a mansion and a Lamborghini, I am sure it will happen. As long as I work my ass off, anything and everything can happen. I just have to wake up, get out of bed, take a shower, go to work, go to the gym, and then hit an AA meeting. My life is like a waltz—one, two, three, one, two, three. On paper, the waltz is a very basic dance but when you put the steps to the floor, you are given a lot of room for improvisation. Outside of the triple time movement, the world is your oyster. You can choose to breeze through the entire room or you can take tight turns or just hover in a corner somewhere. It's up to you. I need the flexibility to be explosive or calmer, depending on my mood. So many dance styles dictate the pace that you should go. Many styles tell you what to do in a sense. If you are a more upbeat person, you can swing or cha-cha. If you are slower and more intense, you can choose the Argentine tango. But the Waltz is controlled by who you are in that moment. No matter who you are or who you want to be, the only way to really have power of any of this is repetition. You have to practice the career you choose, the activity you want to be good at, or a sexual partner, etc. You have to practice. You have to allow yourself to get stuck and then keep trying. You have to be willing to fall on your face and play the fool in order to graduate to the next level. If you are willing to break yourself for something or someone, then you know you love whatever it is that you are doing. So many people never reach this level of personal identity. Many people have no interest in this. But for the people that want to be great at anything, we all have to be willing to do it over and over again. I believe that this is true for people in recovery as well. If you want get better at being sober, you have to want to learn to be better at living and being a human being. It is all tied together. You take things one day at a time and you just do it. Once you become comfortable with failure and rejection, there is no stopping you. For some of us, we pick up on this quickly. For others, we pick up on this slowly. Don't compare yourself to others. Just keep moving forward. Whatever it is that you are trying to achieve, you will get there. Good luck!

25. Low Ceilings

I have noticed a strange phenomenon that occurs after years of sobriety and recovery. Over time, you will pick up new skills and because you have a clear head, you will actually remember what you learned. You will meet more advanced people and you will slowly get rid of the people, places, and things you don't need. You will simply outgrow your old life. This will be very uncomfortable for a lot of people. It's not easy to tell your best friend of eleven years that you need to move on. You will acquire a lot of what pop culture calls haters. As you move up in life, a lot of people that have always been close will also become uncomfortable. At first, their jealousy will be silent, but eventually they will voice their opinions. They will question what you are doing. They will try to convince you not to do something. Maybe you want to move to your dream city. Anyone that tries to sway you otherwise is not a true friend. They will tell you that they just don't want to see you fail, but really they are afraid to see you succeed. There are so many shitty reasons why people don't want you to move on. You have to ignore those people. Just do what your heart tells you. People that can't support you no matter what are just a distraction. Why are so many people so concerned whether you fail or not? You won't die if you fall on your face. If you are from Boise, Idaho, and you decide to move to LA in order to live out your dream as an actress, just do it. If you are married and have three kids, maybe it's not such a great idea. But if you are single and you have nothing tying you down, do whatever you want. There is a big difference between taking a risk and being selfish. If you do not know the difference, failure is definitely on the horizon for you.

If you decide to stay sober for the long haul, I can guarantee that life will not only get better for you, it will also get very different. Everything from the people that you find attractive to the types of jobs you get all the way down to how you chew your food is going to change. For years, I had a slight stuttering problem. Whenever I would get excited, I would stutter. After working the twelve steps of Alcoholics Anonymous, my stuttering eventually disappeared. I will be honest with you and tell you that it wasn't just AA that helped my stutter issue. I did go to a speech therapist once a week for about six months, but I never would have done that without AA. One of my buddies in AA turned me on to the idea of a speech therapist. He went to a speech therapist in his late teens and it helped him out. So, I found a therapist, signed up for a class, and I noticed a huge difference. I have always had a passion for public speaking and my stuttering would hold me back a bit. Ever since I got rid of the stuttering, I have had the confidence to talk in front of larger groups on a more regular basis. It's amazing what a little confidence can do for you. Taking six months of speech therapy actually changed my entire life. I learned that the only way to get better at something is that you have to do it as much as possible. In order to do anything on a regular basis, you need to remove as many barriers as possible. I know that what I just wrote is not even close to being groundbreaking, but at one point in my life, I didn't know this. Actually, I knew that in order to be good at something, I would need to practice, but I never put this knowledge into action. For so many years of my life, I was a lazy person. Once I started showing up, sharpening my knives, carving out my skillsets, and slowly creating a life for myself, *real life* actually started to happen. Life started to become interesting. So many people seem to have a natural understanding of how all this works. The part of my brain that holds this information was asleep. I am not sure what turned it on, but thank God that the switch was flipped.

One of the few downsides to all this growth and forward movement is loneliness. I have already talked a lot about loneliness but the fact of the matter is that for most alcoholics and addicts, regardless of how successful they are, loneliness is simply a part of the deal. What I mean by the deal is loneliness is a part of life. We all experience loneliness, but I have a feeling that addicts feel loneliness a little bit deeper. I remember when I was about ten years' sober, I felt bored of my surroundings. My job no longer challenged me and the city I lived in just seemed slow. I would look around myself and I knew I could do better. But what did that mean? What did 'better' mean at that time? I had no idea what it meant and this was frustrating as well. I knew I could do more with my life and I knew the city of Portland could not provide me with what I wanted. I would go to networking events, but I was simply disappointed. Everybody I met was a small thinker. They just went to those networking events for the free beer and the possibility of meeting the mayor. There was no real wealth and even less sophistication. Nobody had that hunger that someone needs to make real money. From what I could tell, nobody in Portland even cared about making money. Portland is just one long episode of that stupid show *Portlandia*. It rains eight months out of the year, people love naming their chickens that they force to live in their backyards, and every ten minutes, there is a women's march clogging up traffic in the city. How can anyone with half a brain and a little bit of swagger make a million bucks in a town like Portland? I knew I had to get out. The walls were closing in on me. I felt like the ceilings were two inches too short for me and I always had to bend my neck in order to walk from room to room. The last four years in Portland fucking sucked. I felt like only three people really understood me. I wasn't sure if it was because they were as nuts or as brilliant as I was. There is a thin line between 'crazy' and 'genius' that goes back and forth on a daily basis. I think I would have eventually lost my shit in Portland, so I am glad that I got out. I am sure that no matter where I live, these feelings will enter into my being. For now, I feel like I am cursed with the need to be relatively nomadic. Either that or I am only half as brilliant as I think I am, and I will need to move every few years so that I do not piss off the entire city that I live in.

My purpose for writing this is to let you know that it is normal to feel like you don't belong. So many people relapse simply because they can't take feeling excluded. Feeling out of place is a horrible feeling. When you are intoxicated, you can trick your brain into thinking everything is okay. Whatever drug you prefer, I am sure it gives you some kind of relief. The real problem starts when your drug of choice no longer gives you relief. Your only choice after that is to get clean and learn how to live… or die. If you do decide on sobriety, you will eventually experience a wave of emotions that you have been pushing away for many years. Eventually, you are going to have to face these feelings. When you do, I promise that you will live through it. After a while, you will be able to move through life with more confidence and grace, but there is a catch. The catch is that a lot of people that you thought loved you will not be there. The faces of your friends will change. If all the people stay the same in your life, I am almost certain that you will eventually relapse. Why? Because you were once a very sick person and the new healthy you will be unrecognizable. Most people do not like change. You will be different and this will scare people. You will be better than the old you and you will surpass many people that were in your life before you got sober. You will realize that you used to surround yourself with other very sick people. You are going to move forward, but many of the people from your past will not be able to go with you. They will not have the tools that you have to go to the places that you are going to go. Personally, I have had to leave everything I knew behind in order to chase my goals. I have lived in some of the most beautiful and energetic areas of the US, and not one family member has ever visited me. I knew they wouldn't, and I am fine with that.

Even if my family had the financial resources, I do not think they would visit. They couldn't handle the stress of the airports, the cab ride to their hotel, or trying to function in a place outside of what is familiar to them. I have never even bothered inviting anyone from my family to come out to San Francisco. It's a two-hour flight but they just couldn't handle it. If I want to see my family, I will be the one that has to arrange for tickets, transportation, and lodging. No thanks.

This is another part of the book where you might think I am a coldhearted prick, but life kind of has a way of shoving you into a corner. You have to make a decision. Do I go left or do I go right? In the movie *Cast Away*, Tom Hanks tries to swim out to save his best friend Wilson the volleyball. He notices his raft is floating further and further away. Tom's character knows that he has to make a decision. Save Wilson and drown or swim to the raft and live. If you have seen the movie, you know Tom Hanks chooses the raft. For me, Wilson is my family and the raft is my future. The reason why it took me so long to leave is because I was sick. Eventually, the healthy me had to make a decision and that was to leave. The healthier I get, the better my life becomes because I make better decisions. Making the healthier decision isn't always easy. Sometimes, it sucks. Sometimes, you lose a friend or a girl you have a crush on, but making that better decision will improve your life over the long run. I have learned a little trick and I will pass it on to you. When I am feeling really lonely, I will say to myself, "Marques, you are not lonely. You are just not distracted and you want to be distracted right now. Why do you want to be distracted right now, Marques?" I am fully aware that human beings need connection and love. I am not willing to make room for people that simply take up space. I will risk the uncomfortable feeling of loneliness in order to keep room in my life for quality human beings and experiences.

Now if you are my mother or someone else in my family reading this, I am not saying that you are not worth my time. I am not saying that you are not quality people. What I am saying is that I have a life to live. I have a destiny to fulfill. I would love it if you could be a part of my grand scheme, but for one reason or another, you are not. If I were to stay anywhere that I am not meant to be, that would just kill me. I want to live. I want to spread my wings as far as they can go. This goes for all families around the world that have a loved one that is taking a chance that you do not understand. Please keep your resentments and guilt trips to yourself. If you truly love someone, just let them go. Don't call them telling them they need to come for someone's wedding or birthday. It is selfish to try and make someone change their whole life around for you. Just let them fly. If they were meant to come back, they will. Life has a kind of natural pull to it. Just go with the flow. Absence makes the heart grow fonder for most people. Some of us were meant to leave and never come back. Regardless of who and what you are at the moment, I think as long as you try to do your best no matter where you are, you will always be in the best possible place that you could be in. So stop for a minute and take a good look around. Are the walls creeping in on you? Do you keep bumping your head on the ceiling? It might be time to get some new digs. If you don't live in a place that allows you to stand up straight and take on the world, it's time to go. It's okay to be faster and smarter than the guy next to you. You just have to find a place that rewards you for it. I hope that you are strong enough to make the right decision. Not only will you be better off, but everyone around you will profit from these decisions as well. I wonder what the world would be like if everyone made better decisions on a regular basis.

26. Porn

I started watching porn on a regular basis when I was about twenty-eight years old. This was around the time that I wanted to stop sleeping around so much. I am one of the lucky ones and I have never had an STD. I have had so much unprotected sex in the past and I have fucked a lot of questionable characters. Hell, I was a questionable character for years. At twenty-eight, I got a woman pregnant. I had to work really hard to convince her to get an abortion, not because I was some amazing catch but because she was raised in a very strict Christian household. Plus, she was twenty-seven at the time and she wanted children. This was a really scary time. I was in the middle of working with doctors and trying to find the right diagnosis for what was going on with me. Was I bipolar? Was I just imagining everything? Different doctors had different theories. I had to have a serious one-on-one conversation with the young woman that I got pregnant. I told her that my father was mentally ill and he was not able to be in my life. I did not want to follow in my father's footsteps. My father always lived in a constant state of financial poverty. He was always in and out of hospitals for mental breakdowns and severe depression. I did not want my child to go through the same thing with me that I went through with my father. I had to be brutally honest with her and tell her that I thought I was losing my mind, and if she wanted to have children, she should wait until she found a solid man that could be there for her and the child. I was not that man. I could tell by looking into her eyes that she really heard me. A few days later, she got an abortion. I went to the hospital twice that week for depression and anxiety. I was falling apart. Nothing seemed to give me any relief.

Then one night at about one in the morning, I went to a porn shop that I lived a few blocks away from. The only time I felt comfortable enough to go outside was really late at night. I felt that there was something oddly comforting about sex shops. There were people in there, but everything was dead silent. The store that I went to had the AC on full blast, so it was very cool, which is how I like my room to be. I asked the guy at the front desk where their cougar section was. Without even looking at me, he just pointed toward the back of the room. I walked toward the back of the store and there were three isles of 'hot older women for younger men' DVDs. I could feel my brain turn on. A feeling of exhilaration came over me. I also felt a sense of calm. After an hour of looking over every front cover, I picked the one that I would buy. It would cost me sixty bucks. I had very little money at the time, but I had to have that DVD. I remember salivating as I paid for the video. I couldn't wait to get home and just jerk off all night. I walked home at a quicker pace than my usual walking speed. I had not been this excited in a long time. Getting an escort had lost its edge for me and hunting normal everyday women just wasn't my thing. It never had been. Once I realized that I could go to a store and get exactly what I wanted and not have any risk of getting chlamydia, it was as if the world had opened a whole new universe for me. Before this particular night, I think I had only watched porn three or four times. It was never my thing. But at this point, my world had become so small and I had lost all interest in connecting with other human beings on any level. Pornography was simply the natural choice for an addict like me. When I was drinking and using, I was always very social. I never drank alone or wanted to drink alone. Today, I know what everyone means when they say that alcoholism and addiction is a progressive disease. A few years back, I thought it meant that if you keep using drugs and alcohol, your life will get worse. Today, I know that it means whether you stop using or not, things can get worse. The only way to make your life better is by finding the root of the problem and facing it—really looking the boogie man in the face until you are not scared of it anymore and telling it to fuck off. I don't have to drink or use heroin for my life to unravel. I can eat myself to death. I can fuck the wrong woman and get a horrible flesh-eating disease. I can gamble until a couple of huge men knock on my door and tell me to pay them or they are going to break my legs. There are a lot of things that I can do too much and die from. I personally have experienced much darker bottoms without touching booze. I never came close to killing myself when drinking or using drugs. I almost killed myself a few times. I almost killed myself when I was thirty years old and I had not touched a drink in eight years.

Pornography would prove to be a very subtle foe. For years, I would use porn to calm down but only on a random basis. There were a few times when I would wake up exhausted and call out of work. I would call these mental health days. I would stay in bed all day and just relax. I would take a nap, wake up, eat a sandwich, and then take another nap. I would wake up from that nap and watch some porn, eat another sandwich, go to the gym, come home, and watch more porn. When I was about thirty-four, I started calling out from work so I could just lounge in bed and watch porn all day. I would jerk off five, six, seven, or even eight times in a day. I have heard that a lot of porn addicts will jerk off a lot more than this. I have heard horror stories about men needing to jerk off constantly. That is not my story. Once every few months, I needed to escape from the world. I was broke and I was horny, so I watched porn. It never got much worse than that.

It is July 30, 2018, and I am on a brief four-day mini vacation. I am staying at a monastery in Berkeley again in order to rest from the busy summer that we have had at the hotel. I am exhausted and I just need to get away and not talk to people. At midnight, I realized that I was really horny. I have been taking a lot of niacin, magnesium, and nitric oxide, so my body's blood flow and overall circulation has been working better than ever. One of the side effects is that more blood flows to my penis than I am used to. Whenever I think about sex, I get these fucking hard-ons. It's like I am fourteen years old again. It's a great complaint to have, but it can be annoying sometimes. If I don't jerk off, I find it hard for my brain to go into rest mode. If I just jerk off and climax, my brain switches gears and my body wants to go to bed. I think this is how a normal man's body works, but I have never been a normal man with a normal body. I decided to get onto my favorite free porn site and plug in my favorite porn star, Sara Jay, and just get it over with. Right before I came, it dawned on me that it is midnight, I am staying at a monastery, and I am jerking off to pornography. Then it hit me that I came to this monastery not for spiritual purposes and not to heal or meditate or anything like that. I came to be alone. I came to let my true self out. I want space—no noise and no distractions. I just want to sleep as much as I want, eat as much as I want, jerk off as much as I want, and I do not want anyone to bother me while I do it. I don't want to hear any sirens or car alarms or people yelling in the street, or that old lady that collects bottles every night at one thirty in the morning. I just want silence. I want the world to shut the fuck up so I can cum in peace. And yes, I will go to an AA meeting everyday while I am here, but that's it. I am not going to talk to anybody and I am not going to share anything. I will just do my time and then I am going back to my room to do my thing. I have given up on looking for love. I don't care if I meet an interesting person while I am here. I don't even exist right now. I am just passing through. I realized tonight that I have just been passing through for years. I move somewhere, I give people what I think they want for a while, I get bored, and I move on. I am tired of living in fear, but I have not figured out a way to take interest in people for long periods of time. I always seem to get tired of people and their shit. I still cannot wrap my mind around how people keep the same friends for twenty-plus years. After a couple of months, I like to throw away my sheets and buy a whole new set. I like that fresh, clean feel that new things have. I have never been into the whole shabby chic thing. So many people like that worn-in look. Not me. I like fresh and clean. I get a haircut every fourteen days for the same reason I can't go on more than two dates with the same woman. Actually that is bullshit, but it makes total sense to the junky part of my brain. The only problem with the junky side of my brain is that it's shrinking. The healthy part of my brain is growing and it has different needs than the shallow addict part of my brain. My healthy brain wants stability and dependability. My addict brain wants to leave tomorrow and move to Miami and fuck hot Columbian women. I know that is a retarded idea, but I watched a lot of *Miami Vice* as a kid and it looks so fun. But fucking hot chicks in Miami is really hard to do if you don't have a pretty white Ferrari and a yacht with a pet crocodile chained to it.

I keep watching videos about how watching pornography is harmful to your brain. I believe everything these specialists tell me, yet I still watch it. I know that the majority of both men and women in pornography are mentally ill in some way. I am sure many of them are drug addicts and alcoholics just like me. I am sure that many of them suffer from other issues like depression and many other mental illnesses. I am completely aware of this. When I drank and used drugs, I knew that it wasn't good for me, but I still did it. I did it for the same reasons everyone else did. It all felt so fucking good. I still have not found anything that feels better than rolling on ecstasy while getting a blowjob. Smoking heroin was a close second for me. After that, straight fucking comes in third place. Nothing will ever change that for me. And yes, helping a stranger feels good, but it will never compare to cumming while peaking on pure MDMA. It's just impossible. The last time I did this, I was twenty years old. It has been twenty years and I still haven't found anything that feels this good. For years, this pissed me off. When the anger went away, it depressed me. When the depression went away, ten years had gone by and I simply grew out of the need to feel that good. I think time and age play a big role in true recovery. It takes time to develop the depth that it takes in order to even become aware of different forms of happiness. I don't think I really wanted to make a difference in the world until I was thirty-four years old. All I wanted was to feel good. For years, I would have a chip on my shoulder. I would walk by a bar and see people having a good time. I didn't want to drink, but I wanted to sit in a small circle with people and laugh. I wanted to be in a beautiful bar, catch an attractive woman looking at me, go over to her and talk about nothing, and then fuck her a couple of hours later. This stuff never happened for me at an AA meeting. Plus, all the attractive women would only have a few days of sobriety and I would feel like a predator if I hooked up with one of them. Most of the women with a little time of sobriety just don't do it for me. They always become those kinds of women that you see on YouTube videos that march for women's rights. I am not attracted to women that start out every conversation about how they are feminists. I don't fucking care. Plus, San Francisco is the butch straight feminist capital of the world. The only time these women loosen up is after a few drinks and a pump of coke.

So what do I do? Do I have to give up porn too? What else is there? I can't drink, I can't do drugs, I can't watch porn, and I can't eat everything that I want anymore. Am I doomed to go to AA meetings every day, drink my veggie protein shakes, and just get older? I am going to be the younger-looking sixty-two-year-old with forty years of sobriety. If I sleep with a twenty-five-year-old, I will be called a pervert and a monster, and if I stay single, everyone will think there is something inherently wrong with me or I am a closeted homosexual. On top of that, I can't watch porn to take off the edge. Being a guy that believes in a higher power, I can only assume that I have two options. Either God has something better in store for me or He enjoys fucking with me and watching me squirm. Today, I am not sure what to believe. From personal experience, what I do know is that no matter how hard I try to create the world that I want, I will simply get what I am supposed to get. I will get what I deserve. That is a very uncomfortable place to be.

27. Who Are You

Let's say you were on your way to work one morning and you found a piece of paper crumpled up on the sidewalk. You do not know why, but you decide to pick it up. You begin to read what is on the paper. It is a letter that instructs you to answer ninety-nine questions, and if you answer all ninety-nine questions truthfully, your life will change. What would your answers look like? I will play the game if you do.

1. Full name: *Marques Noah Marchand*
2. Gender: *Male*
3. Sexual preference: *eighty-nine percent heterosexual, eleven percent homosexual (Some men are extremely attractive.)*
4. Age: *thirty-nine*
5. Favorite color: *Moss green*
6. Favorite actor: *Tom Cruise*
7. Favorite food? *Pizza*
8. Dream job: *I want Tony Robbins' job.*
9. Dream place to live or visit? *Southern France*
10. How old were you when you had your first French kiss? *14*
11. How old were you when you lost your virginity? *18*
12. Are you currently or have you ever been a victim of sexual, physical, or emotional abuse? Explain. *Emotional abuse.*
13. Describe the kind of person you are sexually attracted to. *Curvy, tan, short, quiet, dark features, most likely Latina*
14. Have you ever thought of hurting yourself? *Yes*
15. Have you ever thought about hurting someone else? *No*
16. What is the worst thing you have ever done? *Disown my family*
17. What is the best thing you have ever done? *I stayed at the hospital all night with someone that I didn't know while they were going through alcohol withdrawal.*
18. If you could have three wishes granted, what would they be? *True love, a house on the coast of Southern France, and unlimited wishes*

19. Would you rather know the date of your death or the cause of your death? *The date*

20. Have you ever been in love? *Yes*

21. What is your favorite song? *Chopin—Nocturne op.9, No.2*

22. What are you most afraid of? *Going insane*

23. If you killed someone, how would you get rid of the body? *Hungry pigs*

24. Do you hate anyone? *No*

25. Is there something you wish you could stop doing but can't? *Prescription sleeping pills*

26. Do you like your mother? *Sixty-five percent no and thirty-five percent yes*

27. What is your biggest regret? *I do not know how to love my brother.*

28. Do you want children? *50/50*

29. Do you like children? *Rarely*

30. What is your happiest childhood memory? *Cooking with my grandmother*

31. What is your favorite smell? *Freshly baked cinnamon rolls*

32. When did you last laugh so much that it hurt? *Last week while talking to my friend Craig after an AA meeting*

33. Describe a perfect ordinary day. *Wake up at noon, get a ninety-minute massage, swim some laps, go to an AA meeting, and have pizza at eleven p.m.*

34. What do you want that you can't have? *Nicole*

35. What is your body telling you right now? *My eyes hurt, but I need to finish this chapter.*

36. Describe your best friend. *Five foot eight inches, ego, face tattoos, genius, emotionally unstable, and kicking ass*

37. What dream have you had more than once? *Falling in an elevator shaft that never ends*

38. Do you collect anything? *No*

39. You are camping with a friend and a bear approaches your campsite. What do you do? *I tell him we need to run. I run faster than my friend and live.*

40. What are you most self-conscious about? *My weight*

41. What is the most embarrassing thing in your room? *My penis pump.*

42. If you consider yourself to be straight, have you ever had a sexual encounter with the same sex? *I have made out with seven men, usually while drunk at a nightclub.*

43. For the next sixty seconds, dance with no music on.

44. Curse as much as you can out loud for twenty seconds.

45. Tell the person next to you that you love them and then walk away.

46. Have you ever seen a ghost? *Yes, four times in my life*

47. When was the last time you climbed a tree? *I can't remember.*

48. Describe your sense of humor? *Very dry. I love making fun of people.*

49. What crime would you commit if you knew you could get away with it? *I would love to be an art thief.*

50. What age do you wish you could permanently be? *Thirty-five*

51. What's your dream car? *1961 Jaguar E-Type*

52. What is you guilty pleasure? *Expensive French food*

53. Where is the most interesting place you have been? *Transgender AA meeting in Cuba*

54. How different was your life a year ago? *I am making more money and I have more self-esteem.*

55. As the only human left on the Earth, what would you do? *Drive as fast as I want*

56. Who inspires you to be better? *Myself*

57. If you were put into solitary confinement for six months, what would you do to stay sane? *I don't think there is anything you can do.*

58. Have you ever saved someone's life? *Yes. A woman was being chased by two men. I yelled at the two men chasing her. I found a brick and threw it at one of the men as hard as I could, knocking him down. Both men stopped and the woman got away.*

59. What's the hardest lesson you've learned? *That life doesn't care how special you are*

60. Do you want to be famous? *No*

61. What are you most grateful for? *I am not crazy anymore.*

62. When did you last cry in front of someone? *October 2016, in front of my ex-girlfriend. I had just moved to San Francisco and I was overwhelmed with all the changes in my life. I collapsed in front of her.*

63. What's the best thing that happened to you last week? *I was able to get four days off work and come to a monastery in Berkeley, California, for a silence retreat.*

64. What quirks do you have? *Disorganized workspaces give me anxiety.*

65. What movie title best describes your life? *Rebel without a cause*

66. Where is the most relaxing place you have ever been? *Brietenbush Hot Springs*

67. What are some things you've had to unlearn? *That God is real*

68. What are you looking forward to in the coming months? *Becoming a member of Les Clef d'Or*

69. What do you spend the most time thinking about? *Money*

70. What do you wish your brain was better at doing? *Math*

71. There are two types of people in this world. What are the two types? *Book-smart and magazine-smart*

72. What are some of the events in your life that made you who you are? *Leaving home at fifteen, sobriety, traveling, and creating a career*

73. If you had to change your name, what would you change it to? *Hans Ulrike*

74. What is something that your friends would consider 'so you?' *Quotes by Napoleon Bonaparte*

75. What challenging thing are you working through these days? *This book*

76. What do you strongly suspect but have no proof of? *Aliens are real.*

77. What do people think is weird about you? *I prefer to be alone.*

78. What are some of your personal 'rules' that you never break? *I do not drink and I do not lie.*

79. What's the best thing about you? *You can count on me to always tell you the truth.*

80. What's the best thing you got from your parents? *They never bailed me out while I was in my addiction.*

81. What is the 'holy grail' of your life? *Sobriety through honesty*

82. If your childhood had a smell, what would it be? *Bean with bacon soup*

83. What's the most immature thing that you do? *I ignore people.*

84. What are you most likely very wrong about? *That most of the female population in California is borderline legally retarded*

85. What keeps you up at night? *I can't turn off my brain.*

86. What lie do you tell most often? *I can't lie.*

87. What do you most often look down on people for? What do you think other people look down on you for? *I look down on smokers and people probably look down on me for being so loud.*

88. What's one thing you did that you really wish you could go back and undo? *I abandoned my brother.*

89. What are you afraid that people see when they look at you? *That I came from a poor family*

90. Who in your family do you wish you were closer to? *My stepfather*

91. Do you think that you can become the person you really want to be? *I know I can and I will.*

92. Do you think you are ugly? *No*
93. Do you want to live? *Yes*
94. Do you love yourself? *Yes*
95. Do you like yourself? *Sometimes*
96. What do you want to be doing at this very moment? *I want to be rich right now.*
97. If you were someone else and you met the person you are today, would you want to be that person's friend? *Hundred percent yes!*
98. Do you believe in God? *Yes*
99. What do you think is holding you back? *Money*

28. Humility

Everybody has his or her own personal Achilles heel. Everybody has that one thing that takes him or her down. For some, it is relationships. For others, it could be expensive shit. I have watched a lot of really smart men and women crumble after a bad breakup. As I watch this happen, I scratch my head wondering why people self-destruct when someone breaks up with them. I have watched people go completely broke because they collect the stupidest shit. I know a guy that is in his mid-thirties and he can't move out of his parents' house because he can't stop buying samurai swords. I have watched him struggle financially and I could never figure out why. One day, I asked him if everything was okay with him because he seemed really stressed out. He told me that he bought a sword for thirteen grand and found out that it was a fake. The guy that was hired to authenticate the sword was in on the scam. The sword was worth maybe four hundred and fifty bucks. I was talking a bit of shit about this friend with another buddy of mine and then he reminded me that I do some stupid shit as well. The one thing that has almost gotten me killed on more than one occasion is my mouth. It doesn't matter if I am drunk or stoned, on acid or stone-cold sober, I have a really big mouth. I have said some things that have ended friendships in less than five minutes. I have yelled at Michelin star restaurant chefs, MS13 gang members, angry city bus drivers, and everybody in between. I rarely get angry. I think I have only been really pissed off ten times in my life. I never become violent, but the things I say to people are simply inhumane. I usually lose my shit after holding in resentment towards someone or an idea about someone. Even with years of sobriety, I will say shit to people that is totally uncalled for. Part of me feels like I should be able to say whatever I want. I can be very sarcastic and flip with people. In the moment, I feel completely justified in my actions, but when I get home and finally lie down for the night, I will go over my day. My mind will immediately zoom in on the person I had offended and I always know that I was in the wrong. I know that I had no business saying the things I said. Why do I feel the need to tell people my opinion on something that they did? Why do I constantly feel the need to air out my harsh criticisms? I have come to realize that I get off on skating that thin line with people. I love pushing certain kind of people's buttons. Ditzy women in their twenties, really conservative dull men, middle-aged lefty cat ladies, and beta males of all ages are some of my favorite targets. If I overhear a girl with a rolled up yoga mat slung over her shoulder tell someone about how they are vegan, I will get on my phone and pretend that I am talking to someone just so I can make fun of vegans while I pass her. For some reason, I love fucking with strangers. Fucking with strangers is one of my last few bad habits that I take complete pleasure in. Offending someone in passing is like eating really salty junk food. You know that it is bad for you, but every once in a while, you just have to dig in and you can't stop until the bag is finished.

Look, I never claimed to be a good person. Hell, being a good person has never been on my bucket list of things to do, not even close. But I am also not a bad person. I am somewhere in the middle. I am like one of those movie villains that help out the hero because we have an enemy in common. The enemy of my enemy is my friend. That is me. I don't wake up in the morning wanting to hurt anyone in any way. I usually wake up groggy, a little bitter that I have to do anything at all, and I just want to have a good time while I am awake. In those waking hours, I might get a little agitated from time to time, usually because of someone that is in my way or said or did something that annoyed me. Whatever it is that pissed me off, it usually has to do with someone or some situation. The easiest way to get back at someone is to simply observe them for five seconds and make some off-color comment about the first thing you notice as you walk by them. This takes a lot of skill, but if you practice enough like I do, you will become quite proficient at this. The person that you offend will not even know why they are offended until it is too late. This is a diabolical skillset to have, but it's fun to use at parties. There is only one downside to behaving like this. It will eat at your soul over time. If you are a human being like I am, being sarcastic all the time will eventually break you down. I personally have started questioning my behavior. Why do I do this? Does it really make me feel good? How did you become this person? When did it start? I waste a lot of time asking myself stupid questions like this, but asking stupid questions is a lot easier than just stopping. At least when I ask these questions, I can pretend that I have some kind of depth or dimension to my character.

The truth of the matter is that throughout my life, I have always lacked humility. I have always been a high-energy person with good intentions but no humility to be found. I think these are great traits to have, but I have also gone through life thinking I deserve something more. If I put a lot of effort into something, I want something back. I tend to be one of those people that keep score. If I call you three times in a row over the course of three weeks, why don't you call me? It's your turn to call, so when are you going to call? My mind will race over scenarios like this. The only time I feel true humility is when I am in a heightened state of agitation or if I am extremely depressed and I decide to get on my knees and pray. I will pray to God and ask him to remove what I am thinking about. On occasion, what I am feeling will go away. The thoughts that I had been obsessing over will disappear. I can honestly tell you that praying has actually taken thoughts out of my brain that I have been grinding over for days. It's completely insane and incredible when this happens. These are the rare moments that I am truly humble. I wish I could feel humble on a more regular basis, but I think a part of me still enjoys the drama of daily life too much. I still enjoy getting ahead of all the traffic that life dishes out. I love the buzz that pushing the limits gives me. Granted, I am always experiencing a form of exhaustion by living like this, but in the moment, it can be a quit exhilarating, even gratifying in some way.

On a rare occasion, I will meet someone and I will get an immediate feeling about him or her. I feel as if I am experiencing their aura in a way. I know immediately that they live in an almost constant state of emotional and spiritual health. I have meet a few people in my lifetime that were more like spiritual athletes than just your ordinary everyday Joe out there trying to keep up with the rat race. The few people that I have met and obtained these special gifts look completely normal on the outside, but if you stand close to them or take the time to look in their eyes while you shake their hand, you will notice something is very different about those persons. I am not sure what the term for these types of people is. They are not spiritual gurus in any way. They are just people that were born with a gift. Or maybe something traumatic happened to them during their childhood. Maybe they lost someone they cared about deeply and the extreme pain that they went through forced them into a state of openness, gratitude, and humility in order to survive and push through that horrible event. But they are here with us now on Planet Earth. You realize this person has special superpowers that you wish you could have but can't. So what do you do? Do you simply ask one of these modern-day indigo children to teach you their ways? That could be a weird question to ask someone. You have to remember these people are after all just people. But maybe it wouldn't hurt to get some pointers from someone that is obviously much more calm and centered than you have ever been in your life. Personally, if I was lucky enough to bump into someone that is always so calm yet strong, full of life, and ready to take on the world, I would simply walk up and ask him, "Excuse me, sir, but I couldn't help noticing that you seem pretty much unfazed by the world around you. I myself experience anxiety on a regular basis and I am not exactly sure where my life is headed. How do you always stay so grounded and self-assured all the time? Will you help me with this? I have to be honest. I am a bit lost, and for some reason, I think you know how to just walk through all this madness in a graceful and dignified manner. Will you tell me your secret? I want humility, but I don't know how to get it. I just need help. I will do anything to learn. I won't be a pain in the ass and I won't get on your nerves. I just want to see how you live your life. Is that too weird? I just want to be humble!"

29. Self-Esteem

Motherfucking self-esteem! What exactly is it? If you don't have enough of it, the world will roll right over you. If you have too much of it, people can't stand to be around you. Self-esteem is a lot like cocaine, but who in the world does just the right amount of cocaine? The answer is nobody!

I think that self-esteem is one of the most important ingredients to living a full and happy life. I also think that self-esteem is one of the most volatile ingredients to achieving any kind of happiness. Recently, it has come to my attention that happiness should not be my main focus in life but happiness is something that I enjoy. I need to look at happiness more like a dessert rather than the main course. I have learned that happiness is more of a side effect of living a life with purpose. I do not think that anyone is simply 'happy' all the time. I have met a few really happy people in my lifetime and I have noticed that all of those people had one thing in common. They all lived lives with purpose. It wasn't their wives or husbands that made them happy. It wasn't all the money they had, but I do want to point out that all of the happiest people I have ever met also had a lot of money. I personally have not met anyone that has taken a vow of poverty that was truly happy. I have met some extremely religious people that have taken a vow of poverty and only one of them I found to be truly happy. The others that I have met were standoffish and kind of rude. One of the most interesting and pleasant people I have ever met is a monk by the name of Vincent. When I first met him, I could immediately tell that Vincent had found his place in the world. Vincent is a friendly, calm, and vibrant man in his early seventies. Has Vincent always been such a great human being? Who knows? Maybe, maybe not. Maybe Vincent was an abusive husband in his early years and he finally turned over a new leaf after destroying everything around him. Maybe he has always been a lot like the Dalai Lama, but I doubt it. All I know is that today, Vincent is awesome. Whenever I see him, he always tells me it is good to see me and gives me a hug. It's not a creepy hug that a lot of people might think a priest or a monk might give another man. I think that priests and monks get a really bad rap. I know that a lot of priests have done some really horrible things to people throughout the years. But a lot of people in general have done a lot of really horrible shit. Not all priests are evil pedophiles and not every guy that works on Wall Street is out to rob you blind. I use the priest and Wall Street example because as a society, we associate these two roles with an extreme amount of negativity and distrust. I have watched a few documentaries and films based on true stories about Wall Street tycoons and priests committing atrocious crimes against people that were weaker than them. We have all seen the film *The Wolf of Wall Street*. This a great movie about a man that starts out with good intentions and eventually loses his shit because of greed, drug addiction, and his manic pursuit for power. I am sure a lot of you have seen the film *Spotlight*. This is an amazing film based on true events where a well-known Boston-based newspaper uncovers a major story about priests in the Boston area molesting young children. Through their research, they develop a list of eighty-seven names and begin to find their victims to back up their suspicions.

Money and organized religion might just be the two most important and powerful ideas in the world. No matter where you go, money and religion are the top dog. I grew up in Portland, Oregon, which is known for having one of the largest atheist populations in the country, but there are churches everywhere and the wealthiest families tend to put their kids in private catholic schools. The longest wars that have ever been fought have all been based on religious differences. Sure, land will always be a part of the equation, but all these wars start because some guy disagrees with some other guy's God. This will never stop—money, sex, and religion. These three things will always make the world go round. But who are the guys that are at the top of these mountains? How do the Donald Trumps, the Dalai Lamas, and the Jeff Bezoses of our time become who they are? I don't think it is as simple as environment, good genes, and money. All of these men have something intangible, something almost magical about them. There are so many geniuses out there that have come from wealthy families but we never hear about them. Why? Because nobody cares. From the very beginning, they simply failed to capture the interest of their peers. From the first day of kindergarten to all the way to their senior year of high school and even further up through their senior year of college, only four or five people gave a shit about them. Why? Because they lacked chutzpah. There are some qualities you just have to be born with. Not everybody could be Elvis Presley or Marilyn Monroe. Only one person gets to have that honor. And yes, I am sure that in Elvis Presley and Marilyn's time, there were plenty of very attractive, smart, and talented people born on the very same day they were born, but they all lacked something. Nobody could shake his ass like Elvis and no other woman had that Marilyn look. Even today with all the technology and industry specialists, nobody knows how to bottle what Elvis and Marilyn had. These industry specialists get close every fifteen years, but they just haven't found that magic wand. Take Donald Trump. Love him or hate him, he is a billionaire and our current president. What do you do for a living? What does the richest person you know do for a living? Do you know anyone as fascinating as Donald Trump? And if you think Donald Trump is not fascinating, you are a fucking idiot. I didn't ask if you think Trump is a nice guy. I didn't ask if you agree with the way he is running our country. I said fascinating. Donald Trump becoming our president is nothing short of incredible. Not impossible, almost anything is possible. There are richer people than Donald Trump. There are smarter people than Donald Trump, but how many people have the complete package like Trump has? How did Donald Trump become our fucking president? Confidence. Donald Trump is probably the most confident man this country has ever seen. Go on YouTube and watch all the old interviews from the early 1980s. Now watch his interviews from the 1990s and then the 2000s. Donald Trump is still the same unapologetically confident man that he always was. He only sleeps a few hours a day, he eats steak for every meal, and on top of that, he doesn't drink. This guy is the pure definition of power and control.

People hate guys like Donald Trump. Donald Trump makes every other man in the room look like a total ass. Every man that Trump stands next to immediately turns into a total pussy beta male. Watch how he shakes another man's hand. Every time, he grabs some guy's right hand and pulls the man in close to him and looks him right in the eye. How many men do you know that do this? The only man I have ever met that shakes hands like this is my stepfather. Every time my stepfather shakes my hand, I immediately wonder if he is going to crush me. I am almost forty and I am finally getting over my fear of shaking hands with my stepfather. I can finally look my stepfather right in the eye. Why did it take me so long to be able to do this? Because for most of my life, I have always believed the voice in my head that tells me I am a piece of shit. For most of my life, I was a pussy. There, I said it. I have always made friends easily, but on the inside, I always hated myself. I never thought I was good-looking enough, I never thought I was strong enough, and I always thought I was kind of a twerp. Once I started traveling, these feelings started to dissipate. Once I hit my fourteen-year mark with sobriety, I started to realize that most people can't do what I can do. I should be more specific. Most junkies can't do what I can do. I can stay sober. How many drug addicts and alcoholics do you know that can stay sober? Millions of people try every year and only thousands succeed. Every time I go to a large

AA event to see a major speaker, someone will lead the meeting by asking the crowd how many people have a year of sobriety. A bunch of people will raise their hands. Then the meeting leader will ask the crowd how many people have five years of sobriety. If you have a crowd of two hundred people, maybe a quarter of the crowd will raise their hand. When the crowd is asked who has ten years of sobriety, you will notice a major drop-off in hands reaching for the sky. By the time you reach fifteen years, you will see maybe twenty people. Maybe fifteen people will have twenty years out of a crowd of two hundred. I have met maybe fifty people in my life with over thirty years and I have only met two people with fifty years of sobriety. Like I have mentioned before, I have been to AA meetings all over the western hemisphere and the simple fact of the matter is that most addicts cannot stay sober. I think that most addicts feel that they aren't worth saving, so what's the point? The only addicts that I have ever met with a healthy self-image are people with years of therapy, twelve-step meetings, and action taken to improve their lives. Most people are not doing these things. Most people seem to try stopping for a while, getting a job, and then getting a girlfriend. These are the wrong ingredients for the type of cake an addict is trying to bake. Money and pussy does not equal sobriety. It never has and it never will.

I actually just looked up the definition for self-esteem. Self-esteem simply means the confidence in one's own worth or abilities—self-respect. Who in the fuck has this? If you are outside reading this or in a crowded area, look around you. What do you see? Do you really see a bunch of people with 'self-esteem' walking around? No, you don't. What you see are a bunch of 'me, me, me' consuming machines. How many people are smoking cigarettes right now? How many people do you see walking with six bags from a high-end clothing store? Do you see any women jogging wearing a ton of makeup? Why in the hell do women jog with makeup on? Maybe it is two in the afternoon and you are walking by an Italian restaurant with outdoor seating. What do you see? You see huge plates of food, pints of beer, and cocktails. It's two in the afternoon, for God's sake! Why in the fuck are you eating four pounds of pasta and drinking three lemon drops? What the fuck is going on? I have to be honest with you. I personally love it when I see restaurants and cafés packed with people eating and drinking. I am a hotel concierge, so when I see this, I know business is good. The more people that I see eating and drinking too much at any given time of the day, I know I will be able to pay my rent and go on another vacation soon. I love my weekly massages just like soccer moms love taking their three kids to lunch. I love my quarterly escorts the same way Britney and Nicole love shopping at Nordstrom's for three hours. These things make us feel good. But why do I need to do these things so often? Why do I need to feel this good on such a regular basis? This is simple, people. Because I have fucking low self-esteem. Of course I am going to follow this sentence up with, but I am getting better. I am getting better at what? I can't exactly measure my self-esteem. I don't know how much self-esteem I had last month versus this month. It's all just feelings. I do know that I have a lot more self-worth today than I did three years ago because my life purpose is much clearer today than it was three years ago. Three years ago, I knew that I wanted to get the fuck out of Portland, Oregon. I knew that I wanted to be a respected hotel concierge and I knew that I wanted to do more public-speaking and I knew I wanted to get paid for it. Out of all that, the only thing I knew that I had to do in order to achieve my goals was to move out of Portland. That's really all I had. So, I took the first job out of Portland that I could get and held my balls in one hand and opened the door with the other. The day I finally left Portland, I was completely ready. I had no reservations. Other than a few friends and family, Portland had nothing to offer me. I was so relieved when my plane finally took off. I remember being in the air and feeling like I was being reborn. I could finally be whatever I wanted to be. I also knew that if the next place didn't work, I could go somewhere else. There were no more rules. This was freedom. I was scared out of my fucking mind, but I knew it was the only solution. I was finally attempting to meet my potential. I had no idea how long it would take, but I was going to find it. I was going to look it right in the eye and I was willing to tear it to shreds if it didn't want to work with me. I was becoming a fucking beast.

Today, I go back and forth between thinking I can achieve anything that I set my mind to, to doubting if I will ever be able to afford a one-bedroom apartment in San Francisco. Yes, I know, a one-bedroom apartment in San Francisco goes for $3,600 a month, but if I become half as successful as I want to be, I should be able to not only rent in San Francisco but eventually buy something. I know that buying a doghouse for under a million bucks is little more than a pipedream, but I am going to give it my best shot. I personally never wanted to be a multimillionaire, but I have always had my eye on becoming one of those six-figures-a-year bachelors, kind of like Jeff Goldblum in the movie *Nine Months*. If you haven't seen it, don't break your back on it, but it's a funny flick.

My major issue with the whole concept of self-esteem is how much to have. I do not understand what the secret amount should be. On top of that, when I am feeling good about myself, I tend to feel a tinge of guilt because I do feel so good about how things in my life are going. One of my mentors told me that people just don't want to hear how great someone's life is when their life is shit. I get where he is coming from, but I personally would want someone to tell me if their life is going great. I would ask them how they made their life so good. I would want to know what actions they took. Over the years, I have asked certain people how they became so successful. What I learned was that their actions were only part of their success. Their mental state was another huge piece of the pie to their success. All of the successful people that I have talked to about this have told me in one way or another that they had to believe what they wanted to happen would happen. They didn't just sit on a couch and wish for something good to happen. They worked their asses off while they visualized what they wanted to happen. They would stay with a general idea. Maybe you want to help people. That's great, but *how* do you want to help people? You want to help find clean drinking water for poor people. That's great, but where do you want to do this? Do you want to work in a small village located in South America somewhere? And how would you help? Would you help build a machine that would filter the dirty water? Would you help coordinate people to join your team? Would you be a laborer? Once you are able to answer these simple questions, I think you are on your way. While you figure these questions out and you take action in order to turn your plan into a reality, you might notice something different about yourself. You might notice that you feel useful and productive. You might even feel happy. Who knows, stranger things have happened. If you are struggling with a disease like addiction, I think feeling useful is a major part of one's recovery. It takes your mind off trying to stay sober. It takes your mind off yourself. It takes your mind off useless questions like, "What does it mean to be sober?" These kinds of questions just produce self-doubt and unnecessary struggle. Just get sober and move forward. Those two things will be the hardest decisions an addict will ever make. The rest is just a giant cherry on top. Sobriety can be a very dull and gray place if that is all you ever have. I never want to be fifty years' sober with nothing else going on in my life but AA meetings. I need to be in the middle of something. I want to talk to people and I want to listen to their ideas. I want to see other people succeed as well and I would love to help them get there. That is my purpose and that is my happiness. That is where I create my self-esteem.

30. Service!

One thing I have learned over the years is how much I enjoy helping people. Granted, I do not like a lot of people, but liking someone and helping someone are two completely different worlds. I help people at work that I simply do not like all the time. I enjoy the exchange. Most of the people I help I would not want to hang out with, but that's not going to stop me from making some kind of difference. Ever since I was a little kid, I have always offered to lend a helping hand. If I was walking somewhere with my mother and we saw a little old lady walking across the street with grocery bags, my mother would demand that I run over and help her. Plus, as I was growing up with my grandmother, she was always having me do random things for her like crawling up into the addict for Halloween decorations or climbing to the top of the dry storage closet for a baking pan. I was always my grandmother's personal bellboy and I was completely fine with that. I have always been a people-pleaser with a golden tongue. If you needed a pallbearer for your wedding, I would show up in a freshly pressed tuxedo. If you need someone to mow your lawn at the last minute, my mother would send me over. I always hated the manual labor jobs and preferred light work around the house or the random party host gigs.

For years, I thought there was only one way to succeed at life and I just didn't have what the world needed. I thought I was destined to be a C-human being with the minimal skills to barely get by. My stepfather was my first teacher. I know now that he had the best intentions for me, but I really had no idea what he was talking about. We didn't speak the same language. My stepfather was and is one of the top minds in the tech field and I barely have a basic understanding of ninth-grade mathematics. Through working with and meeting people from all over the world, I have learned that I have the gift of universal communication. I can talk to anyone regardless of his or her background. This is the one thing that I did really well while my stepfather did it very poorly. My skillsets are geared towards people and his skillsets are geared toward mechanics and tech-focused ideas. I always believed that that my talents and skills were worthless. The first time I was ever told that I could really make a difference in the world, I was thirty-two years old. Maybe people have tried telling me this before and maybe I just never heard what they were saying, but everything really clicked for me in my early thirties. I am sure that a lot of the knowledge that I have accrued throughout the years could be chalked up to 'growing up.' I can agree with this, but I am certain that I never would have grown up if it were not for the spiritual program of Alcoholics Anonymous.

I know I have specified at the beginning of this book that I am not trying to sell you on God or that God is real and I am not trying to convince you to join Alcoholics Anonymous or any other wacky-ass group for that matter. All I am doing is telling you how I have been able to get sober, stay sober, and slowly create a successful life for myself. For a lot of people, what I am writing is nothing more than a madman's rant. Some people will read this and totally know where I am coming from. That doesn't mean that I am right about anything and you are in the dark. I am not more advanced than you or anything like that. I am able to stay sober, nothing more. I would also like to make it clear that many people stay sober in a variety of different ways. The way I stay sober might not work for anyone else. Personally I doubt that, but there is a chance that the way I stay sober could hurt someone else. If what I write helps you or someone you know in any way, then I have done my job. I have found that speaking to people and writing is the best way for me to help people. Actually, the best way I have learned to help people is to ask them what is going on with them and listen. I close my eyes and I just listen. Sometimes, I will start out by telling a fellow addict my story and then ask them to tell me about their story, or I will reverse the process and have the person I am trying to help to start by telling me their story. Some people need to just let it out right away. When I come across this person, I simply let it happen. Once this person is done speaking, I will not give my opinion on their experience. I will just thank them for sharing their story with me. Then I will ask them what they want to do about it? Do they want to stop drinking and using? If they want to stop, I will then tell them my story and tell them how I have been able to stay sober. I will tell them exactly what I have been writing in this book. Sure, I have other life stories to tell, but the basic idea will always stay the same. And yes, I always follow the twelve-step model. Why? Because I have tried so many other methods for living a successful life but the only thing that set me free from the emotional prison that was my life are the twelve steps of Alcoholics Anonymous. I like to make it clear from the start that Alcoholics Anonymous is about living a better life. The drinking and the drugs were only a small symptom of the problem. If all I had to do was stop drinking and my life would just become amazing, I don't think I would have kept working the AA program. I probably would have only gone to meetings for a few months if at all.

Remember, I was eight years' sober before I ever went to an AA meeting. For those first eight years, I was miserable the entire time. I was suicidal for half of those eight years. Before AA, I simply had no idea how to live a good life. Sure, I exercised and I ate really healthy, but this did not cure me. Actually, nothing cures addiction, but for me, Alcoholics Anonymous has helped give me a fantastic life. It has been like winning a lottery, but the rewards that you receive happen over your lifetime. You don't get some check that is supposed to last you for the rest of your life. If you are a true blue addict, you really don't want to be given everything all at once. I have learned that I need things rationed out to me. Even today with all the knowledge that I have been given, I would still have no idea how to handle one big lump sum. Whether it is money or love, I can't have it all right now. I still need things to come at me slowly because I still get easily overwhelmed by certain life challenges. I couldn't image getting sober and then being given a huge fortune a few weeks later. I would totally lose my shit. Over the years, I have come to realize that my AA program and my higher power act as my spiritual accountant. My higher power never gives me more than I can handle. Sometimes I feel overwhelmed but if I stop, pray, or meditate for a minute, I will immediately settle down. I will realize that what I am freaking out about just isn't that big of a deal. And yes, breakups, job losses, and the death of a loved one are no small issues. These experiences crush people every day. People without the disease of addiction will most likely be temporarily destroyed by any of these horrible situations as well. I do not think that alcoholics and addicts have a monopoly on experiencing misery. I just think that addicts have a near impossible time of acclimating to the hard times that they experience. Moving on seems to be next to impossible for addicts. It took me ten years to get over my first love. The occasional resentment towards my parents still pops up, and when a woman rejects me, it will take me weeks if not a couple of months to really get over it. I am not proud of these things, but I have to be honest with you just so you know that I qualify. I qualify hundred percent. But there is a silver lining. Over the past few years, I have learned to get over my resentment quicker. I have learned to spot if someone is not good for me right away. My radar picks up bullshit immediately and I do not put up with it. I have learned that talking to my mother on a regular basis is not a good idea because I do not feel the need to put up with her lies. If I do not allow a friend to lie to me, why would I allow a family member to lie to me? No matter who lies and regardless of the kind of lie, it's all bullshit. It has taken me close to twenty years to just do my own thing and not worry about the consequences. Today, I am freer than I have ever been. Becoming the person that I am today and continuing to improve is the best thing I can do for myself and society as a whole. Continuing to be brutally honest about who I am, what I want out of life, and helping others to become who they want to be is the greatest gift I can give.

When it comes to serving others, just do what you can. Whether it be the decision to stop drinking or using drugs, paying your child support, finishing school, or just helping your next-door neighbor move their couch to the other side of the room, just fucking do it. Don't waste your time thinking about it. If you can, do it. It's as simple as that.

31. God, Are You There?

Have you ever talked to God? Have you ever tried? When I was sixteen, I started taking a lot of acid. I met a guy named Cliff that was a couple of years older than me and he took a bunch of us to a rave in Northeast Portland. We waited in line and a kid about our age asked if we needed anything. Cliff told him that there were seven people in our party and each person needed three hits of acid. We bought what we needed right there and took it immediately. The acid started to hit within thirty minutes. I was dancing and sweating and life was perfect. After an hour of dancing my ass off, something told me to go outside and find a church. I walked outside of the building and walked a couple of blocks down the street. It was about one in the morning. I found a church and saw a window that I could easily fit through if I could just get it open. Of course the window was locked, so I found a large rock and broke the window. I had never destroyed private property before and I would never do it again after this, but something told me I had to get inside the nearest church. By the time I snuck inside the church and found a comfortable place to sit, I was starting to peak on the acid I had taken. I sat in the main sanctuary area of the church. I stared at all the stained glass windows and the large cross with the track lighting hitting Jesus on the cross ever so perfectly. I went over to where all the candles were located and I decided to light them all. I think I lit every candle in the sanctuary. All of the light from the candles and stain glass windows and the gigantic crucifix in the center of the room became overwhelming to me. I lit a cigarette and just took everything in. A wave of emotions came over me and I began to cry. I had nothing on my mind that caused my tears, but I knew that something powerful was happening to me. Everything hit me all at once and I knew that I would never be the same again.

After this experience in the church, I knew that I wanted to know more. I knew that I had experienced God. I never heard any voices, but I felt something very powerful. I felt what I now believe to be all-powerful. I began doing as many different kinds of psychedelics that I could get my hands on. Most of my trips were in the wrong environments. I would take mushrooms in the basement of some random kid's party or at a nightclub in a city. But once in a while, I would get together with some of my hippy friends and we would go to the woods or take a road trip to the California Desert. I think I wanted to be a modern-day Jim Morrison. I wanted to meet God face-to-face. I had some questions and I wanted direct access to the source. I wanted to know the truth. Unfortunately, the truth would never come. I would take mescaline and I would think I found the answer, but I would wake up the next morning with nothing. I would take notes about the night before and I would read the notes the next day only to realize that I was basically insane for six hours. When I was nineteen, I went to a small village outside of Panama City, Panama, with a few friends. We went there with the sole purpose of experiencing a DMT trip. One of my main acid connections knew of a guy that grew up in the States and moved to South America to become a shaman. My buddy had this shaman guy's mailing address, so I sent him a letter and a week later, I received a response. A small group of my friends and I coordinated with the shaman and a month later, we were forty miles east of Panama City. I was out of my mind with fear. I think I had a panic attack that lasted five days. I had only heard stories about people taking DMT and either they lost their minds or they found complete inner peace. At this time, I was also studying and practicing on how to have out of body experiences, so I was hoping that my future DMT experience would help me with this. In the letter that I wrote expressing interest in taking DMT, I also asked if he could help me have an out-of-body experience as well. In his response, he offered to assist me in my quest. I was very excited, but I was afraid that I would never come back to my body and be lost forever in some kind of spiritual purgatory. Remember, at this time in my life, I was on some form of psychedelic on an almost daily basis for about a year. I was out of my mind so things that concerned me on a day-to-day basis were not rooted in the physical reality that we all know. Looking back, I am pretty sure that I was slowly losing my mind.

The night of my DMT trip was kind of like a guy's only camping trip. There were tents and a small fire. Our DMT guide brought out a bunch of strange-looking roots and grass. Everything had already been pre-dried, so he chopped everything into a fine powder. Once the plant material had been turned into a fine-enough powder, he brought out a long straw and packed some of the powder into it. He casually asked who wanted to go first. One of my friends volunteered. Our guide put the straw into my friend's nostril and he blew the powder up his nose. Within seconds, my friend's eyes glazed over, rolled back into his head, and he collapsed. He reached for the sky and started swatting the air as if he were trying to swat a housefly. He seemed to be incapable of speaking and he would just moan. It was as if he had swallowed his tongue. Then he started to smile. I knew that he figured something out and I immediately volunteered to go next. Our guide packed the straw again and placed the two-and-a-half-foot straw to my nose. He told me to inhale with my nose on the count of three. One, two, three, and a rush of powder went up my nose. By the time I sat down on the ground, I immediately felt like I was falling at a hundred miles per hour. I couldn't catch my breath. I felt like I was in a rocket and I was going Mach-three straight to hell. The energy I felt was very aggressive. I felt like I was being shot down a tube and I was about to meet a demon. Whatever it was that was in store for me wasn't good. The forest that I was in was gone. The small fire, my friends, and the tents were all gone. I was just falling. Everything was black and I saw shards of light shooting up and all around me. Had I become the real Dr. David Bowman from the film 2001: *A Space Odyssey*? I was seeing all the same shit that Dr. Bowman saw at the very end of the film, all the color streaks and all the fear. But what was I about to see? Would I be transported to a strange neon-lit room only to see myself as a very old man? After what felt like ten minutes of the horrifying falling, I suddenly found myself at the bottom of what I assumed to be a volcano. I was sitting on a rock that was floating on top of a pool of lava. There was no air or temperature. There was no fear. I did not feel anything. I just knew that I was at the bottom of the earth and there was nothing but red and yellow lava, and I had no idea how long I would be there. Then out of nowhere, a large floating human skull appeared and it began to breathe white smoke. It spoke with a very deep voice. The voice I heard was the actor Tim Curry's voice where he played the devil in the film *Legend* with Tom Cruise. The giant human skull with Tim Curry's voice repeated the words, "The never-ending lives in the never-ending sky." The skull was floating in a perfect circle above the lava and he would just repeat those words over and over again. After a few minutes, I found myself in the back of a minivan under four sleeping bags. I was drenched in sweat, was out of my mind, and shaking with fear. I felt like my brain had been scooped out with a spoon, and all I knew was fear and thirst. I was so thirsty, but I could not remember how to speak. I wanted to yell out to my friends and beg for some water, but I could not make the words come out of my mouth. Finally, my friend Russ came to check on me. He asked me if I was okay and I reached out for him and started crying. He kept asking if I was okay. Finally, I could whisper the word 'water.' For the first couple of times, Russ couldn't figure out what I was saying. I just kept saying, "Water. Please, can I have some water?" Finally, Russ understood what I needed and he brought me a cup of water. I felt like I hadn't had any water for days, but only an hour had actually gone by. My buddy Russ helped me out of the minivan and sat me down in front of the fire. He told me that nobody else in our group took the DMT. When they saw what happened to me, they all decided not to go through with it. Everybody in my group would tell me that I was yelling with my eyes closed and swatting at the air. One of my buddies laughed and said that I reminded him of Indiana Jones in the *Temple of Doom* when Mala Ram gives Indiana Jones that psychedelic tea and Indie loses his shit and becomes temporarily possessed. I think I was briefly possessed that night if there is such a thing.

I only saw my friend that took DMT with me once after that night. He would become heavily addicted to heroin and die a few years later. I always saw him as being a very troubled person and I do not think that he should have been playing with drugs like acid or DMT. I think psychedelic drugs can destroy people with an organic mood disorder such as bipolar or schizophrenia. I think that my heavy psychedelic drug use did a number on me psychologically. I did learn a lot, but I almost didn't come back from a few trips that I went on. On the other hand, I do believe that psychedelic drugs can help to enhance and broaden the minds of some people. I wish that someone like Donald Trump would take acid just once. I really think a guy like Trump could use a little acid. Maybe it would mellow him out a bit. What if Trump, Putin, and Kim Jong-un took a little acid together? Maybe something really positive would come out of it. Of course I am joking… but what if?

I am not sure if I ever connected with God or any other higher power that might actually exist during any of my past psychedelic trips, but I feel like I might have once or twice. Sometimes, I wonder if God is nothing more than a chemical in our brain that makes us think we are communicating with a higher being. Maybe that chemical is nature's way of keeping the human race moving forward. Or maybe there really is something omniscient out there.

For years, I told myself, and anyone that would listen, that I didn't believe in God. Inside, I would curse God. If God were real, why did He give me such a shitty life? For many years, I hated something that I didn't even believe in. When I say that out loud, it always sounds so foolish to me. Why would you hate something that you know is not real? That's fucking stupid. For the first couple years in AA, I couldn't believe in a higher power. I could not rap my mind around this concept, plus I had no interest. I just wanted to feel better. I didn't go to AA to talk about God or to start believing in any God. Even if God was real, I didn't care. I just wanted to be happy. I wanted to make a lot of money and I wanted to start getting laid again. To this day, I do not think that there is anything wrong with that. I started developing faith in a high power simply because I started experiencing things that were unexplainable. I started developing self-worth and I slowly stopped having panic attacks. I stopped hating my parents all the time, and I was able to start traveling and living a richer life. When I gave to the world, I would receive so much more in return. I have been taking mental notes over the years on how my life has improved and the only explanation is that God is real. I know that a lot of people might think I am mentally ill after reading this section of my book, and technically they are right. I do believe that alcoholism is a mental illness, but if all someone gets from what I am writing is that I am mentally ill, then I feel a little pity for those people. I am not even sure why I feel pity for people like that, but I do. If you are living with an incurable disease, what option do you have other than acknowledging that you have a disease, figuring out exactly what the disease is, finding a support group, asking questions, listening, praying to something, and doing whatever else it takes to live and succeed with the time you have left? Other than that, I think your only other option is to just end it. Either end it immediately or just keep using whatever it is that you are addicted to and die a slow and miserable death. Out of those three options, I chose a higher power. The fact that I chose to believe in a higher power was just as powerful as my first AA meeting, my first time using drugs, my first time having sex, and a lot of other first times that I would experience during my life. Out of all my first times, choosing to believe in a higher power has had the longest effect on my life. I have heard thousands of people say this as well. I have experienced God firsthand. This doesn't make me a good person or a better person than you. Even though I have had some major spiritual experiences, I still do things that I shouldn't. I still pay for sex, I still watch porn, I still eat too much, and I still obsess over money. No, I don't think this makes me a dirty sinner. I do think that I cause myself unnecessary turbulence and pain from time to time, and this will continue to happen until I decide to stop doing the stupid shit that I do. Why do I see escorts? Simple. I am lazy and I don't want to put in the effort that it takes to have sex with a 'normal' woman. Why do I eat too much? Simple. When I get hungry, I sometimes eat too much because I feel like I deserve to eat as much as I want. Why do I watch porn? This is also simple. I watch porn because I am afraid to be vulnerable with a woman. I am afraid she will reject me, so I just Google free porn and pick the woman I am in the mood for and satisfy myself until I am done. When will I stop doing this stupid shit? I have no idea. I do know that as long as I do these things, I will remain alone because I know that no healthy woman in her right mind would allow me to see escorts, watch porn at two in the morning, and eat brie cheese in bed after jacking off to porn.

Look, just because I believe in God doesn't mean I am a good person. The best thing I can do is to maintain my honesty. There are a few things that I want to stop doing eventually. Like a good addict, I don't think I will actually put any effort into quitting until I see it as a real problem. If I get into some serious trouble with the law concerning my activities with escorts or if a start to gain some serious weight from eating way too much, then I will really focus on the issue at hand. I tend to approach everything the way I approached my drug and alcohol abuse. I will see that I have a problem and I will eventually do whatever it takes to stop.

My relationship with food is beginning to really trouble me these days and I have been pondering whether I should start praying in order to alter my eating habits. I think I might need to pray when I get my late-night food cravings. The cravings I have for food at midnight are the same cravings that I would have for booze when I was twenty years old. I believe that food can be just as dangerous as drugs and alcohol. Plus, you never see commercials at one thirty in the morning advertising some random beer commercial, but for some reason, McDonald's finds a reason to sell you a Big Mac in the middle of the night. I can't possibly be the only person that sees this as a major problem. Who in the fuck needs a Big Mac at one thirty in the morning? I guess all McDonald's represents is a bad habit. For some people, reading US magazine is their McDonald's. For other people, having sex with ugly girls is their McDonald's. For me, watching porn and eating brie is my McDonald's. Porn and brie is my go-to fast food chain. It temporarily satisfies a part of my brain. It takes away that loneliness that we all try to escape from when it pops its ugly head up. Every time I watch a little porn, I realize after the fact that I forgot to say my prayer. "Marques, you are not lonely. You are just not distracted. Why do you want to be distracted?" I am reaching a point in my life where I must say this prayer every time I get those late-night cravings. My relationship with food is one of those things that I will need God's help with in order to move forward. There are a lot of things that I can improve on my own, but my food cravings are not one of those things. I hate the fact that food is bigger than me, but it is. Now that I think about it, I will probably have to ask for God's help on this tonight. Once I get home from working out, I will make myself one of my famous, ugly, green veggie protein shakes and when I am done, I will need to knock on my floor and say, "God, are you there?"

32. Pulling it all Together

Is getting sober enough? For a true junky, addict, or alcoholic, in the beginning that's all there is. For a true addict, getting sober is like trying to throw a football through the hole of a sewing needle. Staying sober for any length of time is even harder. Learning to live life on life's terms gets even harder than that and learning to actually enjoy your life is even harder than that. By the time you learn to actually enjoy your life, you will look back on your journey and be blown away. It's as if you were given superpowers. But you weren't given superpowers. You have been given a gift. You will realize that many people on this troubled planet are having a hard time, not just hardcore addicts like you or me, or your friend or your next-door neighbor. So many people yearn for love. People want to be loved and they want to love someone else, but they can't or don't think they deserve love. Millionaires, beauty queens, famous sports' superstars and even your local plastic surgeon, all these people need to be loved, listened to, and valued. But how many people feel all of these things? Not many. So many of us bust our asses in our jobs and personal lives trying to be good enough. We work harder, faster, and longer than the next guy and nobody notices. Nobody cares. Then you go home. Maybe you go home to an empty apartment in a busy city or maybe you go home to a house in the suburbs filled with children, a wife, two cats, and a dog. You walk through the door and the kids are running around trying to kill each other and you step in a pile of dog shit. Your wife yells at you for being an hour-and-a-half late. You walk up the stairs and sit on your bed and you look at the closet doors. You just stare at that closet door. You think to yourself, 'I have a handgun in there. I could finally just end it.' Or maybe you sit down on your bed and you feel a sense of gratitude wash over you. You love your chaotic scrambled world. You have been working so hard to build something with someone that you love and you are actually doing it. What's the difference between the guy that wants to blow his brains out and the guy that enjoys all the bullshit that comes with raising a family? It is the same situation but with two completely different mindsets. But why? Well, we don't know. We would need to know the whole story on these men. We would need to know about their childhoods and how they were treated throughout their lives. We would need to know every little detail such as their sleeping habits and their diets. Did they exercise? Did they smoke? Is there a history of any kind of illness in their families? What was the quality of their educations? Once we know all the facts, then we could figure some things out. The only way we can truly know someone is to dig it all up. Take out all the skeletons, uncover all the lies, and find out what really happened. You can't really help anyone until you know all the details and you can't help someone until you have done all of this with yourself. How are you feeling today? Are you satisfied? Have you settled in any area of your life? Do you think you have what it takes to improve your life? What are you willing to do? Are you willing to say that I have a problem and here it is? Would you tell someone all of your deepest, darkest secrets? Are you ready to cut yourself open and throw your guts on the table for everyone else to see? If the answer is yes, maybe you are ready to move forward. Maybe you will have a chance. If not, there is always tomorrow. But what if there are no more tomorrows left for you? Maybe you have run out of luck and corners to hide in. Maybe you have been left with nothing. But what does 'nothing' look like? Is it just a pitch-black room with no way in or way back out? Is it cold? Can you hear anything? Can you even hear the sound of your own voice? Is there air to breathe? Briefly, I experienced this pitch-black room with no possibility of escape, and yet here I am today writing this book. How did I get out? What was it like? It is different for everyone, and if I told you how I got out, you probably wouldn't believe me. Actually, I told you how I got out. Were you listening?

The End